	State	Class	Occupation		n
Product Markets			"Mass" vs. "Batch" markets (Chapter 3)		
Capital Markets		Economic con-centration (Chapter 3)		Conglomeration (Chapter 7)	
Resource Markets	Oil crisis (Chapter 6)				
Labor Markets			Wage contours (Chapter 4)		Deskilling (Chapter 3)

WORK AND INDUSTRY

Structures, Markets, and Processes

PLENUM STUDIES IN WORK AND INDUSTRY

Series Editors:
Ivar Berg, *University of Pennsylvania, Philadelphia, Pennsylvania*
and Arne L. Kalleberg, *University of North Carolina, Chapel Hill, North Carolina*

WORK AND INDUSTRY
Structures, Markets, and Processes
Arne L. Kalleberg and Ivar Berg

WORKERS, MANAGERS, AND TECHNOLOGICAL CHANGE
Emerging Patterns of Labor Relations
Edited by Daniel B. Cornfield

A Continuation Order Plan is available for this series. A continuation order will bring delivery of each new volume immediately upon publication. Volumes are billed only upon actual shipment. For further information please contact the publisher.

WORK AND INDUSTRY

Structures, Markets, and Processes

Arne L. Kalleberg

University of North Carolina
Chapel Hill, North Carolina

and

Ivar Berg

University of Pennsylvania
Philadelphia, Pennsylvania

With a Foreword by
John T. Dunlop

Harvard University
Cambridge, Massachusetts

PLENUM PRESS • NEW YORK AND LONDON

Library of Congress Cataloging in Publication Data

Kalleberg, Arne L.
 Work and industry.

 (Plenum studies in work and industry)
 Bibliography: p.
 Includes index.
 1. Work. 2. Labor supply. 3. Industry. 1. Berg, Ivar E. II. Title.
 HD4904.K294   1987   306′.36   87-2333
 ISBN 0-306-42344-8

© 1987 Plenum Press, New York
A Division of Plenum Publishing Corporation
233 Spring Street, New York, N.Y. 10013

Printed in the United States of America

To the Bergs and Kallebergs here and in Norway

FOREWORD

Work occupies a pivotal role in the daily activities and over the course of a lifetime of members of modern societies. In anticipation, work influences education and training; it has much to do with shaping current earned income and status in the community; and in retrospect, it influences retirement income and activities. It is a powerful force affecting personal associations. In our society work is deeply encased in moral and religious values:

> As Poor Richard says, A Life of Leisure and a Life of Laziness are two Things. Do you imagine that Sloth will afford you more Comfort than Labour? No, for as Poor Richard says: . . . Industry gives Comfort, and Plenty and Respect.
>
> Study to show thyself approved unto God a workman that needeth not to be ashamed.

But few words have as many different meanings and nuances as "work": to forge or to shape, to stir or to knead, to solve, to exploit, to practice trickery for some end, to excite or to provoke, to persuade or to influence, to toil, and the like. A need for precision in meaning is requisite with respect to work, not only in common discourse, but, even more so, in scholarly communication.

It should not be a surprise that work, and concepts encompassing work, have been a central focus in a number of different social and behavioral sciences: economics, sociology, industrial relations, social psychology, and social history. Each of these fields has tended to define the term and to build it into concepts in its own ways for its own purposes. There has been too much isolation and too little common discourse across disciplinary lines. The present volume is designed to make a contribution toward a more integrated approach.

By *work structures,* the authors mean the "institutions, regularities, and arrangements" that characterize work. "These are the rules that many people have agreed on and thus legitimated, for longer or shorter periods, as effective means of solving the economic and political problems of production and distribution. . . . These structures describe the ways in which labor is divided, tasks allocated and authority distributed." The volume focuses on six major types of work structures: nation-states, industries, business organizations, occupations, classes, and unions.

The authors regard the ultimate causes of work structures to be "the various markets within which exchanges take place and the political processes that determine the mix of market and nonmarket initiatives in a society." "Markets are the fundamental complexes of patterned behavior in which one must look for the origins of our work structures and processes." They stress the critical importance of four types of markets: capital, product, labor, and resource markets.

A matrix composed of six work structures and four markets is thus created. The authors stress the interactive effects among the numerous cells of the matrix rather than concentrating, as single disciplines do, largely on a single work structure or a single type of market, failing to appreciate the insight to be gained from recognizing such widespread and complex interactions. These interactions generate processes which, in turn, produce changes in both work structures and in markets.

Consider an illustration centrally related to the analysis of work, the determination of the compensation of labor services and the absence of work opportunities, that is, the problem of unemployment. The discipline of theoretical economics, particularly in recent years, has posited the labor market for occupations and job classification as a bourse in which the wage or salary cleared the market and in which unemployment existed only when (real) compensation was too high. (In the matrix view of this volume such economic analysis is confined to a single cell of the labor market and occupations or industries.) A study of the interactions among other cells in the matrix would recognize the fact that beyond labor markets, compensation is significantly influenced by developments in product, capital, and resource markets, as well as by attributes of work structures other than occupations or even industries. Unemployment is not to be interpreted in terms of labor market developments primarily. Moreover, the feedback and dynamics of the processes of interaction throughout the matrix, or in certain cells, influence the changes in compensation and unemployment.

The same integrative approach illuminates a number of other questions of concern to social sciences and related to work: the impact of economic development on a labor force; the consequences of international competition on industrial relations arrangements; and the changes in the health care system associated with a community aroused over the rates of increase in health care costs, among others.

In all analysis, it is essential to be clear and explicit concerning what is fixed and what is variable (exogenous and endogenous) for the problem at hand. The matrix analysis of the volume should encourage specificity on this matter.

The dimensions of the world of work are appropriately a focus of attention in undergraduate education as well as in the various professional schools. The perspectives developed in this volume should be helpful in considering the full range and consequences of work activities, their interaction processes and dynamics, and the methods of approach to vital issues unconstrained by the imperialism of a single discipline.

JOHN T. DUNLOP

Harvard University
July 1986

PREFACE

Our dedication of this volume, earlier on, reflects those personal dimensions of a collaborative enterprise that so often leaven coauthors' earnest work with pleasure. We are of different ages—and thus of different times—but we have a number of commonalities in our backgrounds as youths in Norway, as adolescents in Brooklyn, New York, as bilingual immigrants, as the offspring of "politically conscious" parents, and as university social scientists. Discussions of these experiences during work breaks left us more than just mindful of the roles of our autobiographies not only in our choices of scholarly pursuits but also in our definitions of situations and our approaches thereto.

We became especially conscious, in our joint labors, of the urges we both have felt to understand better the tensions we experienced from our earliest years between the individualistic search for opportunity, so often and so widely celebrated in America, and the roles of structural and institutional arrangements that block (or mock) some persons' progress even as those arrangements help to reward others' individual aspirations and the tactics chosen to fulfill them.

While the chapters herein do not argue the cases for these two perspectives in any essentially explicit ways, they do, indeed, sum up to a resolution substantially favoring one side of the middle-ground position: While we allow considerable room for examinations of the capacities of individuals to truly serve their own ends, we tend to stress, more urgently, the roles of social arrangements ("structures" and "markets" in this book's language) that impact in ways that help and hinder the self-serving behavior of members of different population groups. Our personal, as well as our professional experiences, accordingly, have made it impossible for us to be dogmatic about either of two of the main logics in the social sciences, but it is evident that we are somewhat less generously disposed toward individual-centered analyses than toward the alternatives.

On a less personal note, we are obliged to report, as most authors are, that we would have done some things differently had we not "released" the manuscript in the form it now appears.

First, the validity of the main thrusts of our argument would have been far more adequately tested had we incorporated much more comparative and historical material than in fact we did. We anticipate, though, that many of these types of tests will be conducted by contributors to the series for which this volume is the initial listing.

Next, the book would have been a better one had Oliver Williamson's *The Economic Institutions of Capitalism* (New York: Free Press, 1985) been in our hands while we were doing revisions in the fall of 1985. His newest work on "transaction costs" constitutes one of the most seminal chapters in the integration of major economic and sociological paradigms.

Third, we were regularly urged, during informal consultations with colleagues, to afford abundant illustrations, and so we have. The price authors pay for these exercises, however, is to lose a certain timeliness or, worse, to tie important points to dated material to the points' disadvantages. Consider that today's college freshmen, now living with what some would like to regard as an "oil glut," were in first grade when sheiks, a shah, and the leaders of Venezuela visited OPEC's cartel-like policies on oil-consuming nations. And the current shortage of "new entry" high school graduates, the so-called Baby Bust cohort, appears to have converted the once lively (and very large) literature on youth unemployment into just so many chapters in recent economic history.

Fourth, we have given insufficient attention to the *labor force* and its human members while hammering away at labor *markets, occupations* and *jobs*. While we note differences among persons—age, gender, ethnic, and race differences among them—we do not weave the data on these groups' members into our discussions of "markets and structures" in any but schematic ways. By according passing attention to segregation and discrimination, for example, we can claim only that our work complements that of colleagues for whom these phenomena are the salient ones.

Fifth, in our future work we will be more attentive than we are here to admixtures of "jobs" and "occupations." The Civil Service System with its GS grades (and the equivalents in the several states and the sprawling Department of Defense) for example, has made occupations—even an occupation—of a multitude of *very* different jobs. Indeed, it is worth noting that the current feminist battle cry, "equal pay for equal work," is really only an echo of an older, popular determination beginning soon after McKinley's assassination, that generated pressures for the Pendleton Act. GS 15s are GS 15, after all, whether they are nurses on a quiet ward at a Veterans Administration hospital in Georgia or tower controllers at busy airports in New York or Chicago; and where the Georgia nurse may be responsible for many patients and expensive facilities in a given year, tower controllers have responsibilities for innumerable passengers' lives and for the safe conduct of many multimillion dollar aircraft on any given morning.

Next, though we have argued the point quite insistently elsewhere, we neglect some very critical structures: large urban labor markets, for example, are by *no* means all of a piece. We pause to make some room for disaggregations of both our structures and our markets, to be sure, but we might well have tested their integrity as "wholes" more often than we did.

Next, by playing down the world systems economy, that is, by focusing on the nation-state as the most "macro" of our structures, we leave out the roles of such forces—many of them with more enduring effects than OPEC—as those that turned the United States around from the Goliath of the post–World War II-period into the struggling nation it became following Germany's and Japan's postwar recoveries.

We should quickly add that our distresses are with our own shortcomings; we have only thanks to offer younger colleagues—readers who helped save us from what would have been, at this juncture, additional misapprehensions. We are accordingly happy to acknowledge the able counsel of Michael Wallace (Ohio State), Karyn Loscocco (SUNY-Albany), and Kevin Leicht (Indiana). We also appreciated a later and valuable critique by Robert Averitt, at a conference at the University of Texas-Dallas in March 1986, which came to us after we signed off on the manuscript. We address his critique, however, in a chapter that will be included in a future volume in the present series, edited by George Farkas and Paula England (UT-Dallas).

Finally, we are much indebted to Jill Birdsall and Vadney Stanford for their encouragement, editorial misgivings, good-humored responses to needs for revisions, and skillful management of the manuscript from drafts, discs, and "hard copy" to negotiations with Eliot Werner and Daniel Spinella, our very helpful colleagues at Plenum.

CONTENTS

INTRODUCTION

The only thing a man can do for eight hours a day, day after day, is work. You can't eat eight hours a day nor drink for eight hours a day nor make love for eight hours—all you can do for eight hours is work.

—William Faulkner

We mustn't forget that property has duties even if other people forget that it has rights.

—Henry Arthur Jones, *The Triumph of the Philistines*, Act I (1895)

Few activities are as fundamental to society and to the individual as work. A pervasive activity, our work produces value for ourselves and for others. Work is one of the main bases underpinning a great many economic and social institutions; it is a force behind industrial development, a source of social cohesion, the main activity linking people to the broader social world, and the major way by which individuals are positioned in society.

Our jobs also determine or substantially affect many critical if somewhat more subtle features of our lives, among them: how and where we live; who our friends, competitors, and adversaries are; the kinds of education our children receive; and how we define and feel about ourselves, our memberships in groups, and our relations with each other and with members of other groups. The centrality of work to society accordingly makes it an important subject for study by both social scientists and practitioners in an almost endless number of social roles. Since work touches upon key themes in all areas of life and society, it is at once something that must be understood in its own right and an explanation for many other interesting and important phenomena.

The organization of work, for example, is often used as a *dependent* variable in sociological accounts of differences among societies in their divisions of labor. Work-related correlates, such as job skills and task demands, meanwhile, are also useful *independent* variables in equations

1

targeted on explanations for myriad outcomes, from economic inequality and other dimensions of stratification to organizational performance and productivity, with stops for the attitudes and well-being of groups and individuals.

Scientists, managers, and policymakers, among others, thus study work and its correlates for many reasons that go beyond mere understanding. Some researchers seek to find work arrangements that will improve organizational effectiveness and efficiency. Others study work primarily to promote greater equality and well-being among workers. Still others find in workplaces research laboratories in which to investigate the essentially social components of a broad range of phenomena including problems in the area of mental health. And practitioners are concerned with practical problems of leadership, productivity, and human resources deployment. Although these concerns have their bases in different perspectives, their hosts all recognize the importance of work to individuals, organizations, a variety of social structures, and societies.

WORK STRUCTURES

From a sociological point of view, work is important because of the institutions, regularities, and arrangements that characterize the activity. We refer to these institutions and patterns as *work structures*. These are the rules on which many people have agreed and thus legitimated, for longer or shorter periods, as effective means of solving the economic and political problems of production and distribution. Work structures also represent the hierarchical orderings of persons and clusters of interests, configurations of norms, and the rights and obligations that characterize the relations among different types of actors in the economy. These structures describe the ways in which labor is divided, tasks allocated, and authority distributed. For example, they point to reasons why doctors' work is different from teachers' and why employers are able, with wide degrees of freedom, to hire and fire their employees.

The importance of work structures derives ultimately from the fact that they have important consequences; structures without consequences are of little interest. In this book, we focus on six major types of work structures: nation-states, industries, business organizations, occupations, classes, and unions. Of these, classes are the most problematic in terms of the precise degree to which they have clearly delineated boundaries and consequences. In general, however, our contention is that work structures, including classes, are key explanatory variables in investigations of a widely diversified array of economic, sociological, political, and psychological questions. They underlie the operation of the economy and the transactions that take place in such systems. As such, they have pervasive influence and basic effects on the individuals who must work to support themselves and others.

In addition to their effects on reality, work structures are central to many theories in the social sciences about this reality; these theories often make assumptions about "systemic imperatives" that generate, fuel, or reinforce social changes. These structural forces are often assumed, further, to affect social development regardless of the cultural dynamics present in the society. Examples of these systemic imperatives, on which we will elaborate later, include the routinization and mechanization of the labor process, trends toward increased centralization and concentration of capital, and tendencies of markets to approach one of several types of equilibrium.

Often, the analyst's motivation for studying work structures is to change them in some way. Indeed, it has been in order to alleviate the (often negative) consequences of structures that many researchers have been so interested in them. The specific type of work structure studied depends on the researcher's values and motivations for investigating the structure in the first place.

For example, management scientists often focus on those work structures that can be altered to enhance organizational effectiveness, such as the design of jobs and supervisor–subordinate relations. In contrast, many sociologists and most economists are more concerned with the macroscopic work structures that lie beyond the control of individual managers, such as national labor markets and economic policies. If these work structures are to be changed, global policies and government strategies addressed to basic social institutions (such as patterns of ownership and property rights) are required.

One way to discover the work structures that analysts see as important is to identify the key problems for which such structures are considered central explanations. Consider that the attention of considerable numbers of writers converges on questions of how work structures generate *inequalities* among individuals and jobs. Thus, they seek to explain why jobs in different occupations, organizations, and industries are differentially rewarded (issues of *positional* inequality); why individuals and groups of workers (defined, for example, in terms of their race, ethnicity, age, gender) are differentially *allocated* to these positions; and why, for example, men and women with similar levels of education and experience obtain unequal rewards in labor market transactions. The work structures we consider in this book are keys to answering these questions related to inequality. They are also important to explanations of a wide range of diverse questions related to productivity, unemployment, labor– management relations, and workers' attitudes and experiences.

The study of work structures must consider how these structures originate. We assume that the ultimate causes of work structures are the various *markets* within which exchanges take place and the political processes that determine the mix of market and nonmarket initiatives in a society. Beyond the attempt to understand their origins, it is also of critical importance to explain the ways in which structures are altered and changed, which obliges us to focus on work and industry *processes*, or the many mechanisms by which people and organizations adjust work structures so as to make them "work better." Just as the Founding Fathers designed methods for formal amendments and adjustments of the social structures and institutions "ordained and established" in the Constitution, so the legitimacy and endurance of work structures depend on the existence of mechanisms for changing them with minimal disruption. These mechanisms are generally a good deal less formal than those defining the rights and privileges of citizens and the roles of governmental units in the "law of the land." The continuing bargaining relationships between union representatives and plant managers between contract expirations are cases in point.

NEED FOR SYNTHESIS

In recent years, there has been an enormous increase in research on class, occupation, organization, industry, and union structures and their consequences for issues such as inequality, labor–management relations, productivity, and workers' attitudes and behavior. Unfortunately, potentially complementary studies have been conducted in isolation from one another; although they are useful otherwise, disciplinary boundaries have been major impediments to fuller understandings of the causes and consequences of work structures and processes. For example, studies have been conducted at many different levels and units of analysis: sociologists typically examine organizational and other work structures but have been less often concerned with why they affect individuals; industrial psychologists generally study work patterns within organizations but rarely relate them to macroscopic work structures; and economists have developed theories of the larger economy but have been less successful in explaining the relationships between economic systems and microscopic work structures and individual behavior, or in explaining short-run shifts among the balances of market forces.

The enormous diversity of phenomena related to work and industry and the rigidity of disciplinary boundaries that have impeded their understanding are reflected in the modesty of efforts to integrate studies into even a vaguely coherent framework. One major effort, involving a long, integrative statement about work structures and well over fifty separate volumes organized around the themes in the original statement, was successful in undertaking, as its architects have acknowledged, all but the concluding synthesis.[1] There have been a few promising attempts to integrate sociological and economic approaches to the study of problems of distribution, production, and consumption, particularly one by Oliver Williamson.[2] Most of these efforts have focused on macroscopic aspects of societies and economic systems, and have been less concerned with microscopic structures related to individuals and the organization of work itself. Others have studied such microscopic structures as organizations and task groups within the firm, but these studies generally neglect macroscopic structures in which organizations are embedded. In general, then, there are few[3] efforts to integrate work structures operating at multiple levels of analysis.

A thorough study of work and industry must draw upon a wide range of theoretical perspectives and value orientations. Work structures are diverse and operate at many levels of analysis: from macroscopic (economic systems) to "mezzoscopic" (occupations) to microscopic structures (jobs). Although we conceive of work structures in "macro-to-micro" terms, however, we postulate that they are not internally homogeneous segments of a whole conceived as a smoothly functioning system. Rather, they are a collection of systems with a few shared properties and many more that are *sui generis*. Thus, they can be compared with and juxtaposed with but cannot be reduced to each other, in familiar Cartesian or other classic reductionist fashions, insofar as they derive from exchange relationships. Advancing our knowledge of the correlates and consequences of these work structures requires efforts working toward syntheses of insights derived from a variety of approaches. Such syntheses are not discipline-bound but incorporate all of the units and levels of analysis involved in the organization and experience of work. While such efforts, finally, are useful in and of themselves, they are also necessary to identify lacunae

---

[1] For a brief concluding synthesis, see: John T. Dunlop, Frederick H. Harbison, Clark Kerr, and Charles Myers, *Industrialism and Industrial Man Reconsidered: Some Perspectives on a Study Over Two Decades of the Problems of Labor and Management in Economic Growth* (Princeton, N.J.: Inter-University Study of Human Resources in National Development, 1975).

[2] Oliver E. Williamson, *The Economic Institutions of Capitalism* (New York: Free Press, 1985). See also, for example, Neil J. Smelser, *The Sociology of Economic Life* (Englewood Cliffs, N.J.: Prentice-Hall, 1976); and Arthur L. Stinchcombe, *Economic Sociology* (New York: Academic Press, 1983).

[3] For one of the most notable among the exceptions, see Charles F. Sabel, *Work and Politics: The Division of Labor in Industry* (New York: Cambridge University Press, 1982).

and discontinuities, thus helping scholars to sharpen their theoretical perspectives.

AIMS OF THE BOOK

In response to the need for synthesis and practical application of research in the area of work and industry, we attempt in this book to provide a conceptual framework that draws together theory and data that inform our understanding of the key work structures and how they emerge and evolve. We illustrate the utility of our conceptualization of work structures by addressing key themes discussed in a wide range of literature. This framework provides a systematic way of studying issues related to work and industry, both within and among societies; the exercise should be a useful one to disparate researchers who share desires to understand specific correlates and consequences of work. Our perspective is primarily a sociological one, though our efforts also crosscut the disciplines of economics, history, political science, industrial relations, and social psychology. We accordingly hope that this volume will be useful not only to researchers of a variety of persuasions but to equally diversified groups of teachers, students, business managers, and practitioners.

PLAN OF THE BOOK

We organize and review the literature on work structures in Chapter 1. In Chapter 2, we present the conceptual framework that guides our discussion in the rest of the book. We outline how work structures are interrelated, how they derive from markets, and the processes by which they change. In Chapter 3, we examine what it is about work structures that makes a difference for outcomes of both practical and theoretical interest. We review key studies of these correlates and present some data to help us understand them better. In Chapters 4 and 5, we consider a variety of consequences produced by work structures: labor market outcomes such as income inequality, careers, and mobility; and labor force outcomes such as work attitudes, work-related behavior, and jobs and skills.

In Chapter 6, we focus on how work structures *change*. Here we consider the role of the state and several distinct eras in American history in a discussion illustrating how, within each period, markets, structures, and processes were interrelated, with special emphases on evolving rules governing the ownership and disposition of property. The final chapter underscores the interdependence among structures, markets, and processes.

CHAPTER 1

RESEARCH ON WORK STRUCTURES

Research on the correlates and consequences of work structures is broad and diffuse, ranging from studies of diverse work settings and their societal and other macroscopic contexts to small work groups, their members, and their members' and leaders' ways and means. In this first chapter, we review studies related to work structures found in various disciplines. We classify these studies by their authors' assumptions about work structures and the processes to which they give rise. A look at the kinds of issues that preoccupy archetypal writers, including what they do and do not regard as problematic, affords us insights into the perspectives from which they view work structures. A discussion of past research thus sets the stage for the next chapter in which we outline our own perspective on work structures in the expectation that the resulting juxtapositions will be instructive.

There are three major approaches to the study of work structures. One tradition does not view work structures as necessary to explain anything at all even though its adherents make assumptions about a number of them as they take them as given in their analyses. This tradition simply postulates one or more of the structures of concern to us as if explanations would not be relevant to analyses of the phenomena they investigate. Studies that do not regard work structures as problematic are discussed here mainly as a point of departure, since we are explicitly concerned with the nature of work structures and their outcomes.

Adherents of a second tradition typically focus on one of our specific work structures and assume that the one specified is the key to explaining the consequences that interest them. Our review of past research will suggest several especially interesting types of work structures—nation-states, industries, firms, occupations, classes, and unions—that can be regarded as embodying several suggestive "general orientations" or loose-knit sets of concepts that help one to integrate much of the literature on work and industry.

The third approach explicitly recognizes the multidimensionality of work structures and investigates their relationships to each other, to markets, and thereby to important consequences. This is the perspective, not often explicitly delineated, upon which we attempt to elaborate and concretize in this book. We discuss each of these three approaches in turn.

WORK STRUCTURES AS "GIVENS"

The first group's labors consist of studies of work, employment, productivity, worker well-being, stratification, and related topics in which our structures figure only implicitly and, as we have noted, are taken as "givens." These authors do not generally assert, in so many words, that work structures are "uncaused" causes. Rather, they simply gainsay the matter almost entirely. Hence, the work structures in which these investigators' phenomena are embedded are not themselves subjected to analysis; they are assumed, moreover, to be constant in their configurations, and differences produced by them in the phenomena under study are ignored. Although these researchers would quickly allow that larger structures may indeed affect outcomes of interest, they assume, *for purposes of their analyses,* that they do not do so. Examples of this approach are found in a variety of disciplines, including economics, sociology, and industrial psychology. The assumption was promoted by its devotees from its estate as a Cartesian metaphor by skipping the acknowledgment of a gratuitous assumption in favor of using a blanket and poetic Latin phrase: *ceteris paribus.* Descartes' philosophical competitors—Galileo, Newton, Mill, and Locke, among them—proposed analagous "reductionist" metaphors, all of which have found their way into explanatory social science theories. In each instance the metaphors have remained reductionist in their essence.

Neoclassical Economics

Most studies by neoclassical economists fall into this group. Neoclassical economic theory,[1] for example, makes a number of key as-

---

[1] See the summary of orthodox and neoclassical economic theories in David M. Gordon, *Theories of Poverty and Underemployment* (Lexington, Mass.: D. C. Heath, 1972). Also, the assumptions of neoclassical economic theory with regard to labor markets are reviewed in Arne L. Kalleberg and Aage B. Sørensen, "The Sociology of Labor Markets," *Annual Review of Sociology* 5 (1979): 351–79.

sumptions about simplicity and universality of labor market mechanisms, such as that: institutional contexts are constant; labor markets are essentially competitive even over short-run periods; workers and employers have adequate information about market conditions; and each party is unable individually to influence the prices of either labor "inputs" or "outputs" it confronts in the market. They posit further that wages respond to changes in supply and demand and that workers can move freely in response to these changes in different sectors or segments of the market. These assumptions have been relaxed by some neoclassical economists who explicitly take into account barriers to competition, inadequate information, and other "imperfections" that inhibit or substantially block the operation of competitive markets. However, although these neoclassical economists may allow for the influences of these market constraints, they take the *structure* of the labor market as given; it is not usually a subject of inquiry. Thus, with few exceptions, economic actors are assumed to make choices within preexisting and unchanging work structures. Chicago's Gary Becker sums it up well in a definition of what he calls the market paradigm: "The combined assumptions of maximizing behavior, market equilibrium, and stable preferences, used relentlessly and unflinchingly, form the heart of the economic approach."[2]

That work structures are often assumed to be constant for reasons of convenience is illustrated in the theory developed by John Maynard Keynes. Smelser summarizes:[3]

> In constructing his equilibrium system, Keynes considered several things as given: the existing skill of the labor force, the existing equipment, the existing technology, the existing degree of competition, the existing tastes of the consumer, the existing attitudes of people toward work, and the existing social structure. All these, if they varied, would affect the independent variables (e.g., the propensity to consume and the marginal efficiency of capital) and through them the dependent variables (employment and national income); but they were assumed not to vary.

---

[2] Cited in Victor Fuchs, *How We Live* (Cambridge: Harvard University Press, 1983), 10. There are, of course, a few notable exceptions among essentially neo-orthodox economists who may be identified with the teachings, in the United States, of John Dunlop. See, for example, Peter Doeringer and Michael Piore, *Internal Labor Markets and Manpower Analysis* (Lexington, Mass.: D. C. Heath, 1971). For useful and recent discussions of the adjustments of economists of different persuasions to the specifics of an overarching theoretical apparatus, see also Lester C. Thurow, *Dangerous Currents: The State of Economics* (New York: Random House, 1983; Introduction and Chapters 1 and 8); and E. J. Mishan, *What Political Economy Is All About* (Cambridge: Cambridge University Press, 1982). More generally, see Robert Lekachman, *The Age of Keynes* (New York: Random House, 1966) and Sidney Weintrub, ed., *Modern Economic Thought* (Philadelphia: University of Pennsylvania Press, 1977).
[3] Smelser, 33.

Status Attainment Sociologists

Some sociologists in the "status attainment" tradition of Blau and Duncan,[4] especially those who seek to explain the way in which incomes are distributed among a population's members, treat the structure of occupations as given and thus afford us another illustration of this general approach. Status attainment researchers assume that occupations differ in their levels of prestige or status reflecting in turn their importance to the functioning of a modern economy. However, the occupational structure itself and the functional significance of its constituent occupations are taken as given, not as subjects of inquiry. As in the case of neo-orthodox economics, there is a hint—more or less faint, depending on the investigator—that what is given (and thus functional) is also a desirable state of affairs: xyz is "good" because it works and it works because it is "good."

While the aforementioned sociologists often take the occupational structure of prestige or status as given, their interpretations of this structure are scientifically attractive, in part, because they are consistent with a variety of alternative theoretical frameworks. One such interpretation, as we have just noted, is the functional one, according to which status or prestige differences among occupations reflect variations in supply and demand as well as the real socioeconomic significance of occupational activities. The status attainment model is also consistent, though, with a much less benign view of social organization, a view favoring conflict explanations of occupational inequality. In this second view, power considerations figure more prominently in determining levels of prestige or status than imputations of a social consensus to passive populations who only appear to view the prestige of a given stratum with equanimity.

Regardless of how one accounts for the effects of occupational status or prestige, the key reason why we classify status attainment researchers in this first group is that they are disposed to assume that there are no discontinuities in the social and institutional arrangements in accord with which people are allocated among distinct labor markets. Like most economists, these sociologists often assume that inequality is generated in national competitive markets the attributes of which are left to others to limn.

---

[4] Key studies in this tradition include: Peter M. Blau and Otis Dudley Duncan, *The American Occupational Structure* (New York: John Wiley, 1967); William H. Sewell and Robert M. Hauser, *Education, Occupation, and Earnings: Achievement in the Early Career* (New York: Academic Press, 1975); and David L. Featherman and Robert M. Hauser, *Opportunity and Change* (New York: Academic Press, 1978).

The educational achievements of labor force participants, for example, are assumed to affect their occupational attainments and the income inequalities characteristic thereof in the same ways in all of the several labor markets of which they are members. The assumption is a grossly oversimplified one, a fact that becomes clear when we recall the considerable differences between the roles of formal schooling in the preparation of professionals in the health industry, the National Basketball Association and the National Football League, the American Bar Association, and the professionals (indeed!) whose talents assure millions of air passengers that wide-bodied jet aircraft are properly serviced and maintained.

Despite our characterization of status attainment researchers as treating work structures as "given," we recognize that this tradition is a diverse one, and that the line between these writers and those we term "structural" sociologists is often blurred. For example, some status attainment researchers arguably could be categorized as representing the univariate occupational approach (discussed later) since they investigate occupational differences in earnings and other labor market outcomes. Moreover, many of the "new structuralists" in sociology, who we shall also discuss, have built on and extended the status attainment approach in what some representatives of this tradition might consider to be straightforward ways.

Industrial Psychologists

Industrial psychologists also take work structures as given.[5] Although these scientists have contributed to our understanding of work in many ways, they often investigate workers and jobs at such a microscopic level of analysis that they totally ignore the broader structures that can indeed produce differences in work and work experiences; these structures are neglected in emphases on explanatory variables—task assignments, work groups' norms, supervisory practices—that are organic to a particular work setting. Others ignore the impact of work structures entirely and assume that workers' reactions to their jobs depend exclusively on their personality characteristics.

The Problematic Qualities of Structures

Researchers who gainsay the utility of taking explicit account of work structures cannot thereby deny that they make implicit assumptions about

---

[5] See, for example, Victor H. Vroom, *Work and Motivation* (New York: John Wiley, 1964); and the articles, generally, in the *Journal of Applied Psychology* and *Personnel Psychology*.

them. The traditions we have just discussed all tend to neglect work structures, regarding them as unproblematic; yet questions about the structural differences that their adherents beg must be addressed in any sensible evaluation of the results they report. As we noted a moment ago, human capital and status attainment researchers, who share views about the roles of education and training, often assume that all workers are rewarded in competitive national labor markets. This view of the labor market has been shown to be problematic in several significant respects: the earnings paid to workers on the basis of their educational achievements and their work experiences, for example, differ among diverse occupational and organizational labor markets.[6] Army and Navy nurses earn considerably more than similarly educated, trained, and experienced nurses at civilian hospitals in Utah, Wyoming, and Mississippi; pilots who flew together in Korea earn different salaries depending on whether they fly intrastate or for national airlines; and university secretaries earn less than secretaries in business "fronts" run by organized crime.

Important discontinuities in the characteristics of different subsets of the national labor market constitute puzzles for the first approach and thus signal a need to investigate these work structures with an eye to differences among them. Indeed, solving these puzzles has been a major impetus to much recent research on work structures using the two other approaches we have identified. Although we recognize this consequence with some satisfaction, it is one of our aims to juxtapose and, where possible, to articulate findings of researchers who use data relevant to different analytical levels without much thought to the work of investigators at other higher or lower levels. Therefore our discussion of these structures will have considerable relevance for critical readings of the work of neoclassical economists, status attainment researchers, and industrial psychologists not less than for readers, otherwise, who seek to understand the utilities of research on work and industry.

UNIVARIATE STRUCTURALISTS

Univariate structuralists, as we may call them, differ from the first group in that they do regard structures as problematic, not as given. A diversified group, its members have in common a focus on one or another

---

[6] See, for example, Ross M. Stolzenberg, "Occupations, Labor Markets and the Process of Wage Attainment," *American Sociological Review* 40 (1975): 645–65; and Paul Osterman, "An Empirical Study of Labor Market Segmentation," *Industrial and Labor Relations Review* 28 (1975): 508–23.

work structure, and they examine the determinants and consequences of this structure to the virtual exclusion of others. We refer to members of this group as "univariate structuralists" because they assume that the logics associated with their favored structure afford the one best way to conceptualize and understand problems related to work and industry.

Although univariate structuralists may postulate the existence and potential importance of work structures other than those that preoccupy them, their disposition is to consider them to be substantially less important than the particular structure upon which they focus. If they do not entirely forsake other apparently relevant structures, moreover, writers in this group generally regard them as derivatives of their own more significant work structure. Our terminology is intended to contrast this approach with the next; our use of the term univariate does not necessarily imply that we consider a particular writer to be guilty of the most simple-minded form of reductionist tendencies.

The structures emphasized or neglected by particular univariate structuralists in part reflect basic assumptions underlying entire disciplines and shared by its members, however pluralistic they may be in the detailed execution of their investigations and however catholic they are about which independent and dependent variables should be chosen for study.

Beyond the choices favored by a given discipline overall, investigators' emphases on particular structures and variables also reflect the diversity of analytic frameworks *within* a discipline as well as researchers' motivations for studying some work structures while ignoring others.

Univariate structuralists conceive of their work structures in ways that convert them into general orientations, or cognitive devices that suggest ways of relating one set of phenomena to another. As such, the work structures are *paradigms* in Kuhn's narrow sense,[7] that is, exemplars or analogies that scientists apply to the phenomena they address in solving such puzzles as why some people earn more money than others. In the broad sociological sense, then, work structures reflect assumptions rooted in the entire constellation of beliefs, values, and techniques shared by members of a particular scientific community.

Two examples of such global paradigms are orthodox or, more commonly, "neo-orthodox" economic theory and Marxist radical theory, a theory with its own orthodoxies. Some of the differences in assumptions about the key work structure are accordingly rooted in broader paradigm conflicts. Such is generally the case in scientific research: the selection of one approach over another depends on a researcher's paradigmatic

---

[7] See Gordon (1972).

assumptions. Although paradigmatic tensions are more problematic in the social, as compared to the physical, sciences, given the plethora of multiple and often competing theories and the often unexamined values embodied in paradigms,[8] the social science community has no monopoly in the matter. Thus, there have been stirrings about the gains and losses in natural science research of dedication to Cartesian versus dialectical models.

In the study of work and industry, the choice between competing paradigms often comes down to whether the researcher assumes, as an important example, that classes or organizations are the key decision-making units in a society.[9] The "class" and "organization" paradigms have their roots in different intellectual traditions, Marxian and Weberian; these traditions also differ in their assumptions about who are the key actors in society as well as about which questions are important to study. Class analysts tend to focus on the societal and historical correlates of class relations in society, whereas organizational analysts generally confine their attention to the workings of specific organizations, to their intramural properties, and, thereafter, to interorganizational comparisons among them, holding one or more properties—size or age, for example—constant.

Often, this commitment to a particular work structure has a fairly prominent ideological underpinning; many of these writers are concerned with promoting the political power of one or another interest group or answering key problems as defined by their personal political orientations. Thus, fiscal stimuli aiding business corporations may be regarded as social investment or social welfare, as can aid directed toward minority youth, depending upon one's political values.

In addition to theoretical issues, the choice of one univariate structural approach over another is also predicated on the values and needs of the sponsors of the research. Audiences and clients influence in part one's range of vision: whether one is concerned with examining (and shaping) macroscopic work systems; or is trying to explain (and alter) specific microscopic structures within one or more workplaces.

Much research by univariate structuralists consists of studies of disaggregated data often taking the form of detailed case studies. These provide us with some of the richest and most insightful extant interpretations of work structures available to aspiring synthesizers. However,

---

[8] On the multiparadigmatic nature of social science research, see Robert K. Merton, *Social Theory and Social Structure* (New York: Free Press, 1957).

[9] See Kenneth Westhues, "Class and Organization as Paradigms in Social Science," *American Sociologist* 11 (1976): 38–49.

unlike the multivariate structuralists (see below), univariate structuralists compare work structures in an "intramurally comparative" way: for example, unions are compared to other unions and companies to other companies. Univariate structuralists generally do not compare different work structures, say, unions to business organizations. Indeed, James R. Hoffa, one of the more astute among lay analysts of organizations, offended industrial relationists not less than fellow trade unionists with his ubiquitous use of the term "this union business" to describe a sector in which he was an influential manager.

The studies we classify in the univariate structural tradition are heterogeneous, reflecting the wide range of structures that apparently influence the nature of work and industry and the social relationships among the many actors in innumerably different types of organizations. As we hinted in our introduction, this literature may be reviewed by considering several major types of work structures: classes, occupations, organizations, and industries. These four types of structures have attributes and histories that allow us to treat them as component parts of a variety of social systems around which integrating concepts can be specified such that we can stitch together many of the different strands in the univariate structural approach.

Univariate Class Approach

One prominent group among those we classify as univariate structuralists includes those Marxists who are primarily interested in *class* as an overarching structure. Studies by self-styled radical economists and sociologists have stressed the role of class-linked strengths and weaknesses of a variety of aggregations of persons (and the organizations and sectors in which they operate) in efforts to assay the circumstances of class members' power, status, and ability to take economic and other initiatives. These studies generally assume that class is the fundamental work structure, that it is theoretically prior to the others. Indeed, they tend to assume that class forms the context within which the other work structures take on meaning.

The univariate class approach in its current incarnation is most clearly illustrated by the work of Erik Olin Wright,[10] who defines *class* in a putatively objective, structural sense: class relations are the social relations between those who exercise significant control over money and over

---

[10] See, for instance, Erik Olin Wright, *Class Structure and Income Determination* (New York: Academic Press, 1979); and "Class and Occupation," *Theory and Society* 9 (1980): 177–214.

physical and human capital, on the one hand, and those who do not, on the other.

Wright argues that relations of control, or class, are different from those among persons in different occupational positions. Consistent with a univariate structural approach, he further assumes that there is a causal relationship between the two, so that the correlates of technical activities (occupations), both behavioral and attitudinal, are determined by control or class relations. Occupation and class may compete as bases of organization for the loyalty of workers, but Wright views the organization of workers along bases other than class, defined either by workers themselves or by social science analysts, as forms of "false consciousness," since they inhibit class formation by distracting workers, for example, from their shared interests across many occupations. Workers thus distracted, meanwhile, are tractable adversaries; that is to say, they are amenable to the overtures of their employers with interests in protecting the particular industries in which they manage.

Univariate Occupation Approach

Most sociologists regard *occupations*, not classes, as the key work structure responsible for many work-related consequences. One group of sociologists has extended the status attainment tradition by investigating why occupations differ in the levels of prestige and status accorded them in a variety of surveys.[11] Their explanations of why occupations differ in status and prestige are closely related to those of stratification researchers that seek to account for inequalities in the economic system.

The univariate occupational approach is well illustrated in the results of a long-term research program directed by Melvin Kohn and his associates at the National Institutes of Mental Health.[12] From a large number of job conditions, Kohn defines several as forming the "structural imperatives" of work, which generally affect the psychological functioning of job holders. We classify Kohn and his associates as "occupational structuralists" since, in marked contrast to the neo-Marxists' emphasis on class, they tend to view all work structures as basically deriving from the occupational structure. Thus, Kohn subsumes under the term *oc-*

---

[11] For example, William T. Bielby and Arne L. Kalleberg, "The Structure of Occupational Inequality," *Quality and Quantity* 15 (1981): 125–50; Paul M. Siegel, "The American Occupational Prestige Structure," (Unpublished Ph.D. dissertation, University of Chicago, 1971).

[12] This research is summarized in Melvin L. Kohn and Carmi Schooler, *Work and Personality: An Inquiry into the Impact of Social Stratification* (Norwood, N.J.: Ablex, 1983).

cupational conditions such diverse work structures as the control over the products of one's labor (i.e., ownership and hierarchical position) and control over the nature of one's work activity (i.e., the closeness of supervision, the degree to which the work is routinized, and the substantive complexity of tasks).

Equating all structural imperatives of work with occupational structure is not a great deal less problematic than equating them with class: the degree of substantive complexity and, even more markedly, the closeness of supervision and routinization are structured within *organizations*; occupations in different organizations differ in their levels of self-direction.

Consider that physicians' practices in proprietary hospitals are far more constrained than those in the not-for-profit sector; that clerical workers in large private universities often receive lower salaries but enjoy far more egalitarian relationships with those they serve than do clericals in corporations of similar size in proximal labor markets; and that some quarterbacks "call their own game," while others' signals at the line of scrimmage are programmed from the bench by the Paul Browns and Tom Landrys in the sprawling sports industry. Moreover, control over the product of one's labor often reflects one's class rather than solely one's occupational position *per se*. Thus, the tax vulnerabilities of capitalists are very different from those of operatives and kindred workers; these differences reflect differences in the degree to which capitalists, as a group, can lobby for sundry "tax breaks."

Univariate Organization Approach

Organizations are key work structures because they are the sites within which work is actually performed and directly rewarded. The structural tradition of comparative organizational analysis illustrates a univariate organizational approach. These students of organization focus on the importance of one or more attributes of organizations for understanding the nature, correlates, and consequences of work. Yet, most such analysts view organizations as virtually closed systems: they measure organizational properties and, believing that their interrelations are important for defining organizational forms and consequences, develop theories of how they are related to each other and to the attitudes and behavior of organizations' members. [13]

This approach to organizational analysis has been criticized by "open systems" writers, who argue that understandings of organizational struc-

---

[13] For example, Jerald Hage, "An Axiomatic Theory of Organizations," *Administrative Science Quarterly* 10 (December 1965): 289–320.

tures and of activities therein require very serious and systematic consideration of *other* kinds of structures as well, especially those operating in the environments of organizations. This critique invites the juxtaposition of studies of organizations and their members with investigations of other work structures, such as classes, occupations, industries, and unions; a highly skilled employee in a steel mill over even relatively short periods of time will see himself alternately as a member of a work crew protected by work rules, as a member of that large segment of the working class victimized by Japan's ever-rising exports, and as a skilled worker chary of the union activities of unskilled co-workers bent on improving their economic lot.

Univariate Industry Approach

Another cluster of univariate structuralists focuses on *industries* as key explanations of a variety of social phenomena. For example, labor economists have frequently studied the correlates of industries, such as their size, competitive character, and modes of technology.[14] They view these industrial structures as indicators of, among other things, societal "development," and an industry's performance.

A clearer example of a univariate industrial approach is provided by Blauner,[15] who argues that the "industry a man works in is *fateful* [i.e., dispositive] because the conditions of work and existence in various industrial environments are quite different." He goes on to say that "an employee's industry decides the nature of the work he performs eight hours a day." This, in effect, equates all work structures with industry structures, an overly simplified assumption because differences in the division of labor and the nature of work are often heavily influenced, as we noted in the previous section, by *organizational* differences.

Indeed, work arrangements of many different types may vary more within industries than among them, as the United Auto Workers Union has been obliged to recognize in auto companies in the United States designed by Japanese as contrasted with those of American owners.

These four examples of univariate structural traditions—based on class, occupation, organization, and industry—have greatly increased our knowledge of the correlates and consequences of these work structures. However, it is clear that more satisfying explanations of a variety of

---

[14] For example, Richard Caves, *American Industry: Structure, Conduct, Performance* (Englewood Cliffs, N.J: Prentice-Hall, 1967); and Leonard Weiss, *Case Studies in American Industry* (New York: John Wiley, 1967).

[15] Robert Blauner, *Alienation and Freedom: The Factory Worker and His Industry* (Chicago: University of Chicago Press, 1964), 166.

phenomena relating to work structures require an *integration* of the more specialized research results to which we have alluded. For example, using the term *occupation* to refer to the specific ways in which jobs are structured within organizations, as well as to strategic dimensions of class such as claims to resource ownership, masks important differences produced, in distinguishable ways, by these diverse work structures. The issue is by no means simply a semantic one: it reflects basic assumptions about how work is structured, how data on these structures should be collected, and, in turn, how the data should be interpreted when issues pertaining to cause and effect are examined. Integrating the insights provided by these almost radically disparate univariate structural approaches is a key problem for the third of the general perspectives on work and industry, the "multivariate structural" approach.

MULTIVARIATE STRUCTURALISTS

Multivariate structuralists are superficially similar to the univariate structuralists in that they do not take work structures as givens but as objects of inquiry; both view work structures as "social technologies" invented by human architects more or less according to a plan.[16] However, unlike those in the univariate group, multivariate structuralists explicitly posit the existence of *multiple* structures and levels of analysis and seek to *integrate* them in accounting for the nature and consequences of work.

Although diverse in many particulars, studies by multivariate structuralists are tied together by several common threads. For example, these writers are "extramurally comparative" in their explicit concerns with the relationships between different types of work structures across multiple levels of analysis (e.g., unions and business firms, occupations and classes). They differ, however, in both the number and types of work structures they consider. Some study all of the work structures we discuss in this book (nation-states, occupations, industries, organizations, classes, and unions). Others focus on only two work structures, such as occupations and classes, unions and companies, industries and organizations, or industries and occupations.

---

[16] The qualification "more or less" is used to leave abundant room for both structures that are very deliberately designed by managers (see Alfred P. Sloan, *My Years with General Motors* [New York: MacFadden-Bartell, 1965]) and those that are often regarded as unplanned or "informal" as in the case of human relationists who, since the days of Harvard Business School investigations at Western Electric (see, for example, Fritz J. Roethlisberger and William J. Dickson, *Management and the Worker* [Cambridge, Mass.: Harvard University Press, 1939]), have stressed the structures invented by workers to flesh out, or subvert, "formal organizations" designed by managers.

Multivariate structuralists are also more inclined to try to integrate insights from both economics and sociology in order to account for work structures. The extension of renewed dialogues between some of the leading members of the two professions can in part be traced to the growing recognition that neither group could ignore the substantial unexplained variance, the so-called residuals, in their separate efforts to account for differences in the growth rates among the economies in both the less well and better developed nations. Since the two groups' studies are informed by rather different conceptions of growth factors and of the prerequisites for industrialization, this new dialogue has been a lively one.

The multivariate approach that we outline in the next chapter grows out of several distinct research traditions. Before we elaborate, we pause to identify the key perspectives that have most informed our own. Despite the risks of oversimplification, we find it useful to consider several distinct multivariate research traditions: the new institutionalists, the new economic historians, comparative researchers, and the new structuralists in sociology.

New Institutionalists

We use the general term "new institutionalists" to refer to a variety of related economists, sociologists, industrial relations specialists, and, not least, legal scholars who focus on the impact of institutional realities on the nature of work and industry. In many cases, they are the intellectual descendants of the economic institutionalists of the pre–World War II era. The scholarly interests of these earlier institutionalists, and of economic historians more generally, dropped well down on the priorities list of professional economists, as a group, as econometric modeling, applicable to both macroeconomic and microeconomic problems, gained growing favor in the period following World War II. Indeed, older, more institutional, behavioral and historical concerns were essentially displaced by purely theoretical and econometric interests.

As economists bypassed older institutionalist interests, sociologists and economists who once had large areas of overlapping interests virtually parted company.[17] They had few common interests until a fair number

---

[17] One leading department, at Princeton, actually housed both disciplines until the principals separated in the late 1940s. That is, they divided their labors between departments informed by marginalist and neo-orthodox theory, on the one side, and by theories emerging from studies concerned with behavioral and managerialist phenomena, on the other. For a revisit to the scene of the "Second Battle of Princeton," see Fritz Machlup's Presidential Address to the American Economic Association: "Theories of the Firm: Marginalist, Behavioral, Managerial,"*American Economic Review* 57 (March 1967): 1–23.

of them "reconvened," in the 1960s, in connection with interrelated studies of poverty, income distribution, demographic changes and labor force attributes, the statics and dynamics of mobility, and especially in connection with studies beginning in the late 1950s of the socioeconomic correlates of education.

The earlier period, in which many interests had brought them together, essentially ended with the expiration, in 1941, of the Congressional mandate afforded to the Temporary National Economic Committee. Although Walter Adams and his associates have published six updated editions of a classic, *The Structure of American Industry* (1950–1982), the volume of studies of what Adams describes as "the economic power relations in society" by economists has been steadily declining in favor of technical economic studies of industrial organization.[18]

The limitations of these impressive technical studies by economists became clearer to intimidated social scientists when they were exposed to the earliest formal effort (by a sociologist, James Abegglen), to understand Japan's postwar recovery. His study, *The Japanese Factory* (1958), made not one mention of economic methods; yet many of his conclusions have been sustained by dozens of later studies of the continuing Japanese "miracle." In contrast, not one pure economic analysis, prior to Denison's 1962[19] study of the role of differential investments in education in explaining differentials in the national growth rates of developed countries, has enjoyed such sustained support. Indeed, warnings by institutionalist Gunnar Myrdal that his colleagues were misadvising the Third World with their emphases on industrialization over agriculture in 1968 were virtually ignored until 1982.[20] It was his argument that heavy industries required social bases that were not part of the Third World's political economies.

The significance of a reemergence of an institutionalist approach in sociology (the names of Domhoff, Useem, Mizruchi, and S. M. Miller— the latter once in the combined department at Princeton—come readily to mind) to would-be synthesizers in which the legal, social, political, and economic dimensions of structures and markets are of concern has been

---

[18] See Walter Adams, ed., *The Structure of American Industry*, 6th ed. (New York: Macmillan, 1982). The best summaries of a highly technical literature on industrial organization (market structures, concentration, and the like) are in F. M. Scherer, *Industrial Market Structure and Performance* (Chicago: Rand McNally, 1980) and, more briefly, in Caves.

[19] Edward F. Denison, *The Sources of Economic Growth in the United States* (New York: Committee on Economic Development, 1962).

[20] Gunnar Myrdal, *Asian Drama: An Inquiry into the Poverty of Nations*, Vol. 1 (New York: Pantheon, 1968), 5–126.

considerable.[21] The boldest statement of this approach is Lindblom's *Politics and Markets* (1977). The most detailed empirically informed statements appear in two works by I. Adelman and C. T. Morris, *Economic Growth and Social Equity in Developing Countries* (1973) and *Society, Politics and Economic Development* (1971).[22]

Another institutionalist tradition includes many of the most prominent students of industrial relations. This research tradition can be readily identified with the work of the intellectual descendents, fairly directly, of the "Wisconsin School" of John R. Commons and, after World War II, the work of Sumner Slichter and even more directly of John Dunlop, the latter before, while, and after he had trained several of America's most notable contemporary labor economists. Dunlop and his leading students, Michael Piore in particular, have long questioned narrow, neo-orthodox economic conceptions of wage determination in favor of examinations of the labor market not as a single market but as congeries of smaller subsets of fairly distinct systems.

Still another distinct institutionalist tradition is organized more around legal philosophy than around data. These writers, from the outset, were lawyers as well as social historians but have been joined by economists and political scientists. Examples of lawyers are Max Weber and Thurman Arnold (the New Deal "trustbuster") in an earlier day; Adolf A. Berle for many years; Judge David Bazelon; and in recent times Ralph Nader, Michael Pertschuk, Christopher Stone, Edwin Epstein, and Paul Blumberg. Among political scientists one can include Theodore Lowi, Robert Dahl, Andrew Hacker, and Robert Lane.

There are also a small number of analyses specifically focused on the implications of the differences, under the law, between *corporate persons* and *natural persons*. The critical importance of this distinction for our purposes inheres in the fact that we live in, work in, and study what James Coleman calls an "asymmetric" society; as Andrew Hacker once put it, a large corporation may be likened to "an elephant dancing among the chickens."

The implications of this asymmetry vary in both qualitative and quan-

---

[21] In economics, for example, from Karl Marx, Thorstein Veblen, Paul Sweezy, Paul Baran, Robert A. Brady, Franz Neumann, and Thomas Cochran to John Kenneth Galbraith, Barry Bluestone, and Bennett Harrison, Charles Lindblom, Neil Chamberlain, John Dunlop, Willard F. Mueller, Douglas Dowd, and Robert Reich. In law, from Max Weber, John P. Davis, Adolf A. Berle, and Thurman Arnold to Christopher Stone. In political science, Robert Dahl, Theodore Lowi, Robert Engler.

[22] Charles Lindblom, *Politics and Markets* (New York: Basic Books, 1977); Irma Adelman and Cynthia T. Morris, *Economic Growth and Social Equity in Developing Countries* (Stanford, Cal.: Stanford University Press, 1973); and *Society, Politics and Economic Development* (Baltimore: Johns Hopkins Press, 1971).

titative terms across work structures and markets. Stockholders, for example, become corporate *personae fictae* but, as laws requiring unions to be democratic suggest, organized workers are individual persons. Since *Commonwealth v. Hunt*, 1842, these organized workers are no longer illegal conspirators against corporate persons, but we strive to secure unionists' rights as persons in ways we scarcely think of applying to stockholders. Furthermore, whereas workers, organized or not, have had to deal with corporate persons virtually from the beginning, corporations were not obliged, legally, actually to deal with workers' representatives, that is, to bargain with them in good faith, until 1935, with the passage of the National Labor Relations Act. The implications for employees operating in both manufacturing product and in labor markets are not exactly elusive, deriving as they do from a situation in which corporate persons are quite clearly "more equal" than natural persons. The most thorough and suggestive modern rehearsal of the issues attaching to the asymmetry may be found in James Coleman's *The Asymmetrical Society*.[23]

New Economic Historians

A second research tradition contributing to modest orders of reunification among sociologists and economists has been sparked by the rapid maturation, in theoretical, methodological, and empirical terms, of what is called the *new economic history*. The new economic historians have many of the instincts of the earlier generation of institutionalists in both disciplines, but they are equipped as well with the skills of macroeconomists and microeconomists, with controls over modern statistical techniques, and with the staples of economic theory. They are also in possession of considerable knowledge of history, *per se*, and they have thus been able to pick up almost precisely where the institutionalists of other days left off.

The interests of these new players have especially been with the history of trade, regulation (and public policy otherwise), finance, economic and industrial organization, and the role of the state.[24] They have also been deeply occupied with shifts in the patterns of economic transactions between the United States and other nations; with demographic changes in the American population, both "imported" and "homegrown"; and with the monetary, fiscal, and other "macro-policy" initiatives of government.

---

[23] James S. Coleman, *The Asymmetrical Society* (Syracuse: Syracuse University Press, 1982).

[24] For a neo-orthodox argument of how much more significant "private sector" initiatives have been to United States growth than state interventions, see Douglas C. North, *Structure and Change in Economic History* (New York: Norton, 1981).

Two major foci of their attentions have thus been on the development of different types of markets in the American economy—their growth, evolving structures, and, related to markets, the distribution of wealth and income and the evolution of private strategies and public policies that have affected American markets along social, political, and economic dimensions.[25] One of these economic historians, Douglas North, specifically and pointedly emphasizes the roles of institutions and of ideologies in a book that has inventively reunited economic and noneconomic approaches to the study of national economies.[26] We will draw heavily on his work in Chapter 6.

In addition to these self-conscious new economic historians, a small number of more conventional economists—those less given to the study of history *per se* but identifiable as of a distinct tradition—have put up a kind of rearview mirror to the *recent* past. Their purpose in these efforts has been better to fathom watershed periods during which the simultaneity of an array of critical social, economic, and political events effectively knocked many a carefully drawn forecast into a cocked hat. One of their principal aims has been to improve the predictive powers of massive numbers of equations describing complex modern economic systems. Thus, Otto Eckstein, a leading econometrician, revisited the years from 1974 to 1975, when "the world economy passed through its most dangerous adventure since the 1930s,"[27] in an illuminatingly illustrative analysis to which we will return in Chapter 6.

These students of the recent past afford substantial statistical support for the view that there is much to be learned about industrial society by examining quantitatively the interactions among developments in diverse markets, on one side, and the evolving structures, macro and micro (the state, classes, industries, firms, and unions) on the other. It is in these structures that the prospective benefits and costs of a variety of judgments are calculated and revised and more or less on the basis of which, thereafter, consequential decisions are made. The effects of these decisions may sometimes be to change the structures, to seek to "reorder" the markets, or to redraw the terms of the transactions among structures or markets, or all of these. The effects of these decisions may at other times

---

[25] For a brilliantly conceived and beautifully written overview of American economic history informed by the best of studies in the so-called new economic history, see S. P. Lee and P. Passell, *A New Economic View of American History* (New York: W. W. Norton, 1979), currently in its fourth printing. Although a rash of new economic history writings on discrete historical-economic issues have appeared since its publication, this volume displays the lively new tradition *per se* in a very effective fashion.

[26] North.

[27] Otto Eckstein, *The Great Recession with a Postscript on Stagflation* (Amsterdam and New York: North Holland, 1979).

be to seek, by legislation, the redirection of regulatory measures or the income and wealth redistributive policies and programs of the state.

Comparative Analyses

A third example of a multivariate research tradition is provided by cross-national studies of differences in work and industry. A major early example of a comparative multivariate structuralist approach is the cross-national studies of Clark Kerr, John Dunlop, and their associates.[28] Their research was motivated by problems related to the recruitment and commitment of labor forces to industrial life, patterns of worker protest in the course of economic development, and the impacts on work structures of the policies and practices of management and the state. They used the terms *industrialism* and *industrialization* as unifying concepts in order to develop a theoretical framework capable of embracing a range of historical experiences over time and space. Despite the considerable diversity that exists among industrial nations in the correlates and consequences of work structures, their studies showed that there is a "logic" of industrialization such that industrial societies are more like each other than they, any one of them, are similar to preindustrial societies. In the course of their research, these institutional economists examined all of the work structures we discuss in this book. In particular, they studied cross-national differences in the nature of industries, occupations, organizations, unions, and classes, and they took considerable account of variations in the roles of nation-states in the economy.

A recent comparative effort by Charles Sabel[29] offers a model that very nearly conforms to our own, and his synthesis incorporates all of the work structures we consider in this volume. He attempts to develop a historical and comparative sociology of workplace relations in industrial capitalist societies by focusing on why skilled, semiskilled, and unskilled workers sometimes—and briefly—unite while they are otherwise in conflict. He argues that markets generate different types of investment strategies that lead employers to create different kinds of jobs. Markets themselves result from extraeconomic developments such as political choices made by governments and nation-states. In general, he finds that differences in work structures among the United States, United Kingdom, Germany, France, and Italy are produced both by the exigencies of in-

[28] See, for example, Clark Kerr, John T. Dunlop, Frederick H. Harbison, and Charles A. Myers, *Industrialism and Industrial Man* (London: Penguin Press, 1973). Another example is provided by Reinhard Bendix, *Work and Authority in Industry: Ideologies of Management in the Course of Industrialization* (New York: Wiley, 1956).
[29] C. Sabel.

dustrial development and by differences in national cultures and personalities.

Comparative multivariate studies frequently hold constant one or more work structures in order to examine cross-national differences in other structures. Only a handful of these can be noted here. Thus, for example, Form[30] controls for industry and class in order to study differences produced by country, occupation, and organization. That is, he compares automobile workers of different levels of skill in terms of their institutional involvements (in family, work group, community, and so on) in four countries varying in their level of industrial development (United States, Italy, Argentina, and India). He finds that in the more highly industrialized countries, skilled workers, compared to other employees, participate more in work-related social systems. He concludes (p. 697) that "industrialization and structural differentiation of society may not homogenize industrial workers but rather create internal cleavages which increase the social power of skilled workers and decrease the possibility of a unified or radical working class movement."

Moreover, a study by Duncan Gallie[31] held occupation and industry constant in order to study the impacts of nation-state structures, unions, and organizations on the nature of work and the experiences of workers. He compared two oil refineries in Britain and France and tested the hypothesis that advances in automation produce similarities in previously diverse industrial relations systems. He found that the structure and dynamics of industrial relations in Britain and France, not advanced automation, hold the key for understanding major differences in the attitudes of British and French workers.

The New Structuralists in Sociology

The multivariate structural approach is also represented by the "new structuralists" in American stratification research.[32] These writers study

---

[30] William H. Form, "The Internal Stratification of the Working Class: System Involvements of Auto Workers in Four Countries," *American Sociological Review* 38 (December 1973): 697–711.

[31] Duncan Gallie, *In Search of the New Working Class: Automation and Social Integration within the Capitalist Enterprise* (New York: Cambridge University Press, 1978). See also Ronald Dore, *British Factory, Japanese Factory: The Origins of National Diversity in Industrial Relations* (Berkeley, Cal.: University of California Press, 1973), a comparison in which industry is held constant.

[32] The term *new structuralists* first appeared in James N. Baron and William T. Bielby, "Bringing the Firms Back In: Stratification, Segmentation and the Organization of Work," *American Sociological Review* 45 (1980): 737–65.

differences among industries, classes, occupations, and organizations and
have sought to incorporate these work structures into individual-level
models of the determinants of income, careers, and other areas of social
life in which there are inequalities. Some have tried to integrate notions
of class with the status attainment paradigm, arguing that both class and
occupation are important to understanding income inequality and other
key stratification outcomes.[33] Unlike univariate class structuralists, they
assume that occupations are not simply derived from class but are distinct
work structures having unique and consequential impacts on a range of
social indicators.

Another example of a new structuralist approach is the *dual econ-
omy/economic segmentation* perspective. The foci of analysts in this tradition range from differences in processes of capital accumulation and
the degree of worker exploitation, to the prospects for conflicts and struggles, rooted in class relationships, that occur across industries. These
phenomena are assumed to underlie or at least to affect the historical
trends in advanced capitalist economies toward the development of qualitatively distinct industrial-economic sectors. The precise character and
force of this trend are often assumed to be governed by immanent systemic imperatives that are held to be operative in all industrial societies
but especially and most palpably in capitalist societies. The differentiation
of capital into large and small economic sectors is further assumed to
divide the labor force into distinct labor market segments. Taken together,
these structures are reported to have important consequences for the
distribution of income, power, status, and other inequalities among individuals and groups.[34]

Many recent sociological studies of labor markets also illustrate the

---

[33] For example, Arne L. Kalleberg and Larry J. Griffin, "Positional Sources of Inequality in
Job Satisfaction," *Sociology of Work and Occupations* 5 (November 1978): 371–401; Arne
L. Kalleberg and Larry J. Griffin, "Class, Occupation and Inequality in Job Rewards,"
American Journal of Sociology 85 (January 1980): 731–76; Neil Fligstein, Alexander
Hicks, and S. Philip Morgan, "Toward a Theory of Income Determination," *Work and
Occupations* 10 (August 1983): 289–306.

[34] Some writers in the dual economy tradition illustrate the univariate industry approach
because they assume that industrial sectors alone adequately represent the structure of
economic segmentation (see, for example, E. M. Beck, P. M. Horan, and C. M. Tolbert,
II, "Stratification in a Dual Economy: A Sectoral Model of Earnings Determination,"
American Sociological Review 43 [1978]: 704–20). Other writers in the dual economy
tradition explicitly recognize the need to combine explanations based on industrial sectors
with those focused on other work structures such as occupations and organizations. See,
for example, Michael Wallace and Arne L. Kalleberg, "Economic Organization of Firms
and Labor Force Consequences," in *Sociological Perspectives on Labor Markets*, ed. Ivar
Berg (New York: Academic Press, 1981), 77–117.

multivariate structural approach since they emphasize the operation of labor markets along both occupational and organizational lines.[35] A key concept used by these analysts is that of *internal labor markets*, which appear in both firms and occupations (see Chapter 3). This concept was retrieved from Dunlop's too long neglected urgings by younger economists[36] who were troubled by the inadequacies of the human capital approach to an improved understanding of income distribution. Since interests in the structure and functioning of these markets invite attention to the processes that match people to jobs, the concept is particularly useful for understanding the dynamics of job mobility and careers.

Other Examples

Our previous research provides two final illustrations of a multivariate structural approach. For example, Berg and others examine the relative impacts of occupational and organizational structures on job satisfaction. They find that correlates of *each* work structure affect job satisfaction in important ways and that *both* are needed to explain adequately differences in job attitudes and behavior. Indeed, workers' distress over the way income is distributed among occupations counts more heavily in shaping their attitudes toward their own employers' ways and means as managers than any of the workplace factors over which their employers actually have considerable control.[37] This finding suggests not only that we must examine contexts other than organizations that affect job-related outcomes but that occupations may offer us a more potent variable than class in explaining these attitudes.

Kalleberg and others analyze the separable contributions of class, occupational, industrial, union, and organizational structures to variations in economic and noneconomic rewards.[38] Since each work structure has unique effects on job rewards, each must be considered in expla-

---

[35] See, for example, Robert P. Althauser and Arne L. Kalleberg, "Firms, Occupations, and the Structure of Labor Markets: A Conceptual Analysis," in *Sociological Perspectives on Labor Markets*, ed. Ivar Berg (New York: Academic Press, 1981), 119–49.

[36] See Doeringer and Piore.

[37] Ivar Berg, Marcia Freedman, and Michael Freeman, *Managers and Work Reform: A Limited Engagement* (New York: Free Press, 1978).

[38] For example, Arne L. Kalleberg, Michael Wallace, and Robert P. Althauser, "Economic Segmentation, Worker Power, and Income Inequality," *American Journal of Sociology* 87 (November 1981): 651–83; Arne L. Kalleberg, "Work and Stratification: Structural Perspectives," introductory essay to special issue of *Work and Occupations: An International Sociological Journal* on "Capital, Labor, and Work: Structural Determinants of Work-related Inequalities," ed. Arne L. Kalleberg, 10 (August 1983): 251–59.

nations of inequality. They argue, moreover, that economic inequality is generated by differences in the *power* of economic actors and that inequalities in job rewards are determined both by work structures that reflect the relative power of employers in product markets and by those that represent the relative power of workers in labor markets.

THE UTILITY OF A MULTIVARIATE APPROACH TO WORK STRUCTURES

Our review of past studies of work structures points to the promising returns of a multivariate structural approach for understanding important phenomena associated with work and industry. Despite the potential fruitfulness of this perspective, one over which clearly we can claim no monopoly, there have been few successful attempts to develop systematically a framework showing how the different kinds of work structures are related to each other as well as to broader societal institutions. The result has been that there are significant lacunae and discontinuities in what otherwise would be more cumulative findings and knowledge about the interrelations among work structures, their origins, their suggestive correlates, and their apparent consequences.

These lacunae result from many sources, some of which we have already noted: disciplinary boundaries that impede easy exchange of ideas and findings among different people studying similar issues; theoretical differences rooted in paradigmatic conflicts over what is important to study and over the basic assumptions underlying social reality; and different motivations for studying work and industry that are rooted in the ideologies of investigators and the diverse interests of research sponsors.

Better developed sensibilities to the range of work structures are necessary for understanding many of the phenomena associated with work and its consequences. More often than not, as we will see in later chapters, the explanations of those who take work structures as given and of the different univariate approaches are *complementary* to a very significant and reassuring degree.

As we implied earlier, for example, neoclassical economists are concerned with the choices people make within preexisting work structures, whereas Marxists focus on the nature of these structures themselves. These two perspectives are complementary since one addresses how work is structured the way it is and the other focuses on why individuals make choices within or among these structures. Such a distinction obtains between studies of positional inequality as compared with individual attainment to which we also alluded earlier. Though different kinds of questions are asked by representative analysts, their observations are often reconcilable. Hence, not only is there a need for their synthesis but a basis for attempting it.

A comprehensive framework for studying work structures would enable researchers and practitioners to know the implications of restricting their focus to one specific structure virtually at the expense of another. This is not to suggest that good studies should incorporate in their explanations all work structures, nor that studies including more work structures are better than those with fewer. As we have argued, holding some work structures constant is often necessary in order to examine the nature and consequences of others. However, researchers studying specific work structures will benefit from an effort to recognize explicitly how their structures are related to others and how these interrelations affect their conclusions and interpretations of research findings. In this book, we suggest a framework that addresses some of the issues raised by a multivariate approach to work structures. As a first step, it is necessary to consider how work structures are related to each other and how they are embedded within different types of markets. We outline this framework in the next chapter.

CHAPTER 2

WORK STRUCTURES

Interrelations, Markets, and Processes

In this chapter, we elaborate on our conceptualization of work structures and offer suggestions about the ways in which they are related. We argue that the origins, correlates, and consequences of these structures must be subjected to systematic analysis, thereby developing clearer understanding of them as causal agents.

It is, of course, not inappropriate to postulate the primacy of some work structures as givens—thus inviting some controversy—in efforts to explain one or another phenomenon. But it is useful to pause, in a global research area, to attempt to fit disparate studies together, an undertaking requiring, though, a recognition that one person's (and/or one research tradition's) independent variable is another's dependent or intervening variable. We are of the mind that there are sufficient numbers of studies of the types implied by the cliché about "one man's meat" to specify juxtapositions with an eye to synthesis. Such efforts should be rewarding for specialized researchers as well as for those of more theoretical bent, even though there is admittedly room for negotiations over "primacies."

Our argument has three main parts. First, we posit that work structures are complementary and interrelated in theoretically meaningful and important ways. Second, we suggest that societal and historical influences, operating through each of four critically important types of *markets* (capital, product, labor, and resource), largely determine the correlates of work structures. Third, we argue that structures' principals generate *processes*, which in turn produce changes in the structures and markets.

31

Thus, although the structures are in the main complementary, some of their constituent elements may be less than fully integrated with one another. For example, craft unions were augmented by industrial unions in the United States in the 1930s and the latter's members were far more interested in using the state's resources for reforms than were members of their craft union progenitors.

The historical specificity of work structures and processes is particularly important when one evaluates their correlates and consequences. As a first step, we present a scheme for conceptualizing work structures and the relations among them.

CONCEPTUALIZING WORK STRUCTURES

Figure 1 presents a heuristic diagram of the interrelations among work structures. We derived this schema from the literature on work and industry, and it represents a "first cut" into our conceptualization of the relations among these structures.

The triangles denote four business *organizations*, which are grouped into two *industries*. We picture three *class* groups within each organization: owners, managers, and workers. There are several kinds of links among these class positions: craft and industrial *unions* link workers in different companies; and trade associations and "interlocks" link owners' agents in different firms. In addition, four *occupations* are pictured within two or more of the organizations. Finally, *jobs* are represented as specific tasks within each firm. We briefly describe each of these work structures; we will elaborate on their major correlates in Chapter 3.

Types of Work Structures

Business Organizations. Business organizations are work systems directed toward the production, distribution, and consumption of goods and services. Their purposes include the creation of wealth, the manufacture of goods, and/or the provision of services. These work organizations are basic units of analysis for studying issues related to work and industry, since the vast majority of people in industrial societies work in them.

As we noted in the last chapter, business organizations are *corporate groups* that enjoy well-defined legal status, can make enforceable claims, have specified rights and liabilities, and can be disbanded or survive as

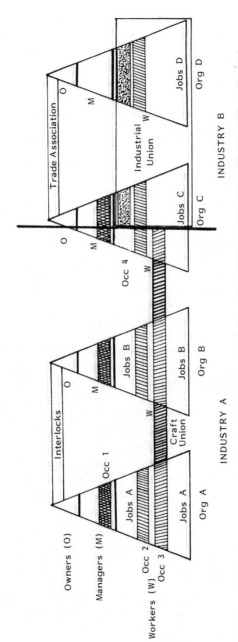

FIGURE 1.   Work structures and their interrelations: Industries, organizations, occupations, classes, unions, and jobs.

a legal person for several generations.[1] In these utilitarian organizations, owners are the prime economic beneficiaries (or, sometimes, the victims) of the activities of organizational members as has been demonstrated in a series of studies since those by Berle and Means in 1932 in which the authors made so much of the increasing separation of the ownership from the control of corporations.[2]

Business organizations vary in size, as measured both by their numbers of employees and by their assets. Hence, the four organizations pictured in the diagram could range from single entrepreneurs, who are the sole members of their firms, to giant corporations such as General Motors. In addition, since large firms often have establishments located at many sites, each triangle could represent *many* business units. The pyramidal shape of these organizations, meanwhile, denotes the concentration of authority and the relatively greater rewards associated with higher levels in the organization.

Firms of different sizes may also differ in their internal arrangements. For example, the ratio of the actual numbers of owners and managers to workers may be greater in larger organizations. These correlates of size are often considered, but only rarely is account taken of what is meant by the term *manager* or of the discrepancies between large numbers of small and small numbers of large stockholders in large "publicly held" corporations.

Industries. A *theoretical industry* is a group of products, sometimes quite heterogeneous, that potential buyers see as close substitutes for each other, and are therefore sold in virtually the same product market.[3] Since business organizations are the primary sellers of goods and services in industrial societies, an industry is, derivatively, a group of firms and of particular divisions of otherwise diversified "parent" firms.

Differences among product markets generate differences among industries in their technologies, cultures, and labor–management relations. In Figure 1, organizations A and B (and part of C) are grouped together into industry A. For example, organizations A, B, and C could represent

---

[1] See Max Weber, *The Theory of Social and Economic Organization*, trans. and ed. A. M. Henderson and Talcott Parsons (New York: Oxford University Press, 1947).

[2] For a classic (1932) statement on the separation of the interests of firms' owners and members, with an updated introduction and revisions, see Adolf A. Berle and Gardiner C. Means, *The Modern Corporation and Private Property*, rev. ed. (New York: Harcourt, Brace & World, 1968). See also Peter M. Blau and W. Richard Scott, *Formal Organizations* (San Francisco: Chandler, 1962); and Amitai Etzioni, *A Comparative Analysis of Complex Organizations* (New York: Free Press, 1961).

[3] Joe S. Bain, *Industrial Organization* (New York: John Wiley, 1959).

Apple Computer, Compaq, and IBM, respectively. All three are members of the personal computer sales and service industry, though IBM is also in many other industries, such as office supplies. We could define these industries broadly, as in the distinction between manufacturing and service industries. Or we can define them very narrowly, as, for example, the pizza and hamburger *subsegments* of the fast food *component* of the restaurant *industry*. The waves of mergers of heterogeneous producers (500 billion borrowed dollars worth between 1979 and 1985!) have made industries increasingly less tractable units for research purposes; not only are industries growing more heterogeneous in terms of their products, and their parent companies becoming more diversified, but they march to diverse financial drummers.

Class. The breadth and diffuseness of the concept of class make the definition of this work structure even more challenging for investigators than that of industry and have led to lively debates about its definition, presumed boundaries, and correlates (see Chapter 3 for an extended discussion).

In our diagram, we represent classes as the relations of control among owners, managers, and workers within each organization. These objective structural relations are *classes-in-themselves,* groups of positions having similar control relationships to others in the organization. Hence, owners control the profits generated by the organization's sale of goods and services, whereas workers usually have little control either over the distribution of profits or over how work is done.

But having said this much, we encounter many complex issues when we move from assertions to the workaday world. For example, there are a large number of possible links among class positions in different organizations, raising vexed (and vexing) questions about the conditions under which classes or their constituent subsets come to act "for themselves," that is, develop something like a shared consciousness of their interests and undertake joint initiatives. These *classes-for-themselves* are represented in our diagram by links among members of similar classes *across* the different organizations. For example, unions link *workers* in different organizations and even in different industries.

We also picture several key links among *owners*: interlocking directorates and trade associations. These groups frequently crosscut industries and afford means, at least putatively, by which owners of different firms can advance their common class interests; the evidence that they actually do so is thin. Indeed, of all of our structures, classes in the modern era are the least coherently organized, for reasons we will discuss later. We have included them partly out of a sense of obligation to colleagues who have focused on class as a component of larger social systems and partly because the *absence* of terribly clear multiple class demarcations in some modern developed economies is interesting in and of itself.

Occupations. As industries classify the activities of firms, so occupations describe the activities of individuals. Occupations are cultural constructions based on structural realities of jobs having wide societal relevance. They are useful for describing the kinds of work done in a society, since they group together work activities that are rather general and transferable among employers and often among industries. Jobs within an occupation perform many similar types of tasks, have similar duties and responsibilities attached to them, and often involve similar working conditions.[4]

We picture four kinds of occupations. Some occupations (2) are sufficiently general so as to crosscut almost all firms and industries. Clerical workers, for example, are found in virtually every industry and in all organizations above a certain size. Occupation 1 is found among managers in three firms but not in a fourth and represents activities such as engineering, accounting, and so on. Not all firms hire full-time managers in these areas, and whether they do so often depends on their size and industry. Occupations 3 and 4 are unique to industries A and B respectively and represent specialized sets of activities (for example, typesetting) that are found only in some industries.

Unions. Unions are organizations designed to represent workers in their transactions with managers and employers. Most unions in the United States link jobs and occupations in *different* firms. Our diagram shows two such unions. *Craft* unions are generally organized along occupational lines (in this case, Occupation 3, which could be electricians) that span firms. In contrast, *industrial* unions usually organize all workers in different jobs, occupations, and organizations within an industry; examples are the autoworkers, the steelworkers, and the mineworkers in deep-shaft mines. Such industrial or *expansionary* unions may also crosscut industries, as in the case of the Teamsters (once an occupational union, it now includes some teachers and hospital workers). And the Industrial Union department within the AFL-CIO Federation now houses the old CIO unions. Not uncommonly, an expansionary union fails; the mineworkers lost surface or strip mine workers to the Operating Engineers Union, whose members drive tractors, bulldozers, and other earth-moving gear.

Union structures also vary by country. In countries such as Japan, for example, company or enterprise unions often organize all workers in

---

[4] Bielby and Kalleberg; Siegel, 8, 149–51; Albert J. Reiss, Jr., *Occupations and Social Status* (New York: Free Press, 1961).

a single firm. This form of union organization tends to tie managers and workers together in a "community of fate" as much as a community of interest and makes labor–management relations less adversarial. Company unions were formed by some large American corporations in the early part of the twentieth century but virtually disappeared as independent industrial unions were formed. Company unions are reemerging, however, and are becoming more common in this country, following a rash of decertification elections in recent years; most such events are soon followed by reunionizing efforts and a growing proportion of the new unions are essentially of the company union type.

Jobs. Jobs are specific tasks within particular organizations. These tasks are not transferable across employers, excepting subcontracting arrangements, but embody firm-specific skills that are often geared to the activities constituting the firm's internal labor market. In the United States, at least, considerable emphasis has been placed historically on the delineation of individual tasks; jobs have thus truly become the ultimately microscopic units of work, since they define precisely the economic activities of *individual* incumbents.

Nation-States. Nation-state structures are not shown in Figure 1 but could be incorporated in a straightforward way by drawing one such diagram for each of the countries in a comparative study. Cross-national studies of differences in work structures are as yet relatively scarce; consequently, we must be sensitive to the possible nation-specific nature of much of the research on work structures. Our arguments in this book apply mainly to *industrial* societies, especially, though not exclusively, capitalist societies.

Nation-states are basic work structures for two major reasons. First, they set nearly all the ground rules for the operations of their citizens' economic, political, and many of their social organizations. Hence, nation-state structures provide the framework within which work structures and institutions emerge and take on their qualities. In some nations, work structures other than those we described in Figure 1 could be important for work and industry. For example, in certain socialist countries such as East Germany and the Soviet Union, membership in particular political *parties* is highly salient and may afford party members, as such, considerable control over the structure of the firm.[5]

Second, the bureaucracies of nation-states constitute important work structures in themselves. In the United States, for example, the government bureaucracy is differentiated in ways that parallel industries, being divided into *functional* units such as Congress (fiscal policy), commerce,

[5] See Bendix.

foreign trade, defense, the "Fed" (monetary policy), and a host of regulatory agencies also organized along functional lines (FCC, FAA, ICC,
and so on), and units, or agencies, that regulate in more organic cross-
industry fashion (the FTC, for example). Despite the fact that they are
public bureaucracies, increasingly larger numbers of decisions in these
organizations are made by appointees (both political and civil service),
not by elected officials.

Assumptions and Implications

Our general assumptions that there are significant interrelations among
the attributes of work structures do not constitute a theory in the sense
of a deductive framework from which a set of internally consistent propositions can be derived. The bases for a formal theory that would be
holistic (rather than reductionistic or Cartesian) are not sufficiently staked
out, a matter to which we return in our two concluding chapters. Rather,
they add up to something like a metatheory that is informed by a number
of definitions, prior assumptions, postulates, and general images of work
structures and the interrelations within and among them. This way of
looking at work structures, we suggest, will be useful in our subsequent
discussions for several reasons.

First, our aggregated assumptions suggest some of the specific ways
in which work structures are related to each other. The complexity—
especially the structures' intramural heterogeneity—and dynamic nature
of these work structures can be understood only if one starts with a clear,
if somewhat gross, picture of their interrelations.

The assumptions represented in the diagram also better equip us to
identify the key correlates of work structures. For example, they imply
that industrial differences are due in part to the number and size of their
constituent organizations as well as to the type of unionization found
within them.

Second, a consideration of the phenomena captured in our diagram
helps us to clarify our assumptions about the multilevel character of work
structures along what we term the macroscopic, mezzoscopic, and microscopic levels. At any given point in time, macroscopic structures generally impose both constraints and opportunities on microscopic ones.
Thus, constitutional provisions that define the terms of trade among the
three branches of our government have relatively more enduring effects
on the relationships among these branches than most specific laws passed
by Congress. However, over time, microscopic processes and structures
may produce changes in macroscopic ones. A recent illustration is the
Supreme Court's ruling that, after more than thirty years, there will be

no further powers of legislative veto exercised by the Congress, a ruling that resulted from the pressures generated by a number of (generally small) conservative "PACs" or political action committees. The actions of Congress and the courts, meantime, have obviously significant consequences for work structures at all of our levels, especially in the three broad areas of fiscal, monetary, and regulatory policy.

Third, the diagram helps point out the intellectual losses of focusing on one of these work structures to the exclusion of the others. For example, there are costs in studying a particular organization at one point in time while holding all else—the industrial, occupational, and socioeconomic historical contexts within which firms operate—constant. Similarly, an exclusive concern with interindustry differences may distract one entirely from important within-industry differences in their respective organizational, occupational, union, and class relationships. Although no investigator can juggle all of these differences at one time, it is fruitful—and self-disciplining—to keep them in mind.

Our model of the interrelations among work structures is accordingly an ideal type, an abstraction against which we can compare the actual links between, say, occupations and unions in different firms. Since it is a simplification, however, we must clarify what the diagram is and is not intended to represent.

Figure 1 assumes, for example, a bureaucratic, organizational model of jobs and work structures: jobs are embedded within firms that are well-closed hierarchical systems. This is a "payroll" definition of business organization. In reality, what constitutes the *organization* is often unclear, since the term is used to refer to corporations, firms, establishments, and business units, otherwise unspecified.

In addition, suppliers and distributors who are dependent upon the firm but are not members of its payroll still constitute important if adjunctive parts of the organization. Subcontracting arrangements, moreover, in accord with which jobs are added and deleted depending on the firm's demand for these activities, are often constructed specifically to avoid the patterns of relationships governing employers and their regular employees. And some giant retailers are the sole purchasers of a supplier's output in what is conceived as a monopsonistic relationship. We will expand on the distinction between these two differentially bounded types of organizations in Chapter 3.

Second, we assume that class relations are rooted in production relations but we do not explicitly represent the social class relations and networks among people outside of the workplace. Such nonproduction relations form a key part of the classlike fabric of modern societies, however, and include clubs, shared background experiences and schooling exposures, common ethnic and other cultural experiences, and so on. Although production relations do affect classes outside the sphere of work and industry and vice versa, we have exercised self-imposed limits on exploring these nonwork relations in this, our preliminary "cut" into work structures. Ignoring the family, religious, and community roles and the commitments that people bring with them to the workplace is regrettably expensive in theoretical terms.

Consider, for example, that a significant portion of the rewards accorded to workers come to them in the form of fringe benefits, the numbers and values of which have become very significant precisely because of workers' urges to meet the costs of health care and to cope with retirement problems; these are defined as much in family and other institutional terms as in terms of individual workers' well-being. Indeed, beyond Medicare and Medicaid programs at the federal level, our private "third-party" health system—including its organizations and the occupations therein—is directly affected by these developments. Further, recent laws establish that a divorced person may very well claim substantial benefits from the ex-spouse's pension plan.

Third, demographic characteristics such as age, race, and gender are not explicitly represented in the diagram. These key characteristics of people differentiate members of the labor force, sometimes very markedly, and are the flesh that stretches over the skeletal division of labor formed by our work structures. Indeed, the rules and mechanisms by which different kinds of people are allocated or matched to jobs are themselves important "structures" in a comprehensive account of the correlates and consequences of work. These rules include formal ones—affirmative action regulations—and informal ones—"homosexuals need not apply." We complete the picture when we later discuss how people of differing ages, races, and genders are sorted and selected into our work structures.

Finally, the diagram is intended to represent work structures and their interrelations primarily here in the United States; it may have to be modified in order to portray accurately the institutional order of the economy in other nations. For example, we have noted that enterprise unions in Japan generally do not link workers in different firms, and the strong ties between Japanese employees and their companies limit occupational links across organizations. Moreover, structures not shown in the diagram—such as party membership, regions,[6] or links between firms and

---

[6] Of course, region constitutes an important work structure in the United States, as well as in Italy and other countries. See, for example, the study of the impact on earnings of local labor markets in the United States by Toby L. Parcel and Charles W. Mueller, *Ascription and Labor Markets: Race and Sex Differences in Earnings* (New York: Academic Press, 1983).

the state—may have substantial impacts on the nature of work and industry in certain countries. In addition, the salience of work structures for particular outcomes may differ across nations. Organizational differences may be more strongly related to earnings inequality in Japan, for example, than in the United States; and union membership may be less important for economic stratification in Norway than in either Japan or the United States (because of a higher standardization of wages between union and nonunion sectors in the Norwegian economy). Though we will frequently allude to such cross-national differences, a systematic comparative analysis of work structures and markets is beyond the scope of our present effort.

With these assumptions in mind, we now turn to a brief discussion of the interrelations among the work structures as implied in the diagram. This discussion will suggest a number of unresolved questions related to work and industry upon which we will elaborate in later chapters.

INTERRELATIONS AMONG WORK STRUCTURES

Central to our conceptualization of work structures is the assumption that they are complementary and related to each other in systematic ways. Despite the often substantial differences in character among them, a grasp, at least, of each structure is necessary for understanding almost all aspects of work and industry.

As general orientations, work structures are useful because they invite our continuing attention to opportunities for integrating insights from diverse theoretical frameworks and from studies conducted at different analytical levels, from macroscopic to microscopic. For instance, these work structures could be viewed as building blocks of other, broader and long well-regarded structures *cum* concepts, such as the division of labor. A fuller appreciation of the significance of the division of labor, for example, requires information on classes, occupations, organizations, and industries because labor is divided in each of these structures in accordance with one or more well-recognized principles.

Nation-States and Work Structures

Differences in the nature of economic and political systems among countries help to differentiate their work and industrial systems. National structures affect the correlates and consequences of the other work structures, especially through their impacts on: (a) markets, (b) legal and political systems, and (c) arrangements for the provision of a variety of goods and services which are not produced by market forces.[7] For example, they affect the preconditions for and the means by which such infrastructures as road building, waste disposal, and public health systems are planned, built, and operated. Nation-state structures may operate at the level of the national economy through such means as tax policies and government programs like the Tennessee Valley Authority (TVA) and Comsat, the satellite corporation. National structures also play some part in spawning national associations in the private sector; examples are the Chamber of Commerce, the National Organization for Women, the NAACP, and organizations in pursuit of the job rights of homosexuals, the elderly, and war veterans.

In addition, cultural differences among countries help to produce differences in their work structures. For example, the lifetime employment system in Japan is clearly an outgrowth of paternalistic elements in Japanese culture. Such paternalism is also reflected in the assistance provided by the Japanese government to firms in particular industries, allowing Japanese managers to think far more in terms of the long run than can American managers. Another example, provided by Sabel, suggests that the high formalization characteristic of French bureaucracies and the low discretion associated with specific jobs therein reflect the low trust relations pervasive in France. In Germany, in contrast, the prevalence of high trust implies less need to limit bureaucrats' zones of discretion, hence the lesser degree of formalization in German organizations.[8]

Within a country, we must quickly add, the state may have different (local) impacts on the other work structures. For example, in advanced capitalist societies like the United States and Japan some industries and industry sectors (for example, such heavy manufacturing industries as autos, steel, oil, and airplane manufacturers) have stronger ties to and receive greater support from the state than firms in the retail sales and personal services industries.

The form of such support varies by country; in Japan, certain industries are targeted, for a time, for direct governmental support while others are left entirely to their own devices, whereas the United States has a series of often inconsistent industry-linked programs, but not a coherent industrial policy. For example, tax benefits are given to one ranking of industries and benefits related to research and development to another: companies in the airline industry have relatively low effective

---

[7] Frederick L. Pryor, *Property and Industrial Organization in Communist and Capitalist Nations* (Bloomington: Indiana University Press, 1973).
[8] See Sabel.

corporate tax rates (19 percent), whereas the aircraft and parts industry has the highest proportion of its research and development funded by the government. Hence, the relationships between the government and United States industries are not coherent ones.[9]

Organizations and Work Structures

Business organizations are social systems; they have structures and cultures that are often *sui generis* in that any one will make adaptations to textbook bureaucratic forms, the better to manage affairs with clients, employee stakeholders, stockholders, and other claimants. Business organizations are not free-standing entities, for they must operate under constraints imposed by various forces, including technological imperatives and the public's interests. But firms' leaders do reserve to themselves (with fairly large margins of public indulgence) many specific choices in both the design and execution of their activities and transactions.

Organizations are intimately related to our other work structures as well, particularly people's class and occupational identities. It is within business firms, for example, that the two-way control relations between workers and their employers are rooted. Organizations, after all, are the sites wherein generic occupational activities are structured in their details and carried out in their particulars. Pilots who fly corporate jets have work lives that are very different from those who fly for the major airlines, and a nurse at Memorial Sloan-Kettering would hardly recognize the circumstances of her colleagues at "M*A*S*H 4077."

To assume that firms are key units of analysis for studying the nature and consequences of work, however, does not require that supraorganizational structures be neglected; these may have important effects on work and industry above and beyond those immanent in organizations. For example, classes, occupations, industries, age cohorts, and gender and race groups span individual firms and, because they are themselves more or less highly organized, they represent distinct units of analysis. Hence, readers of narrowly drawn organizational case studies will reap important benefits if they keep in mind that business organizations are embedded in and affected by other kinds of work structures as well as by firm-specific properties. Pilots in both of the aforementioned settings, after all, must attend to the FAA and to the mandates of tower controllers in critical aspects of their respective employing firms' charges to them. And nurses must come to grips with many challenges that are indepen-

[9] Robert B. Reich, "An Industrial Policy of the Right," *The Public Interest* 73 (Fall 1983): 3–17.

dent of their immediate circumstances. Nurses and doctors involved in triage face the same horrors in setting treatment priorities following disasters, whether in the case of hotel fires or intense combat situations, but they face very different constraints on the degree to which they can otherwise freely fraternize.

Classes and Work Structures

Classes, as we have noted, are related to other work structures, and we discuss their connections to occupations and unions below. In addition, classes-for-themselves span industries and can be organized for longer or shorter periods (by their members or as a result of employers' and political leaders' initiatives) around particular economic and political interests. The ability of passive classes to organize themselves for action may differ across industries, as may powers of one class relative to another. Indeed, such latent capacities as workers have may be untapped for years and years at a time until they feel, at least, that they have been prodded into action by "final straws" heaped upon their backs by employers.

Occupations and Work Structures

Like classes, occupations span different firms within the same industry and often different industries. Occupational associations (e.g., craft unions, professional associations) regularly compete with class groups as ways of organizing the interests of workers in different firms, sometimes at the expense of other occupations. Consider that as blue- and white-collar unionists have won gains in the area of health insurance, and as these have spilled over to their unorganized co-workers, they have reduced substantially the prospects for the rest of the population to be accorded health care benefits through acts of the state.

Occupational differences are highly salient to workers, since it is their occupationally related skills and power that mainly determine their value in the labor market. Of course, there are also occupational differences among managers: some may be accountants and others may be engineers. But it is the *authority* of managers within the organization, and not their occupational activity, that generally matters most. Very few workers, on the other hand, have formal authority in any strict sense, and when they are able to exercise authority it is because their peers, not their employers, attribute it to them as in the case of "straw bosses."

That occupations matter at all among managers reflects disparities in their access to or control over different types of organizationally relevant information, as when comptrollers, treasurers, and accountants have access to financial data of which, for example, industrial relations officers have no knowledge, though these officers may be charged with responsibilities for collective bargaining leading up to and during a strike.

Occupational differences should matter least among owners, who are differentiated primarily by their degree of property ownership and the size and power of their firms.

Industries and Work Structures

In the diagram (Figure 1), firm C is pictured as a member of two industries. This reflects the increasingly important fact that, especially in the modern era in which conglomerates have become exceedingly prominent, a single firm may span several industries. For example, newspaper companies also own lumber mills; Atlantic Richland, an oil company, owns 90 percent of a newspaper, the *London Observer*; and RCA owns television stations, manufactures stereos, and invests in space technology, facts that help account, a little bit, for General Electric's willingness to pay billions of dollars to purchase RCA.

While mergers are not new, the older patterns of consolidation tended to occur within the same or similar industries, through vertical (joining of suppliers of raw materials and distributors of finished products) and horizontal (merging of companies producing similar goods) integration. The newer forms of merger activity have resulted in conglomerations that span traditional industrial categories. These recent trends have created considerable confusion concerning the definition of an industry, as we have noted, and coherent industries constitute key aspects of the environments of fewer organizations now than, say, prior to the 1960s.

To the extent that a particular conglomerate firm produces many different types of goods or services, it may even constitute the most relevant element in the economic environment of an industry the other member firms of which cannot draw upon the subsidies available to a competitor with conglomerate parents during difficult economic seasons.

Industrial environments produce marked differences in the nature of work since they reflect conditions to which organizations must react. But, on another side, firms may also produce changes in macroscopic industry structures. For example, powerful companies may have the clout to generate changes in governmental regulatory policies toward specific industries. Thus, auto companies pushed hard for standards-based emission regulations, thereby preserving the internal combustion engine against obsolescence; the costs of meeting standards could be passed on to customers whereas a new engineering development would require huge outlays and only distant prospects of regaining the costs. The abilities of the leaders of different organizations are enhanced if they are able to act more or less in concert, as when automobile companies banded together to seek reductions in federal air emission standards. The qualification, more or less, is necessary because the courts are chary of imputing conspiracies to managers, in accord with what is known as "the *per se* rule," whose behavior appears to support such a charge. Thoreau once wrote that "circumstantial evidence can be very compelling, as when one finds a trout in the milk," but the Antitrust Division of the Justice Department has lately forsworn such metaphors.

The relations between industries and occupations are also complex. Some occupations—clerical workers and professionals, for example—are found in many different industries and are relatively unaffected by developments in a single industry. Other occupations have evolved out of the development and growth of particular industries (for example, bellhops, among its other occupations, are products of the hotel industry as it evolved, itself, from yesteryear's wayside inns). Finally, some occupational changes may lead to the creation of new industries, as the availability of skilled computer personnel fueled the development of the computer industry; as the availability of barnstorming fliers contributed materially to the emergence of today's giant airline industry; and as the availability of athletes from schools and colleges aided the development of increasingly large segments of the sports industry.

Unions and Work Structures

Craft unionism is an occupational structure, and the restrictive policies of craft unions are significant impediments to working-class organization. Big industrial unions are more representative of the "working class," in commonsense terms, since they link many different occupations and jobs in diverse industries. However, none of the current industrial unions in the United States approximates a true class union like the Industrial Workers of the World, the so-called Wobblies, which in the early 1900s included workers from all kinds of occupations and industries.

Unions may produce changes in organizations. In the United States for example, unions have gone along with—and in some cases actively promoted—technological change, "Taylorism," and task specialization. Other practices have been initiated by management and then embraced by unions, such as cost of living adjustments, or COLAs, reinvented in the 1950s by General Motors, though managers have since pretended that these payments were imposed on them by putatively powerful unions.

(John Dunlop, meanwhile, reminds us that such arrangements existed in the 1880s and were popular in the period 1916–1920.)

A complete understanding of work structures requires us to account for why they were created and how they are maintained. In the rest of this chapter, we briefly sketch the outlines of our argument about the conditions that underlie the origins and changes in work structures, conditions we take to be rooted in the operations of *markets*.

MARKETS

Markets are the fundamental complexes of patterned behavior in which one must look for the origins of our work structures and processes.

We assume that a central feature of all societies is the need for individuals and groups to exchange goods and services with each other in order to satisfy their wants. This leads them to develop means for conducting transactions that economic agents hope will become conveniently routinized. In industrial societies, these exchanges take place in markets. Markets for these exchanges can be arrayed along a continuum from more to less competitive or planned, and they are useful constructs for studying work structures even when they do not fit the economic textbook's perfectly competitive model.

Markets are most highly visible as mechanisms for the distribution of human resources and opportunities in capitalist systems of production, since two necessary conditions that define capitalism are the use of markets as clearing mechanisms for goods, labor, and capital and "commodified" production relationships in which the economic value of the product is determined in markets. But even the economies of advanced socialist countries depend on markets, if for no other reason than that these nations must compete with others in a capitalist world economy. Indeed, in socialist economies many goods and services may more often be exchanged in black markets which, while not legally sanctioned by the state, have been legitimated by long-time practices of their participants as efficient ways to carry out exchanges.

Types of Markets

Exchange relations in industrial societies are complex, and so there are many types of markets. Four major types of markets are especially important to work and industry: capital markets, product markets, labor markets, and resource markets (we consider a fifth market—that for political influence—in Chapter 7). These markets vary in the commodity being exchanged (money and credit, goods or services, labor power, raw materials and other resources). They also differ in the actors (the buyers, sellers, and traders) involved in the exchange: for example, organizations may trade with other organizations as well as with individuals. In addition, each market may be disaggregated into various subtypes (see the matrix printed on the back endpaper). Moreover, the four markets are interrelated: for instance, the operations of capital markets, through their allocations of credit and financing, have significant effects on investment decisions and thereby help to shape the nature of product and labor markets. We briefly discuss each type of market in turn.

Capital markets are markets in which the key actors are buyers and sellers (and their agents) of: (1) cash, (2) credit, (3) capital claims (stocks and bonds), and (4) "futures" of different types. The buyers in these markets are those individuals or organizations with sufficient resources to participate. The lenders or sellers in capital markets are also a diverse lot and include banks and other loan agencies, the government, stockholders, and even hard goods manufacturers and sellers who offer credit to consumers. Capital markets indirectly affect labor and product markets. For example, investors in pension funds such as TIAA-CREF, the key pension fund for academics, or members of employee stock ownership plans (ESOPs), because of their passivity (based in part on their well-founded belief that they are not responsible for investment decisions) and their great volume, may regularly if indirectly create or eliminate jobs through their encouraging dispositions toward mergers and acquisitions and thus their occasional contributions to plant closings and relocations.

Product markets are markets wherein goods and services are bought and sold. In advanced industrial societies, sellers in product markets are generally organizations, ranging from highly specialized small entrepreneurs to giant corporations selling many different types of products. The buyers in these markets are also diverse and include individual consumers, other organizations, and governments (both domestic and foreign).

Most people in industrial societies earn a living in a third type of market, the *labor market*. The term *labor market* refers broadly to the institutions and practices that govern the purchase, sale, and therefore part of the pricing of labor services. They are the arenas in which workers exchange their labor power, creative capacities, and even their loyalties with employers in return for wages, status, and other job rewards. Hence, these are the markets wherein labor force inequalities are most directly generated. These inequalities result from the interplay among the major actors involved in labor market processes: the individual worker, the individual employer, workers' organizations, associations of employers, and the government.[10]

Finally, *resource markets* refer to the buyers, sellers, and intermediaries of: raw materials such as land, water, fuel, ores, crops, and natural resources; infrastructures (for example, communities offer resources to companies such as zoning adjustments, tax abatements, access roads, and no-cost or low-cost water and sewage hookups in order to attract firms to their precincts); other organizations (buying and selling plants as in the case of mergers and acquisitions); and ideas (patents, copyrights) and other products of the "knowledge" industry. Because of the public nature of many of these products, exchanges in resource markets are often subject to especially close monitoring by government and nongovernment representatives of the public. The fact, too, that resources involve international as well as intranational issues adds to the need for monitors, sponsors, negotiators, even protectors (acting in the public's name) as when "the flag follows trade."

Market Constraints, Fears, and Preferences

If our markets operated according to textbook principles of perfect competition, there would be little need to examine the structures that emanate from them since these would only be temporary imperfections in otherwise competitive systems. But in reality markets are not perfectly competitive and there are *constraints* under which they operate. These constraints affect the degree of competition present in the markets and give rise to social institutions and structures designed to deal with them. A central concern of our analysis, then, is to specify some of the conditions under which markets do and do not become constrained.

Although the nature and form of these constraints will differ among markets, there are certain common patterns that are present, albeit in varying degrees and in different ways, in each of the four markets. For example, each market is associated with a variety of *regulatory* mechanisms that proscribe (e.g., unfair competition or trusts) or prescribe (e.g., safety inspections of drugs, childrens' pajamas, and aircraft) certain types of behavior.

Markets are also characterized by many types of *nonregulatory* patterns: the degree to which returns on investments are problematic as to

[10] Herbert S. Parnes, "Labor Force: Markets and Mobility," in *International Encyclopedia of the Social Sciences*, ed. David L. Sills (New York: Macmillan and Free Press, 1968), 481–87.

rate or time; the extent of barriers to entry (for example, the amount of capital investment required to start a business); the risks involved in the market and the amount of control the actors have over these risks, including the degree to which they are able to minimize risk and price competition by obtaining government subsidies; and the transferability or flexibility of what is being exchanged (for instance, medical degrees are more flexible than barbers' licenses in that they can be transported from one community to another; similarly, money is more mobile than land).

These constraints produce *fears* among the actors in each of the four markets. These fears reflect conditions that hinder the ability of actors to realize their interests in market exchanges and are understandable constraints on their behavior.

The specific nature of these fears will of course differ among the actors in different markets, but there are some general fears that actors (especially the "haves") in each of the markets have in common. For example, the advantaged group in each market opposes many public initiatives of one kind or another, be they higher taxes (capital markets), interference generated by affirmative action laws (labor markets), labeling and safety regulations (product markets), or actions of environmentalists (resource markets).

Moreover, the advantaged actors in each of the markets have similar *preferences* or desires, which reflect opportunities for them to realize their interests in market exchanges. For example, the privileged actors in every market generally favor subsidies for themselves and allied actors, social order, research and development, education, unrestricted mobility of capital, and the reduction of regulations generally. Often, one person's fear is another's preference. For example, economic actors generally abhor competition but are pleased when others are more vulnerable to competition than they are.

These fears and preferences lead actors to search for ways to protect their interests in market exchanges by designing structures and processes to facilitate or otherwise influence the various types of transactions. We shall return to this theme in Chapter 6, when we consider the adaptations and processes that modify the operation of markets and work structures. At this point, though, it is important to note that the innumerable contests implied by the foregoing allusions to likes and dislikes can be distilled with the proposition that few of us live at all comfortably with high levels of price competition but then, again, we cannot live without them.

The Robinson-Patman Act, for example, was intended to prevent cutthroat competition and to keep prices from being too low. On the other hand, various kinds of antitrust laws keep prices from being too high and constitute real barriers to the pooling of energies among organizations and occupations. Hence, economic actors and their agents and organizations seek to reduce risks (or *externalities* in the market) by tempering the worst extremes of price competition. This is often done by socializing risks to a greater or lesser degree or otherwise by redistributing them and by moving away from price to nonprice competition, for example, in product-related services and delivery dates.

The constraints on the operations of markets also lead to the creation of submarkets or market segments, which differ in their mechanisms of exchange and their terms of trade. Market segmentation is found in each of the four markets and must be taken into account in explanations of the origins of work structures. For example, labor market segmentation implies that the ways in which people are matched to jobs and the bases on which they are rewarded differ among subtypes of labor markets. In between firms' internal labor markets and the labor market conceived as a nation's workforce are many segments and wage contours that operate in accord with their own logic and often, especially in the shorter run, with considerable independence from one another. For example, the fire, police, and sanitation workers of the major cities in the United States operate with weather eyes open to each others' circumstances rather more than to circumstances outside the so-called uniform services. Professors and doctors, meanwhile, typically see themselves in truly national labor markets. Clearly, these distinct labor market segments pose barriers for would-be organizers of social classes and confront theorists determined to work from the neoclassical market perspective with formidably confounding facts.

Markets and Work Structures

A basic assumption underlying our approach is that the origins of work structures are found in the complex nexus of forces operating in the various markets that characterize industrial societies. The matrices that are printed on the front and back endpapers of this book illustrate the relationships between markets and structures. The matrix on the front endpaper is formed by cross-classifying our basic four markets with our six work structures, while the matrix on the back endpaper represents the crossing of our six structures with key subsystems of these four markets along with the addition of a fifth, the market for political influence. The examples in the cells illustrate the *interplay* between markets and structures: for example, conglomeration is an organizational outcome of developments in capital markets; the oil crisis in the mid-1970s was a national resource market problem; and "deskilling" was a labor market phenomenon that accompanied the weakening of craft unions' power. These matrices thus help to underscore our theme that there are sufficient data available in the research literature on the interactions of developments among small clusters of the cells in this kind of "input–output" table to encourage a move away from excessively reductionist and toward more "holistic," synthetic thinking.

Our assignment of conceptual and temporal priority to markets gains specific support in the findings of the analytically distinguishable bodies of research and legal scholarship that we reviewed in the last chapter. Collectively, the work of these investigators and writers suggests several principles the recognition of which helps direct analysts' attention (a) to the sources of stability and change of a given market as a system of socioeconomic transactions; and therefore (b) to sources of stability and change in that market's key work structures. We can summarize these insights in terms of four propositions:

1. We may assign something very much like temporal priority, in understanding many (though clearly not all) of the relationships alluded to in the cells of our matrix, to key features of distinguishable markets and thus to key differences among markets. These features take on their particular colorations in part from the institutional frameworks that came to govern (i.e., constrain) particular groups' options in a given nation-state. The frameworks, in turn, are legitimated by ideologies that range between the most collectivist and the most individualistic of social philosophies.

2. A preference for equal-interval continuous data scales, in analyses of socioeconomic developments, can usefully and with small cost to rigor, be relaxed to make empirical room for systematic consideration of fairly discrete events that turn out to be points or watersheds both within relatively short and over longer time periods. Such a relaxation makes more legitimate room for intertemporal analyses by social scientists from related disciplines, encouraging sociologists to see a place for their work side-by-side with economists and vice versa. World War II, with its embargoes, wage and price controls, and the rationing of food and many consumer goods, was a watershed, as was in turn the American Revolution, the passage of the Fourteenth Amendment (with its "due process" clause), and the passage of the National Labor Relations Act.

As we will see, the effects in 1973 of judgments by a small number of oil exporting nations' leaders and of dramatic weather conditions on the world's crops—exogenous shocks, as economists call them—generated enormously significant discontinuities in the markets for oil and for farm crops and thus in the energy and food markets, respectively. But it is clear that government policies—the state—played heavy roles in both instances. One policy, during Nixon's tenure in the White House, effectively removed the seven largest oil companies from their long-time position as architects of our foreign policy vis-à-vis Arab oil producers. A second policy in that presidency, that we should liquidate large grain stockpiles (by sales overseas), exacerbated problems associated with a considerable decline in agricultural output across the globe. A third policy, that the Alaskan pipeline from Proudhon Bay be postponed following the completion of lengthy environmental impact studies required by the Environmental Protection Act, was endorsed by the president. The first policy helped *generate* the first discontinuity while the second and third policies significantly *magnified the effects* of the second of these discontinuities.[11]

3. Our four markets differ rather remarkably along a long list of consequential dimensions reflecting significant differences, for example, in their evolution, the legal status of their principals, their key work structures, their vulnerabilities, and their national and international loci. Therefore, farmers, producers of raw materials, jobbers, organized workers, and large manufacturers do not confront all of the same opportunities and constraints.

Markets' structures, meanwhile, reflect differences in the relative importance of coherent collectivities, loosely organized collectivities, and of individual natural persons. Their functioning differs depending on whether given markets are essentially populated by coherently linked corporate persons, pluralities of corporate persons, organized natural persons, unorganized natural persons, or combinations thereof. (The attribution, in many nation-states, of some of the rights of real or natural persons to corporations knows a long history and, as we will see in Chapter 6, has fascinating implications.)

4. The economic agents in our structures have all sought and continue to seek to mobilize the policies and programs of the state to assist them in arranging that markets be hospitable to their interests and either neutral or inhospitable to their economic—and thus social and political—

---

[11] About the oil case, see Jack Anderson, *The Great Fiasco* (New York: Times Books, 1983). Oil companies had long kept Middle East nations at bay by having excess oil producing capacities in each major producing country. "Misbehavior" by any one oil producer could be corrected by shifting production to another country. The "Seven Sisters" simply acted, in political-economic terms, on the market power available to them as oligopsonists—a small number of large buyers—in the Middle East crude oil markets' structure. See also Stanley H. Ruttenberg, *The American Oil Industry: A Failure of Anti-Trust Policy* (Washington, D. C.: Marine Engineers Beneficial Association, 1973); Anthony Sampson, *The Seven Sisters: The Great Oil Companies and the World They Shaped* (New York: Viking, 1975); and Robert Engler, *The Politics of Oil* (New York: New American Library, 1977).

adversaries. In the most simpleminded terms, liberals and conservatives, as we have come to know them in the United States, disagree far more vehemently over what the state should do for whom and with whom than over the abstract need for a state-enforced system of laws, "webs of rules," and specific regulations, as such.

We illustrate these propositions throughout the book. Our efforts should enable the reader to provide his or her own illustrations of the cells in the matrices printed on the front and back endpapers of this volume. In the next section, we illustrate some of the key interactions among these cells.

The Nation-State and Markets. Nation-state structures, operating through economic and political policies, have profound effects on the nature of markets and the work structures that emerge from them. Hence, nation-states may be said to "cause" the operation of markets.

Three key characteristics of nation-states in particular have important effects on the functioning of markets. That is, modern states vary in the degree to which they are self-governing democracies, in the degree to which all or most critical political power is centralized and, finally, in the degree to which the main lines of economic, wealth-producing activities are disciplined by free competition, in accord with one or another politico-ideological schema.

In addition, industrial societies vary along four other key dimensions that affect the operation of markets: the degree to which they are rich in one or in many critical resources; the degree to which their cultural traditions endorse the deferral of gratifications, a propensity to "get by" or save, and what we commonly think of as disciplined work habits; the degree to which producers, consumers, and their national leaders look generously upon the use of credit for the purchase of goods and services; and, finally, the degree to which a society's age structure and immigration policies (and other factors affecting a nation's demography) change with consequences for the adequacy of the fit of labor supply with labor demand. These dimensions along which industrial societies vary relate, fairly obviously, to the way in which our market types operate and to the ways in which the actors in our work structures both operate intramurally and interact with each other.

Consider that the use of credit by all economic agents entails their mortgaging a portion of their future productivity. A prerequisite for such forms of exchange is a willingness on the part of both creditors and debtors to take risks and to live with uncertainties. In their transactions, these agents must feel reasonably confident that they can, in the future, collect from borrowers and, in turn, repay their own creditors. Indebtedness, meanwhile, can have other consequences. Thus, all things being equal, well-"leveraged" consumers who belong to unions are probably less likely than debt-free persons to be militant and to risk strikes that compromise their short-run or middle-run capacities to pay their creditors.

There is some truth in the line in the song Janis Joplin made famous to the effect that "freedom's just another word for nothing left to lose"— among them houses, cars, cottages, boats, vacations, childrens' tuition, and other credit-burdened purchases. Over the short haul, indebtedness can have disciplining effects on workers *cum* consumers. And, in the United States, the state has encouraged a great deal of lending and borrowing by all economic agents and agencies (including the state itself) by income tax rules, for example, permitting interest payments to be deducted from earnings otherwise vulnerable to levees—a categorical tax expenditure by the Congress. In other Western-type democracies, states have not encouraged the proliferation of consumer credit arrangements nor have the populations expressed nearly so much interest in them as have American producers and consumers. Consumer indebtedness, meanwhile, has contributed little to public misgivings about corporate mergerers who borrow heavily for their schemes.

Among the more significant consequences of the expansion of credit, beyond those that may bear on industrial discipline, are the heightened concerns in this country about prevailing interest rates, their determinants, and these rates' own effects, in turn, on the structure and functioning of modern economies. The credit habit can be encouraged or discouraged, of course, but since not all debts are of short term the habit cannot simply be turned off; the resulting "lag factor" leads to perils in the making of decisions in both public and private sectors, as the market for money adjusts to different circumstances, or as the market is "tuned" by the combination of the actions of public and private decision makers in banks, government agencies, and producers' organizations.

Consider, further, that resource-rich societies, whether an Arab nation with large oil reserves or the United States with many abundant resources (including highly productive available land—a critical resource at this time), enjoy what economists call comparative advantages. Many of a society's economic actors gain benefits in their market transactions because of their possession of exploitable resources. Indeed, many citizens in such nation-states gain all the more if their national governments recognize and enhance the options of those who actually mobilize, control, and exploit these resources in servicing a nation-state's ends. The role of oil-producing nations' governments, in 1973, in "cartelizing" both the output and pricing of much of the industrial world's oil supply needs no rehearsal here.

In the matter of capital markets, only a little less familiar are the roles that appear to have been played (rather amateurishly) by American bankers in the management of most of the credit advanced in recent years to so-called Third World nations. Bank auditors of the United States and its fifty state governments were apparently not very much more alert than internal bank auditors to the fact that the credit-worthiness of many of these overextended nations was, at best, problematic. And, back home in Third World countries, leaders are stewing, nervously, over their constituencies' impatience with austerity programs prescribed for them by the international banking community in response to pressures on this community to "clean up their acts."

Finally, we may remind ourselves that an indeterminate but clearly not insignificant part of the economic growth in countries such as the United States, Germany, and Japan was due to their investments in the educational achievements of their work forces. In this country, these so-called human capital investments—many, obviously, by the government through research grants, student loans, GI bills, health care programs, school lunches, dormitory bond issues, teacher training, and many other such measures—quite evidently impacted upon the attitudes, ambitions, skills, and imaginations of labor force participants. By allowing corporations to deduct (until very recently) from their taxes all the dollars they spend on workers' education and skill development in hundreds of thousands of company-sponsored programs, the nation-state once again helped to shape the supply of human resources. It also shaped, in part, the changing capabilities of the members of many occupations, from apprentice bricklayers to professors with postdoctoral grants to airline maintenance mechanics who must regularly be retrained to serve new generations of wide-bodied aircraft laden with "high tech" controls and evolving FAA safety requirements.

These national marketing programs, or policies regarding resources, products, jobs, and dollars, separately and in different combinations, affect industries, occupations, organizations, and unions both directly and indirectly and are thus of critical interest to us. And note, once again, how substantially subversive of class-based types of interest groupings are these congeries of incursions by the nation-state into different types of markets.

Classes and Markets. Class relations are found within each of the four types of markets. However, at least in the United States, there is little overlap in class membership among these markets. This makes it incredibly difficult, especially in the absence of strong political parties, for any of the conflicting class groups to sustain themselves as coherent entities.

This is true even within specific markets. For example, in the United

States, the conflict between creditors and debtors in capital markets has subsided over time, while, in the same time period, creditors have become differentiated and even antagonistic toward each other. The financial sector itself has become a mass of cutthroat competitors, such that the interest rates banks can charge are kept low by law but the price of financial services provided by such nonfinancial institutions as Sears Roebuck can be relatively high. At the same time, the disadvantages associated with being a debtor have decreased through inflation and the ability of debtors to deduct interest from their taxes. This has reduced the significance of class differences within capital markets in the United States and has made other work structures—occupations, organizations, and unions—more important than class in explanations of work and its consequences.

Occupations and Markets. Occupations are most directly affected by labor markets, whether conceived in national, sectoral, or organizational terms, since these markets are the arenas in which occupational activities are bought and sold. Indeed, "the search for structure in the labor market [as distinct from the labor force] is a search for the mechanisms that differentiate jobs."[12] Occupations are also influenced, though less directly, by product markets, since the production of particular goods and services, given the technology associated therewith, requires certain types of workers. Moreover, some occupations have become more dependent on capital markets in recent years; for instance, more doctors need credit to set up practice and to pay for their education; they also use credit markets for patient treatment, as when patients pay their fees by Master Card. Also, occupations are becoming increasingly dependent on resource markets: the dependence of firms in some industries on raw materials can affect their hiring practices and hence the distribution of people to particular occupational groups.

Organizations and Markets. Business organizations participate in all four of our market systems: they acquire and invest money and credit (capital markets); they sell their goods (product markets); they purchase raw materials (resource markets); and they hire, fire, and promote employees (labor markets). If possible, firms act in concert to achieve their interests in market exchanges. For example, companies may act as oligopolists (controlling prices as sellers) in product markets or as oligopsonists (controlling prices as buyers) in labor markets. However, their ability to obtain such advantages is limited by public scrutiny of their activities in each of the types of markets.

---

[12] Marcia K. Freedman, *Labor Markets: Segments and Shelters* (Montclair, N.J.: Allanheld, Osmun, 1976), 6.

Industries and Markets. Industries are most directly affected by the operation of product markets. One reason for this inheres in our historical concern with price competition: we sought to regulate against the formation of trusts that were, by definition, conspiring against customers for a given *product* by using their market power to influence weaker competitors' prices. Industries are also affected by the operation of capital markets, which determine *what* will be produced, and labor markets, which affect *how* goods and services are produced. For example, American auto companies have recently lost ground in the worldwide automobile market to Japanese firms. The increasing threat of foreign competition has created marked changes in the nature of domestic auto product markets (the production of smaller, more fuel-efficient cars) as well as in the nature of labor markets (the rise in "outsourcing" and the hiring, otherwise, of nonunion sources of labor). In one case the normal operations of capital markets were augmented by federally guaranteed loans to one large automobile manufacturer as in the cases, earlier, of such loans to an airplane manufacturer and, at this writing, to one of the nation's larger banks.

Resource markets are used by industries to help their member organizations: for example, the American Banking Institute provides training for people in the banking industry; the American Newspaper Publishers Association helps their members to obtain resources such as the latest in printing technology; and the Supermarket Institute is both an interindustry and intraindustry research and marketing apparatus that also serves the big chains by decreasing predatory competition, maintaining good relations with other industries, and conducting retreats in which they can lobby with their suppliers. Such industrywide groups also seek to obtain key benefits for their members, through political means, as in the agribusiness industry, where dairy farmers, as an example, receive payments for *not* producing milk.

Unions and Markets. Although unions are organized primarily within labor markets, they are affected by changes in other markets as well.

When unions invest their members' pension funds, for example, they are acting as buyers in capital and resource markets, and union leaders must often react, as workers' agents, to developments in these markets. For example, bankruptcy is a solution to the labor problems of many companies that is generated within the structures of capital markets by forces operating well beyond employers' precincts: Johns Manville filed under the Section XI bankruptcy law to evade asbestosis claims; and Continental Airlines rid themselves of their binding contract with unions with the substantial help of bankruptcy proceedings. At this writing, the

House and Senate are working out differences in amendments to the bankruptcy law, and it seems certain that union agreements will not, in the future, be as readily voidable by an employer's bankruptcy filing as was allowed, in the spring of 1983, by the Supreme Court. Union agreements will very likely be treated by legislators somewhat differently from an employing firm's agreements with its *creditors*; creditors, after all, build bankruptcy prospects into their reckonings.

These examples highlight the complexities of the relations between markets and work structures. We will expand on these relations in Chapter 3, when we consider the correlates of work structures and, in Chapter 6, when we discuss historical eras in American society in which the relations among markets, structures, and processes underwent considerable changes.

WORK AND INDUSTRY PROCESSES

In addition to markets, an understanding of the correlates and consequences of work structures requires us to pay close attention to the initiatives (and the responses thereto) undertaken by groups of people in order to realize their interests. We refer to these initiatives as work and industry *processes*. These processes themselves often become emergent structures; it is thus necessary to investigate the sociohistorical contexts and conditions under which processes do and do not become institutionalized. For example, in reaction to the wave of strikes in the United States immediately after World War II produced by deferred worker demands, the Taft-Hartley and Landrum-Griffin Acts were passed to amend or deinstitutionalize some of the conditions of collective bargaining created by the Wagner Act of 1935. In this case, processes at one point in time became structures in subsequent historical periods; the Department of Labor's bureaucracy was augmented to apply regulations related to unions' financial and electoral procedures.

Interest Groups

The *interest group* is the key concept by which we link structures to processes. Interest groups represent initiatives by members of particular work structures that seek to link their own specific concerns with those of the public good. Work structures are often able to sustain themselves as interest groups to the degree that they can persuade the public that it can benefit by giving them what they want.[13] Interest groups may be formal as well as informal, and they represent both reactions by actors to the initiatives of others and actions designed to fill lacunae resulting from other actors' lack of initiative. Indeed, our political parties emerged in response to the needs for social arrangements—"social technology"—that could link the demands of constituents to the formal machinery of the government structure outlined in our Constitution, although several of that document's major authors, Madison especially, deplored parties.

The formation of interest groups may be explained within a resource mobilization framework, as many scholars have found it useful to do in studies of social movements. Interest groups are often formed by members of work structures such as occupations, organizations, classes, and unions. For example, professional associations are interest groups if, to some reasonable degree, they are able to clothe their concerns in the public interest, as have been the cases when established professions have received "licenses and mandates"[14] to control their own activities. Moreover, unions are interest groups when they seek to act in ways that benefit people other than simply their own members. For instance, unions have been recently concerned with decreased federal funding for poverty programs and the opening of other holes in social "safety nets" that were intended in the main to protect people who are unable to compete successfully in the economic system.

Interest groups may also crosscut work structures, as in the case of "peak" associations, which span industries (e.g., National Association of Manufacturers—NAM). Moreover, occupations, classes, and unions may compete as bases of interest group formation with each other and with those rooted in members' demographic characteristics such as age, race, or gender. Thus, women and blacks might apply pressure as members of the National Organization for Women (NOW) or the Congress of Racial Equality (CORE) on the unions, to which they also belong, to be more responsive to their rights to expanded opportunities and to unions' own opportunities to end discriminatory practices.

Types of Work and Industry Processes

In this section, we briefly outline some of the most critical work processes or initiatives. We group them according to the actors who are

[13] For a discussion of interest groups that closely conforms to our own, see Graham K. Wilson, *Interest Groups in the United States* (Oxford: Clarendon Press, 1981; New York: Oxford University Press, 1981).
[14] Everett C. Hughes, "The Study of Occupations," in *Sociology Today,* ed. Robert K. Merton, Leonard Broom, and Leonard S. Cottrell (New York: Basic Books, 1959), 442–58.

responsible for these illustrative initiatives: the formation of regulations by governments; the undertakings of business firms, industries, and trade associations; the initiatives of leaders representing occupations, trades, and skill groups; and the initiatives of nongovernmental interest groups.

The Government. Initiatives are often made by members of the government acting as representatives of the people at national, state and local levels. The initiatives of these public agents are either responses to complaints from one or more groups or to opportunities they identify to serve society. Such initiatives often affect the nature of markets and work structures. For example, the government may enter capital markets "in the public interest," to reduce interest rates; it thereby has profound effects on demand in both product and labor markets.

Among the most substantial capital market intrusions are loan guarantee programs—affecting education and construction, for example—their consequentiality being often overlooked because they involve large transactions that do not appear on governments' budgets. Other examples of government initiatives are: fiscal and monetary policy, publicly supported research and development, education, licensing, tax abatements, regulation and deregulation (from general issues such as antitrust, which is an adaptation designed to preserve industries' members by avoiding monopoly, to specific regulations such as OSHA), tariffs, and other welfare programs in the more popular sense of the term.

Business and Industry. Initiatives are also taken by business firms, acting either singly or in concert. These are often designed to counteract or forestall initiatives made by governmental and nongovernmental representatives of the public and by occupational groups. Collective actions by firms range from initiatives made by agents of business in general (National Association of Manufacturers—NAM) to the initiatives of specific industries (the American Newspaper Publishers Association and other trade associations). The kinds of work processes initiated by the private sector include: some research and development and associated technological changes; employee stock ownership plans (ESOPs); interlocking directorships; tariffs; conglomerates, mergers, and acquisitions; divestiture and capital mobility; collusion to fix prices; "make-work" programs (Works Progress Administration—WPA); franchising; human relations and work reform movements; selective "social responsibility" initiatives reflected, for example, in donations to specific charities; and subcontracting.

Occupational Groups. Representatives of workers include occupational groups such as professional associations and craft unions as well as industrial unions, families, and other social strata. For example, in some basic American industries we have three tiers of collective bargaining activity by workers. Thus, one auto negotiation will set the tone for contracts in the others among the "Big Three," that is, "pattern bargaining." Thereafter, the skilled and unskilled in a given multiplant corporation will scrap over differentials, that is, wage contours. Finally, the companywide agreement will be augmented by local agreements, especially plant-level work rules. Other examples of workers' initiatives in the invention of work structures include: arbitration procedures; strikes and job actions; grievance machinery; output restrictions; licensing; ESOPs; and the use of relatively structured third-party referees, informants, and "shape-up" mechanisms to secure jobs and career advancement.

Nongovernmental Public Representatives. A final set of initiatives is made by nongovernmental representatives of the public. These initiatives are often prompted by those of the other groups we have discussed. For example, citizens' groups may try to counter initiatives of government and/or business leaders. Initiatives made by nongovernmental public representatives include: Common Cause; public interest research groups (INPIRGs); right to work committees; "Nader's Raiders"; the American Red Cross; the Salvation Army; the National Rifle Association in activities aiding arms makers; and other citizens' groups and voluntary associations.

SUMMARY

In this chapter, we have presented a conceptual framework for studying *work structures* and their interrelations. We have argued that the fundamental origins of work structures are the exchange relationships that take place in different kinds of *markets*. We have also outlined some *processes* that produce changes in work structures. This discussion has raised a number of important questions in the study of work and industry. We must now consider structures in more detail and ask what it is about them that makes a difference to various consequences. In other words, we must examine the *correlates* of work structures. These are the subjects of the next chapter.

CHAPTER 3

WORK STRUCTURES AND THEIR CORRELATES

STRUCTURAL CORRELATES

In order to appreciate the "hows and whys" of work structures as specific independent and dependent variables, it is necessary to specify in detail the attributes of work structures and thus the dimensions along which they differ. These attributes we conceive to be their correlates and we conceive these correlates, in turn, as being wrought or shaped by nation-state policies and by the operation of the four market systems discussed in the previous chapter. We are concerned with the correlates of work structures that make a difference, and the features of work structures most worthy of discussion are those that appear in the literature to have enduring value to those who seek to explain a very large number of phenomena.

There are two main kinds of structural correlates. One type refers to how work structures are *differentiated,* or what distinguishes one structure from another along some dimension, such as size. The delineation of the ways in which work structures are differentiated is often the major concern of the univariate structuralists, who emphasize the attributes associated with their structure of interest. A second type of structural correlate refers to the ways in which work structures are *interrelated,* that is, their configurations. Multivariate structuralists are especially concerned with these interrelations, since they posit the need to integrate work structures in order to explain particular consequences.

In this chapter, we outline the major attributes associated with the work structures of interest in this volume: nation-state, class, occupation, industry, organization, and union. Our treatment will highlight some of the most frequently observed correlates of work structures that make them important to study. This will provide a foundation for our discussion in later chapters of both the consequences of these structures and how they change in response to each other and to developments in the larger society.

CORRELATES OF NATION-STATES

Nation-states are born of historical and cultural forces in response to which constitutional and governmental apparatuses are designed by one or more generations of founding fathers. These systems of government are influenced by the social contexts from which they emerge and, in their modern guises, began to take on the shapes they have today—geographic boundaries and reasonably well-respected sovereignty over their destinies—in the eighteenth century when, in Western Europe, clusters of principalities began to unify around a few basic sets of shared interests. These interests included those in trade, defense, interboundary policy (later foreign policy), coinage systems, law and order, common languages (usually, but not necessarily), loosely shared beliefs and apprehensions (and thus prejudices), cultural traditions, and a variety of religious, philosophical, and political demiurges.

Generally, the founding fathers of today's nation-states have emerged out of the upper strata of the middle classes with well-developed interests in the formation of legal systems that would reduce ambiguities in the relationships, rights, privileges, and immunities among property owners, creditors, and those obliged to sell their skills in return for cash, goods, services, and claims to resources.

These classes of traders, farmer-owners, and goods producers have regularly been joined by military leaders, members of the so-called free professions, including clerics, and by survivors of the thinning ranks of aristocratic groups. The members of these classes and status groups shared an interest in protecting the wherewithal of "haves" against what they took to be the predatory (and what they otherwise feared would be the communitarian) impulses of "have nots" to redistribute a society's wealth and resources downward.

In modern times, nation-states vary in several major ways that have an important impact on work structures. First, they differ in the balance of influences over the instrumentalities of government (especially the instruments of coercion) that are allocated to central, national governments, on the one side, to subordinated entities—states (in the United States), communes, counties, and the like—on a second side, and, on a third side, to "the people" and their incorporated and unincorporated agencies—firms, partnerships, associations, clubs, caucuses, unions, and other legally constituted but private collectivities.

Second, nation-states vary in the degree to which they are organized around democratic principles.

Finally, nation-states differ in the degree to which their more organized economic activities are essentially planned by public officials.

The issues attaching to the balances among jurisdictions in the central state and in noncentral agencies and jurisdictions are of particular interest to us because, in joining them, one comes face to face with one of the major sources of the variations in all of the work structures that concern us in this volume as we move across international boundaries. To the extent that controls over social, economic, and political instrumentalities are centralized in the state, in all but a few totalitarian systems like the Soviet Union, to that degree: (1) class divisions become more marked and significant structures; (2) the correlates of occupational groupings become somewhat less significant; (3) organizations become appreciably less autonomous in their treatment of resources; (4) industries become more strategically important as policy-implementing vehicles; and (5) unions become more political and in their local organizations less potent as mechanisms for serving rank-and-file workers' interests.

Conversely, as public and private agencies outside the central government are invested with rights, privileges, and immunities, they tend to proliferate and to become potent as mechanisms for serving interests that lie beyond a central government's purview. Thus, in the United States we have fifty separate bodies of state laws, most of which touch importantly on issues joined as well by the federal Congress, by the enforcement agencies collectively known as the executive branch of government, and by the federal courts. In the United States and in a few other countries, we have, in addition, counties and municipalities of different types with additional overlays of influence or power over innumerable matters on which federal and state governments also have jurisdiction. The balances among central and noncentral loci of powers range from the relatively decentralized system in the United States to the centralized systems, for example, in England, France, Japan, and Scandinavia. Our brief characterizations of work structures in the more and less centralized state systems accommodate these divergent cases rather well.

When we turn from our work structures to our four markets, we see a similar picture. Seen in the perspective of political economy, a reemergent specialty in modern economics departments, nations may be crudely classified in terms of the relative importance of central planning mechanisms, on one side, and market forces on the other. In contemporary France and Japan, the activities in all four of our markets are very substantially influenced by state-level agencies and by monetary and fiscal policies of the government majorities or governing coalitions *whether or not* conservative critics of central governmental activism and the so-called positive state are in power. In the United States the shifting fortunes of our two main political parties are associated with marginal but not trivial increments (or decrements) in the overall use of the federal government as a major partner in the economic drama, but the overall balance in the United States is toward less formal use of government than in Japan or France. Of course, both political parties in the United States promote the use of government, though they differ over the extent of this use and, otherwise, in respect of the particular clusters of interests they feel should thereby be served.

We will expand on our discussion of how nation-states affect the correlates of the other work structures in the subsequent sections of this chapter. As we will see, central governments have profound impacts on classes, occupations, organizations, industries, and unions.

CORRELATES OF CLASS

Social class is one of the fundamental concepts of sociology. As Erik Wright has described the pervasiveness of class: "Sociology's one independent variable is a chameleon which blends into virtually every sociological tradition."[1] Since the meaning of class has been widely and often hotly debated, we must examine the different theoretical assumptions about the nature of class groups before we can identify what about class makes a difference.

We begin by reviewing the two major approaches to class: the Weberian and Marxist traditions. In both of these perspectives classes are conceived as systems of social relations that are complex and multi-dimensional. Their adherents differ, however, in their assumptions as to whether these class relations originate in markets or in productive enterprises.

Weber saw classes as originating in the nature of exchange relations in markets.[2] In his view, classes are bases for potential communal action

---

[1] Wright, *Class Structure and Income Determination*, 3.

[2] Max Weber, 1922, *Economy and Society*, ed. Gunther Roth (1922; reprint, New York: Bedminster Press, 1968).

rooted in peoples' market-related interests. Since the economic order is complex, being composed of many markets, so are the numbers of potential class groups. Wiley,[3] following Weber's approach, argues that there are as many bases for class differences as there are major forms of exchange relations in the economy. He identifies three markets, each of which has its own form of conflict between the two fundamental class groups of propertied and unpropertied. In the labor market, the basic conflict is between wage earners and employers (owners or owners' hired managers) over issues such as the price of labor. In commodity markets, the key conflict is between buyers and sellers of goods; and in credit markets, the basic conflict is between creditors and debtors. The degree of class cohesion and/or conflict in a society is determined by the extent of overlap among the groups in each of these markets. Such overlap varies across countries and time, depending on the degree of industrialization in the society and the period of the business cycle. For example, Wiley argues that the United States has a very inconsistent class structure, marked by low degrees of overlap between the dominant and subordinate classes in each of these markets, accounting in part for the often contradictory or paradoxical aspects of American politics.

In contrast to the Weberian perspectives, some Marxists assume that classes are defined by social relations within *enterprises*. Markets are important since they are the arenas in which class conflict often occurs, but these Marxists assume that markets are not the *bases* of class formation. Hence, the postulated absence of markets, as in some forms of socialism wherein markets are largely replaced by planning, does not mean that there are no classes: *all* societies have firms that produce goods and services; consequently, there will be "classes" even in socialist economies because of the presence of relations of domination and subordination within organizations. These relations are complex and Wright's three major dimensions of class are similar to Weber's three markets: (1) control over money capital (credit markets), (2) control over physical production (product markets), and (3) authority or relations of supervision and discipline in the labor process (labor markets).[4] These multiple bases of class formation imply that many potential classes, often having contradictory interests, may coexist for long periods of time.

Another way of classifying diverse conceptions of class, and one that crosscuts Weberian and Marxist approaches, is according to whether analysts emphasize "class-in-itself" or "class-for-itself"; in other words,

[3] Norbert Wiley, "America's Unique Class Politics," *American Sociological Review* 32 (1967): 529–41.

[4] Wright, *Class Structure and Income Determination*.

by whether they see class as a *structure* or a *process*. In much recent research in the Marxist tradition, like Wright's, classes are viewed as objective structural relations. Such structural conceptions of class naturally lead to questions about the boundaries of class groups: What are the structural categories that define the class maps of advanced industrial societies?

In contrast, some Marxists and Weberians focus more on the formation of class-based interest groups (classes-for-themselves) that derive from objective class structures. Classes-for-themselves are class groups whose members are aware of their interests vis-à-vis other classes and are mobilized into actions based on these interests. Unlike classes-in-themselves, which are simply taxonomic categories constructed by social scientists, classes-for-themselves are social actors capable of impacting upon and even transforming society and the nature of work and industry. As Przeworski has argued, it is necessary to concentrate on the processes of class formation, that is, the creation and destruction of links between and among class positions.[5] E.P. Thompson, the leading historian of class, has noted, for example, that

> I do not see class as a "structure," nor even as a "category," but as something which in fact happens (and can be shown to have happened) in human relationships . . . and class happens when some men, as a result of common experiences (inherited or shared) feel and articulate the identity of their interests as between themselves, and as against other men, whose interests are different from (and usually opposed to) theirs.[6]

To view class as a process is to raise important questions about how members of common economic positions develop organizations that act as interest groups in pursuit of their goals. Key issues here include the degree of overlap among classes in different markets and whether property owners and the nonpropertied, as defined within a multiplicity of markets, act as classes that have identifiable correlates. For example, employers may join together in cartels to advance their interests, while workers may band together in unions. To the extent that these unions are not restrictive (as craft unions in the United States historically have been) and seek to include members of the nonpropertied class in general (as do some industrial unions and as did the International Workers of

---

[5] See, for example, Adam Przeworski, "Proletariat into Class: The Process of Class Formation from Karl Kautsky's *The Class Struggle* to Recent Controversies," *Politics and Society* 7 (Fall 1977): 343–401.

[6] E. P. Thompson, *The Making of the English Working Class* (New York: Pantheon, 1963), 9–10.

the World or the Knights of Labor), we can speak of *working-class organizations*.[7]

Our view of class incorporates insights from both Marxist and Weberian traditions, and we see class as both a structure and a process. Corresponding to Marx's notion of class-in-itself, we have defined class as a work structure: the objective, structural relations of ownership, nonownership, and control within enterprises. Corresponding to Weber's view of class, we have assumed that markets *cause* work structures: whether classes-in-themselves become interest groups depends on the nature of markets and their particular intramural development within a given economic and political context.

The Class Structure

The class structures of advanced industrial societies are complex. We first examine differences in ownership and then look at class boundaries in the labor market.

Ownership. There is broad agreement among both Marxists and non-Marxists that ownership of private property is the key defining criterion of class position. A basic way of distinguishing members of the labor force with regard to their class position, then, is by whether they are self-employed or wage and salaried employees. In the United States and other advanced industrial nations, there has been a decline in self-employment during the past century. For example, in 1948, 16 percent of the American labor force was self-employed, but as long ago as 1979 only 8 percent of the labor force worked for themselves or, in the cases of franchised businesses in automobiles, fast food, shoes, drug stores, and gasoline dealerships for example, as independent agents of larger corporate complexes.[8]

Ownership of productive enterprises, furthermore, may be more or less concentrated. *Economic concentration* refers to the degree to which

---

[7] It is not clear, though, what we might best call joint ventures between employers' cartels and working-class organizations as in Mussolini's corporate state and Hitler's National Socialist system.

[8] The incidence of self-employment varies by occupation and industry. White-collar workers are more often self-employed than blue-collar workers; and professional and technical workers, managers and administrators, craftspeople, and farmers are the occupational groups with the highest levels of self-employment. Moreover, those in construction, retail trade, and service industries are more likely to be self-employed than people involved in the manufacture of goods. See T. Scott Fain, "Self-employed Americans: Their Number Has Increased," *Monthly Labor Review* 103 (November 1980): 3–8.

money, credit, and the sale of goods and services in a society are controlled by many or few agents or agencies. (We will later discuss a closely related concept, industrial concentration, which refers to control over product markets.) One way to measure economic concentration of manufacturing wealth is by the percentage of assets controlled by the top 100 and 200 manufacturing firms. Evidence from advanced industrial societies documents the trend toward increased concentration in the economy. For example, in the United States, these percentages have increased from 36 percent (100) and 46 percent (200) in 1927 to 48 percent (100) and 61 percent (200) in 1984. These increases have not been linear, since they have fluctuated with parallel swings in the business cycle. So, for example, the percentage of assets controlled by the largest American manufacturing firms dipped during World War II (for example, 40 percent [100] and 47 percent [200] in 1942, down from 44 percent and 51 percent respectively in 1939) and increased again during the postwar recovery.

Simple dichotomies, such as those between owners and nonowners, are attractive enough but they belie the complexity of the class structures of modern industrial societies. Property owners can not be said to constitute a coherent class in the United States, for example, since groups are both constantly shifting and generally highly *issue-specific*. Moreover, large firms have many owners, whereas some individuals may own all or part of many smaller firms. In addition, people without substantial ownership claims may differ considerably in their control over the conditions and fruits of their labor. The legal "owners" of most large firms are stockholders who, in formal terms, have the ultimate say in the selection of boards of directors, the governing bodies of firms. The control of corporations implies the power to select such boards; however, there is often a lack of significant coalitions to do this, and so managers may in fact have day-to-day control over the enterprise for relatively long periods.[9] Although they are not owners, then, managers often possess effective control and hence may be viewed as exercising power. It might be added, though, that in an age of takeovers not a few managers spend considerable time fighting "sharks" while looking for protective "white knights."

Class Boundaries in the Labor Markets. Debates about class boundaries focus mainly on the divisions between the *middle* and *working* classes. These debates center around cleavages in *labor markets*, since the nonpropertied earn their living by working for others and depend upon capitalists for their jobs, working conditions, and job rewards. In the Weberian view, class boundaries within labor markets are based on

[9] Caves.

occupational differences such as skills and other market capacities. Hence, Weberians differentiate members of the working class on the basis of their occupational membership and skills. Some authors have equated working-class membership with manual (blue-collar) occupations; others have included white-collar employees as well in this group. Giddens[10] has extended Weber's view of class by arguing that there are a multitude of attributes which give one person a greater market capacity than another (e.g., education, skills, contacts).

Even in the relatively circumscribed circles of Marxian theory,[11] there is considerable debate as to the most correct definition of class boundaries. Like the Weberians, some Marxists see the middle and working classes as differing primarily in their levels of *skills*. For example, some Marxists argue that the roots of the new middle class are intellectual knowledge, which has become a form of property. Thus, professional-technical workers and many managers and other white-collar employees form the professional-managerial class (PMC).[12] A spouse of one such person recently won her claim to the value of one half of her ex-husband's medical practice license for supporting his learning in medical schools; lawyers are not slow to identify property!

In contrast, recent Marxian discussions, especially those of Wright and Carchedi,[13] have argued that reducing the concept of class to occupation and skills corresponds only loosely to traditional usage. In contrast, they maintain *control*, and not skill, is the key source of class boundaries and the basis for defining the middle class. Moreover, social relations within enterprises, according to Wright, reflect relations of *exploitation*, not simply agreeable relations among superordinates and subordinates. Unlike Dahrendorf,[14] for whom authority relations in any organization constituted bases of potential class formation, Wright argues

[10] Anthony Giddens, *The Class Structure of Advanced Societies* (New York: Harper & Row, 1975).

[11] See, for example: Nicos Poulantzas, *Classes in Contemporary Capitalism* (London: New Left Books, 1975); Francesca Freedman, "The Internal Structure of the Proletariat," *Socialist Revolution* 26 (1975): 4–83; Albert Szymanski, "Trends in the American Class Structure," *Socialist Revolution* 10 (1972): 101–22; Erik O. Wright, "Class Boundaries in Advanced Capitalist Societies," *New Left Review* 98 (July–August 1976): 3–41; and Bertell Ollman, "Marx's Use of Class," *American Journal of Sociology* 73 (1968): 573–80.

[12] Barbara and John Ehrenreich, "The Professional-Managerial Class," *Radical America*, Part I (March–April 1977): 7–31; Part II (May–June 1977): 7–22.

[13] Wright, "Class Boundaries in Advanced Capitalist Societies"; G. Carchedi, "Reproduction of Classes at the Level of Production Relations," *Economy and Society* 4 (1975): 361–417.

[14] Ralf Dahrendorf, *Class and Class Conflict in Industrial Society* (Stanford, Cal.: Stanford University Press, 1959).

that classes are rooted only in productive organizations such as business firms.

Consequently, Wright distinguishes classes from occupations. That is,

> occupations and classes . . . designate qualitatively distinct dimensions of the social organization of work. Occupation broadly designates the technical content of jobs; class designates the social relations of domination and appropriation (that is, control over investments, decision-making, other people's work and one's own work) within which those technical activities are performed.[15]

In delineating the boundaries among the component parts of the American class structure, Wright identifies three groups of managers differing in their levels of authority, two groups of workers differing in their autonomy over their own work, and two types of employers differing in their number of employees. His assumption that one's class is distinct from one's occupational membership is supported somewhat by his data: members of particular class groups are found in many different occupations; and one's class membership cannot be predicted from knowledge about one's occupation and vice versa.

Nevertheless, the distinction between *class* and *occupation* is often unclear. For example, while managers are found in many occupations, they are concentrated in occupational categories such as foremen and managers and officials. Does *manager* designate a class, an occupational position, or, as in the view of some, simply because of its expanding size, a work force unto itself? By definition, managers supervise others and exercise control as part of their occupational activity, and here distinctions between the technical division of labor and social relations of production become fuzzy.

Similarly, it is unclear whether semiautonomous workers and ordinary workers are really two distinct classes. Semiautonomous workers are primarily found in the professional occupations (especially teachers) and enjoy considerable autonomy over their own work. Since autonomy is closely related to an occupation's skill and power, it may not be useful to call semiautonomous workers a separate class.

Clearly, the nature of industrial organization is affected by what capitalists do, and the way work is organized is determined in large part by the actions of the owners and managers of capital. However, we argue that the correlates of class can often be explained by references to forces in other of the types of work structures we consider in this book.

---

[15] Erik Olin Wright, Cynthia Costello, David Hachen, and Joey Sprague, "The American Class Structure," *American Sociological Review* 47 (December 1982): 709–26; quotation from 719.

For example, if unionized workers do not organize across industries with consciousness of widely shared interests, their unions are not agents of the working *class*. Similarly, if managers do not act as a class, studies of managers might better focus on their behavior within specific firms or other social aggregates, especially since managers increasingly do battle with each other and with "corporate raiders."

Managers are perhaps the most problematic group to conceptualize in class terms, since a number of mechanisms serve to hinder the formation of their class interests as property owners or as owners' key agents. For instance, managers are rewarded, in part at least, on the basis of their loyalty to specific firms, and their interests are tied more often to their own companies and employers than to the fates of managers, at least in the nearer run, in other firms. Hence, some managers actually have more in common with their subordinates than with their peers in other companies, even in the same industry.

Some managers want tariffs, for example, and some do not; the Lockheed bribery scandal pitted this airplane manufacturer against its competitors, and managers of defense and nondefense companies often hold very different views about government spending. In addition, although managers often join organizations that span firms–trade associations (NAM), the Business Roundtable, or personnel managers' associations—these stand for relatively narrow, non-class-related issues such as patriotism, a benign view of collective bargaining, information, and/or service.[16]

Class Processes: Conditions under Which People Act as a "Class."

One key issue in the analysis of class has to do with the ways in which people become truly conscious of their shared concerns and develop organizations to promote these class (as opposed to occupational or firm) interests. It is not easy, however, to specify the conditions under which classes come into conflict and those under which they collaborate. As Thompson points out:

> We can see a logic in the responses of similar occupational groups undergoing similar experiences, but we cannot predicate any law. Consciousness of class arises in the same way in different times and places, but never in just the same way.[17]

---

[16] See Sar A. Levitan and Martha R. Cooper, *Business Lobbies: The Public Good and the Bottom Line* (Baltimore: Johns Hopkins Press, 1984), 12–64.
[17] Thompson, 10.

The extent to which class is salient for work and industry also varies across national boundaries. The most strategic ways in which central governments abet or subvert truly class-linked behavior have to do with the degree to which they are actually engaged in the allocations of income among social groups by the use of transfer payments, subventions, public investments, and tax expenditures not recorded in budgets among groups, interests, and organizations in a society. Put crisply, central governments vary among themselves (and, over time, *within* their nations), in the force and extent of the roles they play in the distribution and redistribution of wealth and the revision of laws and rules concerning property rights.

We would suggest that what the late C. Wright Mills once called the "democratic demiurge" has been sufficiently well developed in Western-type nations that genuinely class-linked initiatives have become weakened by innumerable *progressive* reforms and central governments' interventions that have contributed: to long periods of economic growth— thus a larger economic pie; to income (or in-kind) transfers through loan and income guarantees, antipoverty measures, old age insurance, unemployment insurance and the like; to public investments in education, health, housing, and recreational activities; to public employment; to subsidy programs including incentives and protective tariffs on products or resources; and, finally, to civil rights programs and other similar efforts on behalf of groups victimized by obnoxious prejudices. It should be noted that many of these redistributive programs are designed not to *eliminate* inequalities in "final outcomes" regarding the distribution of wealth. Rather, many are designed substantially to reduce inequalities in access and opportunity and, to a lesser extent, to reduce the inequalities in the holdings of "haves," "have-littles," and "have-nots."

It is also notable that not all redistributive programs are designed to be progressive, in the conventional sense that they will reduce inequality. Indeed, several costly programs have (and are designed to have) upwardly targeted effects. These programs add to the claims of individuals, groups, and organizations whose members are quite comfortably situated before the facts of government largesse. The tax deductibility of mortgage interest payments on a condominium at a ski resort in Aspen, Colorado, or on a cottage at Martha's Vineyard will surely favor construction workers in Colorado and Massachusetts, semiskilled workers in ski-boot and wind-surfer factories, and the hostesses on airplanes who serve cocktails to would-be skiers and swimmers, respectively. But the longer-term and direct beneficiaries are mortgage lenders and the executives who borrow therefrom while they make their money from the successful mergers of perfume makers with manufacturers of odiferous chemicals.

The point is not a whimsical one: it is arguably the case that Americans have not even come close to a revolution since Daniel Shays frightened creditors, nearly to death, when he led a rebellion of indebted farmers in 1786. His rebels helped materially to spark the astoundingly rapid conversion, in the newly independent United States, from the radicalism implicit in the Declaration of Independence to the spirit of law and order that was written, soon after, into the United States Constitution!

Nor did we come close to a revolution during the Great Depression. It could also be argued that it has been part of our genius (and luck?) to grow in economic terms and to redistribute and redistribute, yet again, the fruits of our prodigious work such as to give most Americans a stake in the status quo and an inclination to see themselves as members of a middle class with many property ownershiplike claims. It could well be argued, further, that the single most important correlates of the state in Western-type democratic societies are reformlike programs that reduce prospects for erstwhile or would-be classes to engage in serious conflicts, a matter to which we will return in Chapter 6.

Class formation in the United States has been hindered by several additional factors. First, there has been a proliferation of status, as distinct from class, groups. When Americans identify themselves they both seek and, in multifarious ways, are encouraged to see themselves, in terms other than just their employment and property relationships—for example, as consumers, members of ethnic and other groups, members of professions, and ascribed members of heterogeneous race, sex, and age groups.

Second, population density in the United States has never been as great as in Europe while the constantly expanding American frontier tempered the salience of covetous interests in property acquisition.

Third, there have been relatively high rates of occupational and social mobility in the United States produced in part by the industrialization of an agrarian economy and in part by considerable opportunity for education. Bolstered by the American emphasis on individualism, the belief in individual access and the actual existence of a fair degree of access have helped to distract citizens from concerns with what might otherwise have been more collective class interests. These factors all contributed to what Edwards[18] has called "class fraction" politics in the United States; these politics pit members of the working class against each other and hinder the formation of cohesive and effective class groups.

Several theorists of the relations between the working and middle

[18] Richard C. Edwards, *Contested Terrain* (New York: Basic Books, 1979).

classes assume that the boundaries between these groups are weakening and that classes are becoming more homogeneous. One group of these theorists holds that the working class is undergoing "embourgeoisement," becoming more like the middle class as mass-produced goods make it easier for differences among consumers, for example, to be blurred. According to Zweig,[19] the riches produced by capitalism in the United States after World War II were so great and fairly distributed that workers began to emulate the consumption habits of the middle class. The closer workers got to the middle class, the more they wanted to become part of it and its culture. In Blauner's[20] version of this thesis, the waning of revolutionary consciousness was not due to a rise in the standard of living but to changes in the division of labor: automation increased workers' self-direction, which linked them increasingly to their superiors in a community of interests.

In contrast, the theory of *proletarianization* argues, almost in reverse, that the middle class is taking on interests that are more compatible with those of the working class. This increased solidarity between skilled and unskilled workers is due both to decreased social mobility and the destruction of crafts as formerly skilled middle-class members come to resemble more closely their unskilled counterparts.

A central problem, then, and one that we will address repeatedly throughout our discussion, is to identify the conditions under which classes do and do not take form. We pause here only long enough to note that the propertied rich and the poor are separated, much as are boxers by referees, by a very large middle group who, as de Tocqueville noted, have "much to lose and little to gain" by revolutions. As this reform-minded and compromise-prone population diminishes in size and the gap between have-littles and have-nots becomes more palpably great, these groups' class identities may become more self-evident. That the buffer group will shrink appears at this writing to be quite likely as automation thins the ranks of the better paid workers in the manufacturing sector while the "service economy," with its large numbers of modest jobs, expands.

However, Americans are almost unique in their limited preoccupation with class. Europeans, for example, generally have a more well developed sense of class consciousness, articulated especially in the formation of labor parties designed to represent the interests of the working class. Many of these countries, much earlier, had aristocracies. In Ger-

---

[19] Ferdynand Zweig, *The Worker in an Affluent Society: Family Life and Industry* (London: Heinemann, 1961).

[20] Blauner; see also Sabel, 2–3.

many, Yugoslavia, Norway, France, and Sweden, for example, class has had a profound impact on economic and legal policies and thereby on the correlates of work structures.

One way in which class affects work structures in these countries is through the participation of workers on boards of directors of corporations. In general, if broad-based labor parties emerge, the chances for the participation of workers on such boards are increased. Thus, in Germany, Sweden, and Norway codetermination is mandated by constitutions or laws derived therefrom. At the same time, such participation rarely reflects the outcome of class struggle. In France and Italy, for instance, it seems apparent that worker representatives are placed on boards of directors in order to co-opt them and thereby defuse class-based grievances. In contrast, working-class representatives forced their way on boards in Norway and Sweden. But in these countries there are also national labor parties with only modest local bargaining roles. Hence, the representatives on corporate boards more often become subject to the importunings of labor *parties* than the working classes directly in these countries.

The relative lack of class consciousness in the United States is illustrated by the absence of signs thereof in a cross-national survey of individuals in eight countries (Britain, West Germany, Netherlands, Austria, United States, Italy, Switzerland, and Finland). Class was measured by the objective class positions defined by Wright (i.e., big and small employers; top, middle, and bottom managers; semiautonomous workers and the proletariat) and subjective class awareness was measured by the person's stated class membership (upper middle, middle, and working class).[21] The proportion of people who did not regard their class identification as salient (measured by the percentage of people who did not give a subjective class identification without being prompted a second time by the interviewer) was lowest in the United States (38.2%) and Switzerland (37.3%). Further, Americans, once prompted to choose among the three subjective class categories, had the highest proportion identifying themselves as members of the upper middle class (15.8%); this is the case regardless of the person's objectively measured class membership. These results parallel the findings of similar studies beginning soon after World War II. The relative lack of classes-for-themselves in the United States has left abundant room for our other work structures to become more important in accounting for problems related to work and industry. One such key work structure is occupation, the correlates of which we consider next.

[21] Data supplied by Michael Wallace in personal communication.

CORRELATES OF OCCUPATIONS

Occupation is the dominant work structure studied in American stratification research, and occupations are the building blocks for most non-Marxist conceptualizations of social structure in industrial societies. For example, Blau and Duncan[22] suggest that the occupational hierarchy is "a major source of the various aspects of social stratification in industrial society." This assumption is grounded in Weber's arguments about the importance of occupations to the formation of differentially prestigious strata, classes, and power structures.

Classifying Occupations

Since occupations are aggregations of jobs that involve similar tasks, the categories used to classify them should be relatively homogeneous with respect to the functions of their incumbents. Unfortunately this is not the case, and the major way of grouping occupations, the Census Bureau's occupational classification, does so on the basis of attributes of jobs other than simply skills or functions. This scheme was developed in the early part of the twentieth century by Alba Edwards and, with modifications, is still widely used today. Indeed, Edwards's conceptual arrangement of occupations has had such a profound influence on the way social scientists and others have thought of them that Udy, reflecting a popular view, refers to it as the "Edwards paradigm."[23]

In Edwards's classification, occupations are grouped into broad status levels (professional, white-collar, blue-collar) rather than into skill groups. These major occupational categories are divided in turn into progressively finer detail depending on the nature of their constituents' functional activities (for instance, professionals include engineers among others, who in turn may be classified as chemical engineers, mechanical engineers, and so on). The 1970 version of the United States Census detailed classification contains 584 titles; in some cases, broad occupational titles (e.g., operatives, laborers) are further subdivided by industry categories in order to achieve greater homogeneity, within subsets, in the kinds of tasks performed.

---

[22] Blau and Duncan, 7.
[23] Stanley H. Udy, Jr., "The Configuration of Occupational Structure," in *Sociological Theory and Research: A Critical Approach*, ed. Hubert M. Blalock (New York: Free Press, 1980), 156–65.

Changes in the Occupational Structure

In Table 1, we present the percentage distributions of United States labor force members in ten major occupations for the years 1900, 1930, 1960, and 1980.

During this century, important changes have occurred in several main types of occupations. First, the proportion of farm-related occupations has been drastically reduced.

Second, there has been a large increase in the proportion of people in professional and technical occupations. For example, there are now more engineers, medical and dental technicians, personnel and labor relations specialists, nurses, and social and welfare workers.

Third, the clerical occupational category experienced a marked increase in membership over this period, during which many new types of clerical occupations were created. Those experiencing particularly high

TABLE 1. Occupational Distributions, 1900–1980

Occupation	1900[a]	1930[a]	1960[a]	1980[b]
White collar	(17.6%)	(29.4%)	(42.2%)	(52.2%)
Professional, technical	4.3	6.8	11.4	16.1
Managers, officials, proprietors	5.8	7.4	8.5	11.2
Clerical	3.0	8.9	14.9	18.6
Sales	4.5	6.3	7.4	6.3
Blue collar	(35.8)	(39.6)	(39.7)	(31.7)
Craftsmen, foremen	10.5	12.8	14.3	12.9
Operatives	12.8	15.8	19.9	14.2
Nonfarm laborers	12.5	11.0	5.5	4.6
Service	(9.0)	(9.8)	(11.8)	(13.3)
Private household	5.4	4.1	2.8	0.6
Farm	(37.6)	(21.2)	(6.3)	(2.8)
Farmers, farm managers	19.9	12.4	3.9	1.3
Farm laborers, foremen	17.7	8.8	2.4	1.5
Total	100.0%	100.0%	100.0%	100.0%
(N, in thousands)	(29,030)	(48,686)	(64,537)	(97,270)

[a] SOURCE: United States Bureau of the Census, *Historical Statistics of the United States, Colonial Times to 1970, Bicentennial Edition, Part I* (Washington, D.C.: U.S. Government Printing Office).
[b] SOURCE: United States Department of Labor, Bureau of Labor Statistics, *Employment and Earnings* (Washington, D.C.: U.S. Government Printing Office).

increases in employment include bookkeepers, cashiers, stenographers, typists, secretaries, office machine operators, and bank tellers.

Fourth, there has been an increase in the proportion of workers in service occupations. Occupations with the largest increases include practical nurses and hospital attendants; waiters, waitresses, and other retail workers; janitors, cleaners, and cooks; policemen, accountants, lawyers, teachers, and beauticians.

What accounts for these occupational changes? Three general trends in American society provide important explanations. First, industrial changes led to occupational changes: the increases in professional, technical, and clerical occupations resulted directly from the dramatic expansion in business services (advertising, accounting, banking), social services (medical, legal, educational, and governmental) and professional staffing needs in large manufacturing firms (personnel experts, trainers, forecasters, sales and marketing analysts).[24]

Second, some occupational changes were due to technological innovations and changes not directly related to shifts in the industrial structure but in the organization of production *within* industries. The transformation in the content of clerical work is a notable example: word processors have effectively changed many clerks into computer operators. Moreover, technological changes made many manual jobs obsolete, such as the virtual elimination of hand compositors in the printing industry.

Third, occupational trends partially reflect changes in the composition of the work force. By far the most dramatic of these has been the increased participation of women in the labor force since World War II. (The proportion of the United States labor force composed of women rose from 28 percent to over 40 percent during the postwar period; and over 50 percent of all adult women are now in the labor force.) The recruitment of women and the occupational structure's nature were mutually reinforcing: the influx of women fostered both the development and design of work that was not physically demanding and required little training (e.g., clerical work); the increased labor force participation of women, in turn, was due in part to the availability of occupations (e.g., clerical and service) that provided relatively clean work, conformed to expectations about sex role behavior, and could be performed part time as well as full time.

These occupational changes have resulted in a blurring of the distinctions between blue-collar and white-collar occupations: there has been a "blue-collarization" of the service sector and a "white-collarization" of

[24] Joachim Singelmann and Harley L. Browning, "Industrial Transformation and Occupational Change in the U.S., 1960–1970," *Social Forces* 59 (September 1980): 246–64.

the manufacturing sector. Both now share problems of unemployment, the first time in history that both suffer equally from joblessness and inflation. Indeed, the white-collar share of unemployment has actually *increased* faster than its share of employment.[25]

Since blue- and white-collar workers have more in common, this provides the basis for a potentially unified working class in the United States, the split between manufacturing (blue-collar) and services (white-collar) now being reduced.

These societal trends, in turn, are affected by national policies and structures operating through markets, both directly and indirectly, that have important effects on the correlates of occupations, as we will see in the next sections.

Nation-States and Occupations

There are several different ways in which central governments foster occupational differentiation and hence affect occupational structures. For example, one of the first acts of Congress following the ratification of the Constitution was to pass the first of many protective tariffs. In the process, these political founders started what Lipset has called the "first new nation" down—or up—the path of modernization and, further in the process, helped change a predominately agricultural society into an industrial one with an occupational structure that was gradually blue-collarized until the mid-1950s. We thus moved, in well under 200 years, from a nation of small farmers or yeoman, small artisans and tradesmen, in the eighteenth century into a manufacturing society in which, following the development of mass production techniques, there were armies of workers in semiskilled and unskilled operations and in "otherwise unclassified" occupations. The Civil War, we may remind ourselves, pitted a northern industrial region benefiting from protective tariffs against a southern agricultural region the citizens of which paid higher prices for finished goods because of the federal protection afforded their Yankee antagonists. The battles were along regional and occupational lines, and not nearly so clearly along class lines.

Next, a government's policies toward labor as a national resource will have indirect as well as direct implications for a nation's occupational structure. While space does not permit a detailed analysis of United States immigration policies, it is clear, for example, that the industrialization

[25] James W. Kuhn, "The Labor Force," in *Inflation and National Survival*, Proceedings of the Academy of Political Science, Vol. 33, No. 3, ed. Clarence C. Walton (Montpelier, Vt.: Capital City Press, 1979), 101–12.

process, predicated on the rapid development of labor-saving capital equipment, added to the expansion of demand for the semiskilled and unskilled ranks of the labor force, demand that was filled by an early version of Europe's modern *gastarbeiter* (guest workers). And after their daily work was done, the new producers were consumers whose purchases fed what nowadays we call aggregate demand—the customers for expansion-minded producers of goods and services—and thus they helped fuel booms in the economy.

Although our federal government came relatively late to play much of a part in occupational licensing, other government units (the several states in particular) were persuaded by their meritocratic pretensions and their anticompetitive dispositions to certify the members of a great many occupations—barbers, beauticians, lawyers, physicians, teachers, nurses, plumbers, and electricians, among them. Members of such groups—free professionals and craftworkers—further helped to segment and fragment the potential members of cohesive classes. These sanguine workers learned, as organized labor later did, that the state or its subordinate jurisdictions might just as well be utilized, peaceably, to their advantage, as not. The results, once again, were to encourage still other groups to seek to expand the concept of property ownership as a way of achieving democratic aims or redistributing advantages in more egalitarian directions.

If it is among nearly all governments' fundamental purposes to protect property and to afford due process, then it has apparently made sense to many Americans to emulate those whose contracts are enforceable and whose property is constitutionally protected and, with the help of one's occupational confreres, to secure similar rights and claims. We may note that for every strike called by a labor union there will be at least one hundred legal suits to enforce fair labor practices, seniority and other work rules, minimum wage laws, and "trigger prices" to protect the occupations in a given industry (not less than the industry itself) against foreigners' temptations to dump their below-cost exports on our markets. Additionally, many occupations are assisted by the passage of specifically relevant legislation enacted by a variety of governmental jurisdictions but especially by federal lawmakers.

Labor and tax laws thus create booms in demand for accountants and lawyers, and laws pertaining to education understandably affect the demand for teachers. Regulatory laws shape the demand for public employees whose salary structures and pension benefits often differ from their occupational counterparts in private-sector bureaucracies.

Public policies related to defense, meanwhile, have variable and very large impacts on the demand for (and to some extent the supplies of) human resources. On the military side, governments can recruit more or fewer members of the armed forces and impart many different types of occupational training to them. If the armed forces are voluntary and a "Baby Bust" birth cohort is the one to be tapped, as is now the case in the United States, the possible results are: (a) to bid up the prices both for unskilled workers and soldiers, (b) to reduce overseas adventures, (c) to force changes in tactics or strategy in favor of weaponry over manpower, (d) to return to the involuntary Selective Service System, (e) to enact significant changes in immigration laws, or (f) some combination of these alternatives.

On the civilian defense side, assertive foreign policies spark increases in defense spending such that, even in a high unemployment period, manpower bottlenecks develop. These occur when defense contractors bid up the prices, especially for skilled labor. The prospects for class-conscious behavior by workers, once again, are not very great in a society in which, during the years when the Vietnam war was deplored by many blue-collar unions, other unionists were "hawks" because their economic interests in defense contracting firms were satiable only by expanded defense budget outlays for weapons and other militarily useful products; some readers will recall the angry remonstrances of "hard hats" against critics of the war in Vietnam.

Central governments, alone or together with those in other jurisdictions, thus have numerous impacts on the size, composition, training, rewards, and stability of many occupations. By their impact on laws affecting the relationships between members of some occupations and their employers, central governments can shape substantial numbers of strands in what Kerr, Dunlop, and others characterize as "the web of rules," of which more later, that link managers and the managed in industrial societies.[26]

By their industrial policies, whether formally by planning or in less explicit ways, by programmatic interventions (tariffs, tax laws, research and development programs, and the like), central governments shape the demand for skills of different types and hence impact upon the configurations of occupational structures. And within particular occupations, members have varying degrees of control over their career options, work standards, and the entry requirements for membership depending upon whether the market for these occupational skills is "tight" or "loose." Young professors are thus persuaded that their older colleagues would not likely have earned their comforts had they been judged in accordance with what the new generation bemoans as today's higher standards, now

---

[26] Kerr, Dunlop, Harbison, and Myers, *Industrialism and Industrial Man.*

that baby boom support for the demand for professors has long since ended.

The policies discussed in this section are, in the United States, generally the responses of congeries of ever-changing governmental agencies, the Congress, and core governmental branches to the initiatives of a variety of collectivities and interest groups. As the political fortunes of the initiators change, so do the balances among various types of initiatives. Thus we observe nation-states acting more or less supportively toward many different proposals favoring widely disparate groups or clusters of groups. Such support has quieting or disquieting effects on the members of occupations whose leaders are themselves parties to the frays.

For example, the United Auto Workers were the beneficiaries of only a slight increase in the import quotas for Japanese cars in 1983 at the same moment that Mr. Reagan's administration took on the Professional Association of Tower Control Operators (PATCO), to the total disadvantage of the latter. Further, corporate mergers were accorded the president's blessings while his own attorney general obtained an injunction (in January 1984) against the merger of the Screen Actors Guild with the American Federation of Theatrical and Recording Artists.

With these illustrative impacts of the nation-state on occupations in mind, we now examine the correlates of occupations or the things about them which make a difference. Occupations differ in three main ways: the skills, power, and prestige of their members. These occupational correlates reflect the requirements, resources, and rewards associated with occupational activities.

The Differentiation of Occupations

Occupational Skills. Since occupations are groups of jobs involved in similar technical activities and having similar training requirements, their members' level and types of *skills* are key correlates of occupations. A major way of classifying occupations with respect to skill and related dimensions is the United States Department of Labor's *Dictionary of Occupational Titles* (DOT), of which there are four editions.[27] The DOT categories are based mainly on: the technology used in the occupation; the industry wherein the occupation is most commonly found; and the materials and/or services produced by the occupation.

For example, the fourth edition of the DOT contains 12,099 occu-

---

[27] See, for example, Pamela Cain and Donald Treiman, "The *Dictionary of Occupational Titles* as a Source of Occupational Data," *American Sociological Review* 46 (June 1981): 253–78.

pational categories and rates them on over forty dimensions of worker functions. These include: "complexity of work with data, people, and things"; the amount of training needed to perform adequately occupational activities; a host of attributes required of *workers* to perform the occupation (aptitudes such as motor skills, physical demands, interpersonal skills); and the nature of working conditions. In the DOT classification, occupational characteristics refer both to attributes of tasks *and* to differences among the people who do these tasks. This underscores a fundamental point: skills inhere both in the occupation's activities and in the individuals who perform them.

Since skill is central to defining an occupation, changes in skills are key topics for research on occupational correlates in studies in which investigators tend to augment rather than subvert each others' results. Thus, it is widely agreed that technology and automation have and will continue to alter the conditions and nature of occupational activities in fundamental ways, though there are disagreements over how fast these alterations take place and about the potency (or impotence) of forces targeted on softening their effects. The question is whether these changes have created skilled "knowledge" workers, "deskilled" servants of machines, or a combination of the two. We discuss the research on this issue in greater detail in the section on jobs and skills of Chapter 5.

Occupational Power. Occupations also differ in the *power* of their members.[28] As we discussed in relation to the nation-state above, occupations provide their members with differential access to the kinds of resources they can bring to bear in the workplace and in the market. For example, members of some occupations enjoy such rights as to enter into contracts and to license themselves, thereby maintaining their position and the right to train their would-be members. Others—apart from those in very small establishments—can claim compensation for job-related injuries and minimum wage payments.

Differences among occupations in their power or their resources otherwise, meanwhile, are closely linked to their skill and training requirements. Indeed, control over the supply of skills is a major way by which workers are able to obtain leverage over employers and other workers. Consequently, although occupations are defined largely in terms of technical activities, their members are invariably embedded in far wider social relations; the observation serves to underscore the fuzziness of distinctions between class and occupation.

The effects of occupational skill requirements and resources on re-

---

[28] See William H. Form and Joan A. Huber, "Occupational Power," in *Handbook of Work, Organization and Society,* ed. Robert Dubin (Chicago: Rand McNally, 1976), pp. 751–806.

wards (both intrinsic and extrinsic) are the main subjects in theories of occupational inequality. A considerable body of neoclassical economic theory,[29] not less than functionalist sociological theory, suggests that inequality in occupational rewards is due to differences among occupations in their requirements for entry and performance.

Davis and Moore,[30] in a now classic statement, asserted that unequal rewards "unconsciously evolve" to motivate individuals with the requisite talents and training to enter the appropriate positions and to perform them adequately.

Empirical evidence suggests, however, that neither is inequality in occupational rewards completely technical in origin nor is its evolution essentially unconscious. Rather, the differential power and resources of occupational groups are important for generating inequalities, since occupations differ (1) in their claims upon the value of the output of the production process and (2) in the controls they can exercise over the production process itself.[31]

Differences among occupations in their members' power and skills underlie explanations of the emergence of labor market "shelters" and their near-relatives, *occupational internal labor markets* (OILMs).[32] The fact is that some occupations create internal labor markets for their members, such that senior incumbents of occupations not only influence the entry of potential new members but also govern their mobility, training and training time, wage rates, and sometimes their social relationships off the job as in occupational communities—miners, loggers and, in some measure, professionals. Importantly, members of occupational internal labor markets often change employers and firms as they progress up job ladders within the occupation. Occupational internal labor markets encourage mobility within, rather than between, occupations, for example. We discuss occupational internal labor markets in more detail in the section of Chapter 4 on careers and mobility.

The resources that help determine whether an occupation is able to establish an internal market include: (1) organized bargaining power reflected in the ability of occupational incumbents to control licensing and entry into the occupation, and thus the supply of and demand for their labor offerings and the returns thereto; (2) the cohesiveness of

[29] Jacob Mincer, "The Distribution of Labor Incomes: A Survey," *Journal of Economic Literature* 8 (1970): 1–26.

[30] Kingsley Davis and Wilbert E. Moore, "Some Principles of Stratification," *American Sociological Review* 10 (1945): 242–49.

[31] Form and Huber.

[32] See Althauser and Kalleberg; Freedman.

occupational members and the ease with which incumbents can mobilize into interest groups; (3) the vulnerability of occupations to unemployment (both in terms of its duration and its frequency) and related correlates of business cycle fluctuations; and, finally, (4) the extent of competition with other occupations for access to or control over scarce resources.

Occupational Status and Prestige. The most often used correlate of occupations in empirical stratification research is occupational status or prestige. These are distinct concepts and are measured in different ways: by aggregating individuals' perceptions of the overall desirability of the occupation in the case of prestige; and by computing a linear combination of the income and education levels of occupations in the case of status. However, the empirical correspondence between them is so high (on the order of .95–.98) that we can regard them as tapping a single correlate of occupational structure, one which derives primarily from the education required to perform the job and the economic rewards that occupational incumbents receive.

Occupational status or prestige is used by status attainment researchers to rank occupations for purposes of studying mobility and occupationally related achievements. Although some argue that status or prestige really reflects deference in the classic sense of the term *prestige*, this occupational correlate is better viewed as an overall measure of the "goodness" (as contrasted with the "badness" or disagreeable aspects) of occupations.[33] As such, an occupation's status or prestige results from all of the other ways in which occupations differ: from their requirements, rewards, and resources. Some of the earliest empirical investigators of work structures examined the prestige and status rankings of occupations, which, they observed, could be relatively constant within a society over time and relatively similar across countries.[34]

The reasons why these rankings are relatively constant, however, are not so well known. For example, people might carry around with them "cognitive maps," more or less isomorphic, of the rankings of different occupations. It is probably more likely that occupations in different countries have similar configurations of requirements, rewards, and resources, especially in national economies that are more tightly integrated into what some call the world economy and as ownership itself becomes international in its character, through "outsourcing," cross-national in-

---

[33] See John Goldthorpe and Keith Hope, *The Social Grading of Occupations* (Oxford, England: Clarendon, 1974).

[34] See, for example, Alex Inkeles and Peter H. Rossi, "National Comparisons of Occupational Prestige," *American Journal of Sociology* 66 (1956): 1–31; and Donald J. Treiman, *Occupational Prestige in Comparative Perspective* (New York: Academic Press, 1977).

vestment, international development agencies, and the internationalization of higher education.

That occupational prestige differences are a part of the reality of social structures is illustrated by a study of the relations between prestige rankings and measures of occupational skill requirements, resources, and rewards.[35] The investigators found that occupations with greater skill requirements had higher levels of prestige. Moreover, occupations located in bigger organizations were also ranked higher in prestige, as were occupations the members of which had higher levels of authority. These findings suggest that prestige rankings of occupations reflect the technical nature of occupational activities as well as their resources in a social division of labor and social norms governing the evaluation of hierarchical relationships.

We next consider the correlates associated with the specific organizations wherein occupational activities are actually performed.

CORRELATES OF ORGANIZATIONS

As we noted in Chapter 1, there are two very general theoretical perspectives on organizations. The *closed system* approach is rooted in Weber's conception of bureaucracy as a "legal-rational" apparatus consisting of roles, rules, standing procedures, and personnel policies designed to achieve the goals of its leaders. Writers in this tradition focus on the internal structuring of organizations and have developed a variety of theories to explain their correlates and consequences.

We can classify writers in this tradition into several distinct groups: (1) "management" theorists, who attempt to understand how organizational efficiency may be increased;[36] (2) univariate organizational structuralists, who study the interrelations among organizational properties;[37] (3) "individual" theorists, who are concerned with integrating individuals into the organization and in studying the impacts of organizational structures on people;[38] and (4) "technology" theorists, who investigate the

---

[35] Bielby and Kalleberg.

[36] Frederick W. Taylor, *Principles of Scientific Management* (New York: Harper & Row, 1911); Elton Mayo, *The Human Problems of Industrial Civilization* (New York: Macmillan, 1933).

[37] Hage; Derek Pugh, David Hickson, Robert Hinings, and Chris Turner, "Dimensions of Organization Structure," *Administrative Science Quarterly* 13 (June 1968): 65–104.

[38] Chris Argyris, *Integrating the Individual and the Organization* (New York: Wiley, 1964); Frederick Herzberg, Bernard Mausner, and Barbara Snyderman, *The Motivation to Work* (New York: Wiley, 1959).

impact of technology on organizational structures.[39] In all these approaches, the focus is almost entirely on the *internal* workings of the organization.

In contrast, writers in the *open system* approach argue that organizations are embedded in larger structural and social contexts which must be understood in order to explain internal organizational structures and processes. Compared with the closed system writers who use organizational goals to define the activities of organizations, those in the open system tradition emphasize the importance of the *environment*. Moreover, they often view the organization as a "natural system," containing a number of arrangements that may deviate from its formal structure in ways that both subvert and augment it. Proponents of this view have accordingly been given to study the informal and often nonrational aspects of organizational behavior.[40] This approach is illustrated in the writings of those in the institutional school, a sociological perspective on organizations that analyzes them as "wholes" in the contexts of more macroscopic social structures.[41]

The distinction between closed and open system approaches is sometimes hard to draw, in part because of the difficulties both have in defining the boundaries of the organization. We suggest that one important distinction resides in the fact that some of the people critical to an organization's capacities and well-being are on its payroll whereas others are not. Among the most significant of the latter are subcontractors and franchised outlets. Those considered outside of the organization and part of its environment on the basis of a payroll definition may well be part of the organization if the second definition is adopted. Uncritical acceptance of people's labels about organizational definitions may often lead to faulty conclusions.

For example, Stinchcombe's[42] classic treatment of how an organization's age affects its structure defines organizations in payroll terms. Hence, he overlooks similarities among organizational forms he considers to be very different, such as the marketing of autos and oil in the 1970s, a modern-day variant of the putting-out system initiated by business in the goods-producing sector in Europe in the nineteenth century. An

---

[39] James Thompson, *Organizations in Action* (New York: McGraw-Hill, 1967).

[40] Alvin W. Gouldner, "Organizational Analysis," in *Sociology Today*, ed. Robert K. Merton, Leonard Broom, and Leonard S. Cottrell (New York: Basic Books, 1959), 400–28.

[41] For example, Philip Selznick, *TVA and the Grass Roots* (Berkeley: University of California Press, 1949).

[42] See Arthur L. Stinchcombe, "Social Structure and Organizations," in *Handbook of Organizations*, ed. James G. March (Chicago: Rand McNally, 1965), 142–93; and Ivar Berg, *Industrial Sociology* (Englewood Cliffs, N.J.: Prentice-Hall, 1979).

acknowledgment of these similarities raises questions about an otherwise attractive argument that, over time, organizational forms have linear evolutionary qualities.

What constitutes the organization, moreover, is often ambiguous even if one adopts a payroll definition with reasonable confidence. One key distinction is that between the *firm* and the *establishment*. The firm is the basic corporate group and is a useful unit of analysis for studying issues such as profitability, economies of scale, and so on. On the other hand, the establishment is perhaps the most relevant organizational unit for addressing many issues related to labor markets and other aspects of work: it is the establishment in which people are linked to the overall company, where internal labor markets "live," mobility occurs, and the careers of long-time employees (especially those in blue-collar occupations) often unfold. As the sizes of firms have increased through mergers and other forms of consolidation, there are likely to be many establishments within a firm. As we will see later, small establishments appear to generate more new jobs than larger ones, but when we consider small establishments as parts of their parent firms we see a different picture.

We first look at the ways in which nation-state structures affect business organizations.

Nation-States and Organizations

Central governments, sharing varying degrees of responsibility with lesser jurisdictions depending on how centralized the system, have most of the same types of impacts on business organizations as they have on classes and occupations. Thus, the prospects of an organization's members for becoming part of large, class-based reference groups, like those of the members of an occupation, are influenced by an enormous number of public undertakings, at one extreme, in the name of the governed and at the other by tyrants' agents who claim they act for the people.[43]

In the United States, though, most managers see themselves as the legitimate exercisers of authority over working populations that accord them reasonable orders of deference simply because, as managers, they are legally constituted agents of owners, because they are driven by market forces to act reasonably and in accord with professional standards,

[43] Lest we think that the latter initiatives are restricted to the Nazi Germanies or the Soviet Unions, we may remind ourselves that the FBI is not infrequently obliged to make visits even to corporate executives' homes. Older readers will recall the stock market crash in October 1962 after midnight calls on steel executives following President John Kennedy's outrage over steel price increases he felt were in violation of antitrust laws.

and because their charges have come to believe in the reasonableness of the processes—education among them—by which managers come to their positions.

If any managers consider their employees to be members of the working class, meanwhile, they rarely fret about the possible revolutionary implications of such a characterization. Indeed, employers are far more conscious of the competing claims of their employees, given the differences in the sensibilities among their workers about their age, seniority, skill, gender, ethnicity, and race identifications. These differentiated sensibilities, managers reckon, can be heightened by central governments' responses (or lack thereof) to the organized initiatives of workers' many possible reference and interest groups, from the National Organization of Women to the NAACP. And workers' expressions of their interests are far, far more often couched in gender, race, age, and seniority terms than in terms of "us" and "them."

Leaders of firms often share many concerns about the abilities of employees who belong to other organizations or occupations to limit their options in designing and managing their human resource policies. Hospital and university administrators, for example, worry about physicians' and faculty members' loyalties to their professional colleagues and to their professional societies.

The interests of corporations that more or less unite them in their dealings, for example, with employees, customers, creditors, and other relevant population groups, meanwhile, are those that have to do specifically with corporate managers' desires to maintain or expand their rights and privileges and to resist expansions of their vulnerabilities and outright liabilities. These interests lead corporate organizations' leaders to be ever vigilant concerning the conditions of their legal status and the prospects that their own freedoms as buyers, sellers, traders, or resource users will be threatened by the ever increasing rights and claims of stockholders (and the "raiders" who claim to serve them), stakeholders (including workers, suppliers, and dependent customers), and even their competitors.

Indeed, there are increasing instances of professional managers doing battle with the stockholder-owners of their firms, as when managers resist takeovers; some of the yields of merger bidders' tactics go to shareholders (who, most typically, care not a fig for managers or employees) in the form of elevated stock values. Increasing numbers of managers thus favor the introduction of more federal restraints against mergers, that is to say, effectively, they favor restraints on competition in capital markets; the best way to calm merger waves is to restrict the amount or quality ("junk bonds," for example) of credit that may be used in acquisition efforts.

Among the fundamental legal statuses of corporate organizations are those that enable them to enter into binding contracts and to bring suit to protect their interests therein. These statuses enable corporations to survive, as *personae fictae*, beyond the lives of their shareholders and to enjoy limitations on their liabilities such that the corporate property (and not its property owners or managers themselves) may be sued for allegedly illegal actions. An aggregation or collective of shareholders thus takes on some of the valued attributes we associate with real persons in ways that make corporations literally superhuman.[44] The business firm is, accordingly, one of the most extraordinary types of social technology ever invented by man. And the most important tools in the construction and protection of this entity are nation-states and the government jurisdictions thereunder with the constitutionally sanctioned authority to charter corporations.

In most countries, the corporation is the creature of the nation-state. In the United States, however, the enabling legal act—incorporation by charter—is performed by the several states. When New Hampshire's leaders tried, in 1819, to vacate a contract between Dartmouth College and an Indian tribe, the United States Supreme Court gave a federal constitutional imprimatur to all contracts "legally entered into" by legitimate corporations, an imprimatur that the chartering state could not erase.[45] One might argue that subsequent corporations' often generous gifts to higher education are grateful symbolic repayments to Dartmouth College, Daniel Webster's client and alma mater, for securing for corporations the sanctity of their charters and thus the sanctities of their contracts.

A number of the particular requirements, rights, privileges, and immunities attaching to newly chartered firms in the United States, meanwhile, will vary depending upon the corporate laws of the chartering state. Critics of modern corporations—Nader's Raiders most notably—have argued that the capacities of corporations to "venue shop"—to select chartering venues in accord with their needs for particular advantages—should, and could, be constrained by legislation requiring that corporations be federally chartered. Congress would then have an implicit mandate for specifying a variety of public interest-serving performance criteria as conditions for a corporation's receipt of a charter. In the process, the federal government would, in other words, have "hands-on" control of the levers of the machinery that drives corporate behavior.

---

[44] For a comparison between real and corporate persons and the implications for American social structure, see Coleman, *The Asymmetric Society*.

[45] *Trustees of Dartmouth College v. Woodward* 4 Wheaton 518; 4 L. Ed. 629 (1819).

The issues surrounding the matter of corporate chartering are significant at all of our analytical levels, but they are most acute at the level of organizational structures, for it is essentially at that level that the parties to economic exchanges and transactions—buyers, creditors, owners, employees, managers, union members, consumers, and leaders of peak and trade associations—really and truly converge.

It is in the corporate organizational establishments, after all, that employers make products, sell, borrow, profit (or lose), hire, promote, reward, punish, and bargain with workers' representatives. And it is organizations that managers lead, lawmakers regulate, judges (for the most part) cite for one or another sort of miscreant behavior, try and fine, and reformers seek to change.

Surprisingly, however, studies of organizations have essentially been conducted by: (1) economists and antitrust lawyers who aggregate them by product market or industry; (2) corporate law experts who focus on detailed legal questions and whose interests are driven by contesting and therefore interested clients; and (3) social scientists who are almost always interested in the *intramural* properties and problems of organizations. Few look at organizations in their cultural and institutional contexts. The few social scientists who look both intramurally at organizations and at the forces in their wider sociopolitical and socioeconomic contexts and who do so in systematic fashion will, we hope, be pleased with our modest efforts to lend some credibility to and enthusiasm for the ascendingly significant theoretical status of their model.

Among other significant correlates of the state to be observed in organizational settings are: (1) the expansion of "white-collar overhead" in a firm's workforce attributable to requirements that the firm withhold income, sales, and social security taxes, comply with safety and other workers' protection requirements, engage obligatorily in good faith bargaining, and comply with reporting and disclosure requirements to the National Labor Relations Board (NLRB), the Securities and Exchange Commission (SEC), the Federal Trade Commission (FTC), and other regulatory agencies with specific industry-linked jurisdictions (the Interstate Commerce Commission, the Federal Communications Commission and the Department of Housing and Urban Development, for example); (2) attributes of firms reflecting the degrees to which they are either driven by competitive forces monitored by the state (forcing them, thereby, to be efficiency-conscious) or are protected by the state through research and development allowances, "bailout" credit guarantees, tariffs, subsidies and subsidylike federal purchases and licenses, permitting them to earn what economists call "monopoly rents"; and finally (3) organizations' own obligations to pay their share of the nation-state's expenses (after taking allowable deductions) through income and "use" tax payments, fees and the like. The correlates of the state's initiatives are variable in their effects, depending on differences among firms in their size, market circumstances, industries, vulnerabilities or opportunities (for mergers, for example), and borrowing capacities.

For example, federal policies in the United States regarding labor and collective bargaining generate differential effects depending on a firm's significance to the nation's health, welfare, or safety. Thus the Congress empowers the federal courts to determine whether a strike—say, in steel or stevedoring—should be enjoined for an eighty-day cooling-off period under provisions of the Taft-Hartley Act, because, if continued, the strike's effects would harm the public's interest. Companies whose economic or defense roles are not demonstrably critical do not benefit from such public interventions against strikes by their workers.

With these impacts of the nation-state in mind, we now turn to a discussion of the correlates of business organizations. We classify these correlates as either intraorganizational or interorganizational structures. This distinction parallels that between closed and open system perspectives and suffers from similar limitations and ambiguities. In particular, it assumes a payroll definition of organizations. Nevertheless, since this broad distinction is the basis of most research and data collection on business organizations, it provides a useful way of classifying their key correlates.

Intraorganizational Correlates

Structures internal to the organization are both formal, designed by organizational leaders, and informal, emergent from the interactions of organizational members. Informal structures have been the subjects of many case studies that illuminate how organizations "really" work. While not officially part of the organization, in the short haul, these structures are nevertheless needed; they are the grease that lubricates the workings of the firm. However, their shadowy qualities, in the short haul, make them difficult to discuss and measure in comparative terms. Therefore, our discussion focuses primarily on the correlates of formal organization structures.

Size. A key correlate of organizations is their *size.* This can be measured in different ways: the number of employees; the total number of organizational members; and the organization's assets, financial scope, or scale. As we noted above, we must distinguish between the size of the establishment or plant where workers are directly tied to the company and the size of the parent firm or larger corporate group. And, of course, we must also distinguish the size of the organization's actual payroll from the larger numbers of persons who are effectively dependent on it, though they earn neither salaries nor wages therefrom.

Sociologists and economists often assume that organizations have become increasingly larger, and often paint a picture of most people working in very large organizations. However, in one of the few systematic discussions of the history and significance of the size distribution of business organizations, Granovetter[46] argues that this view is misleading, since the majority of labor force members have and continue to work in relatively small establishments.

He reports, for example, that the proportion of employees in United States manufacturing establishments with less than 1000 employees decreased only slightly in this century, from 88.1 percent (1904) to 72.5 percent (1977). The notion that workers are members of much larger operations now than fifty or seventy-five years ago more accurately describes firms than establishments. But, once again, four of ten Americans still work in firms with fewer than 100 employees, and six of ten work in firms with fewer than 1,000 employees. However, all these conclusions assume a payroll definition of organizations. The results are dramatically different if we view size as an ownership pattern (for example, number of subsidiaries). For example, using a definition of 100 employees or less as small, Birch estimates that most new jobs are produced by smaller establishments but 60 percent of these new jobs are, in fact, generated by establishments that are subsidiaries of larger organizations.[47]

The importance of the distinction between establishments and firms differs among industries. For example, it has the greatest significance in manufacturing and the least relevance in services, since single-establishment firms account for a far smaller proportion of employment in manufacturing than in service and other industries. The sizes of establishments also vary by industry, from an average of 60 people per establishment in manufacturing industries to 8.1 in construction.

Despite the apparent straightforwardness of the concept, the correlates and consequences of size have generated about as much debate in the organizational literature as class has in research on stratification.[48]

[46] Mark Granovetter, "Small Is Bountiful: Labor Markets and Establishment Size," *American Sociological Review* 49 (June 1984): 323–34.

[47] "Small Is Bountiful," *New York Times*, March 13, 1983, 83.

[48] See, for example, John Kimberly, "Organization Size and the Structuralist Perspective: A Review, Critique and Proposal," *Administrative Science Quarterly* 21 (December 1976): 571–97; and James N. Baron, "Organizational Perspectives on Stratification," *Annual Review of Sociology* 10 (1984): 37–69.

For example, big organizations have many advantages over small ones. In general, bigger organizations can better manipulate and control elements in their environment. Hence, they are more likely than small firms to engage in long-term planning because of their greater control over suppliers and distributors and to experience more stable demand for their products and services. Large firms are also better able, up to a point, to achieve increasing economies of scale and thereby to earn higher profits.

Firms are differentially vulnerable to corporate income taxes, and larger firms are better situated to take advantage of public policy incentives specifically enacted as tax expenditure packages, a term denoting uncollected taxes. Similarly, small firms are less readily capable than larger ones of exploiting allowances of different types designed by the state to encourage research and development projects, the returns from which cannot be realized very quickly.

An organization's size is also a good predictor of its vulnerability to union organizers' efforts and of its union's vulnerabilities as well; union members in small firms are more likely to decertify their unions and these firms are themselves less likely to be organized in the first place. Moreover, bigger firms tend to occupy more favorable market positions and, whether organized or not, to pay higher wages and more ample benefits and, over the short run, to pass on cost increases to their customers.

An organization's size has also been shown to be a major predictor of a number of features of its internal structure,[49] though the exact nature of these relationships may vary depending on the type of technology and other environmental characteristics. For example, larger organizations are more *complex*. Specifically, they exhibit both greater *horizontal complexity*, that is, the ways in which tasks are divided among segments of the organization (specialization) and *vertical differentiation*, or the ways in which authority is distributed among positions in the firm, such as the number of supervisory levels and the supervisors' spans of control.

Larger organizations also have higher degrees of *formalization*, with more written rules and regulations, and a greater degree of *standardization*, with more "set ways" of doing things and "SOPs" (standard operating procedures). In addition, larger firms are more likely to have multi-establishment plants and other structures. Each of these establishments could be relatively small, as in the chemical industry. These structural correlates of size often introduce problems of coordination and control, since communication becomes more difficult as the number of organizational members increases.

---

[49] See Baron and Bielby, "Bringing the Firms Back In."

Organizations of different sizes also vary in the nature of their *control systems:* large organizations more often rely on *bureaucratic* control systems, in which workers are directed, evaluated and rewarded on the basis of formal rules and institutionalized practices built into the structure of the firm. And larger firms are more likely to use *technical* control systems, whereby workers' activities are directed, in effect, by machines that time jobs, pace work, and read back workers' mistakes. In contrast, small firms more often use *personal* control systems, wherein owners and managers directly supervise and evaluate workers.[50] In addition to their size, the types of control systems adopted by firms differ by country. For example, in Germany the ratio of managers (and lawyers) to production workers in manufacturing industries is far lower than in the United States. The differences, one reasonably supposes, are rooted in cultural variations in the ways in which authority is exercised and held to be legitimate, work is organized, and innumerable social relationships are defined and conducted.

Firm Internal Labor Markets. Firm internal labor markets (FILMs) are key components of bureaucratic control systems. FILMs are job ladders, with entry restricted to lower levels and progress upward linked to the acquisition of greater skill and knowledge and the evolving rules that govern how work is done, requirements for advancement, and the like.[51] These structures are used by employers to motivate their employees, offering them possibilities of advancement in return for their commitment to the firm. FILMs are not found only in large firms, however, as they may be located in firms of all sizes: relatively small firms are often characterized by well-developed internal promotion systems. There may also be many FILMs within a firm (for example, finance, production, and sales ladders); not all jobs in a firm may be linked as part of a single, overarching internal market. Indeed, the fact that they are often not all of a piece has made for problems in an age of affirmative action and equal employment opportunities: women and minorities have found themselves stymied, at the top of one ladder, from earning promotions that would require their moving over to the rungs of a different ladder.

FILMs are useful for addressing a key issue among sociologists and economists: how and why people move among jobs. Internal labor markets are the structures underlying career mobility, which can occur in different ways. For example, people can move among jobs within the same firm, or they can move, by means of mobility channels among firms, within the same occupation across employers. As we indicated earlier,

---

[50] See Edwards.
[51] Doeringer and Piore; Althauser and Kalleberg.

internal labor markets exist within some firms as well as within some occupations, and analyses of their progress in both are necessary in order to understand differences in the careers of the citizens of many economically developed nations (a matter to which we will return in a section on careers and mobility in Chapter 4).

Explaining Differences in Intraorganizational Structures. A major theoretical debate concerns the general question of why organizational structures and their correlates arise. There are two major perspectives on this question: *technical imperatives* versus *social control.*

The technical imperative approach argues that organizations, as microcosms of society, will become increasingly rationalized as they become more thoroughly differentiated, adopting principles of technical efficiency. According to this reasoning, which parallels that behind the neoclassical economic microtheory of the firm, the organization of work results from efforts by managers to increase technical efficiency by maximizing the outputs produced by different combinations of factor inputs. The mix of factors used and thus the nature of job design reflect decisions based on the relative productivities and prices of different factors of production.

In contrast, Marxists have argued that the organization of work results not only from firms' needs for technical, *quantitative* efficiency, but also from the needs of capitalists to exert social control over the work force. Gordon[52] refers to the latter as *qualitative* efficiency, or the degree to which the organization of work reproduces the social relations of production. FILMs, for example, are designed to motivate workers as well as to undercut their nascent desires to combine against employers. This argument assumes that efficiency is not a value-neutral goal in capitalist economies but rather reflects processes and structures associated with the social relations of production. In support of this, Noble and others have shown that technological developments such as machine design and deployment reflect existing power relations in the capitalist firm.[53]

These two theoretical perspectives lead to different assumptions about how technological change affects the organization of work: the technical efficiency theorists tend to see technology as beneficial to both workers and employers, increasing both skill levels and productivity. Those theorists who emphasize social control focus on the negative consequences of technology, such as decreased skill levels and diminished opportunities for self-direction on the part of workers.

---

[52] David M. Gordon, "Capitalist Efficiency and Socialist Efficiency," *Monthly Review* 28 (1976): 19–39.

[53] David Noble, *America by Design* (New York: Oxford University Press, 1977).

Williamson synthesizes these two explanations of work organization by an approach that stresses the role of "transaction costs."[54] He argues that the modern corporation is the product of organizational innovations that have had the purpose and effect of economizing on transaction costs, resulting from technical factors, on one side, and the need to recruit and motivate employees, on the other. The use of markets and hierarchies are alternative ways by which employers can organize work, and the one chosen depends on the nature of information and other sociological and economic constraints that exist within a given market or organization.

Interorganizational Correlates

The open system perspective seeks to understand how organizations are linked to each other and to larger societal structures and institutions. It complements the closed system approach by focusing on how internal organizational arrangements are influenced by external constraints. As Hall summarizes the main assumptions of this approach:

> Environmental and technological factors, together with the related consideration of the nature of the personnel, traditions, decision-making, and other internal considerations, determine the form of the organization at any point in time.[55]

The boundaries of firms are regularly penetrated in nations that need organizations to mobilize and coordinate the uses of the factors of production, but whose national leaders must also balance claims, rights, and activities of producer organizations that have consequences deemed to be problematical compared with others' needs and claims. For economists, these consequences of organizations' initiatives are conveniently lumped under the rubrics *social costs*, *social benefits*, and *externalities*.

These costs and benefits include such good and bad developments as improved consumer goods and polluted air.

Indeed, government apparatuses at the level of the nation-state are, to a remarkable degree, the results of public representatives' urges to promote the good and minimize the bad effects produced by corporate creatures that have been chartered by national governments themselves or, with their blessings, by the nation-state's federal partners or its subordinate jurisdictions. Thus, organizations differ in their vulnerability to

---

[54] Oliver E. Williamson, *Markets and Hierarchies: Analysis and Anti-trust Implications* (New York: Free Press, 1975); see also his "The Modern Corporation: Origins, Evolution, Attributes," *Journal of Economic Literature* XIX (December 1981): 1537–68.

[55] Richard H. Hall, *Organizations: Structure and Process* (Englewood Cliffs, N.J.: Prentice-Hall, 1972), 171.

being "invaded" by the public interest, for example, by obligations to appoint affirmative action officers to represent and monitor compliance with federal requirements. The nature of organizational forms is also limited by the type of technology available, the types of workers that are supplied in the labor market, antitrust laws, and industrial correlates such as product differentiation and barriers to entry.

The substantial effects of external conditions on internal organizational structures have spawned a "contingency theory" approach to explaining organizational correlates: the *appropriate* structure for a given environment is not given but depends on the nature of the environment and technology. Thus, the Weberian model of bureaucracy is rational only when the environment is relatively stable and certain and the products are standardized and routine. In turbulent environments and thus in situations fraught with high orders of uncertainty and low standardization, nonbureaucratic organizations that are decentralized, flexible, and professional may be more rational.

The environmental factors that affect the internal workings of firms are the subjects of the "population ecology" model.[56] A key insight of this theory is *resource dependency*: organizations, to the extent that it is possible, seek to avoid dependency relations by introducing as much certainty as possible into their interactions with other organizations.

This can be done, for example, by vertical and horizontal integration, which provided the impetus for the major merger movements of the 1887–1904 period.[57] Since the 1950s, the dominant form of merger activity has been, as we have discussed, conglomeration. The emergence of all of these organizational forms can be traced to the efforts of large firms to minimize their dependence and to exploit their comparative advantages, their accesses, their market power, and, of course, their environments.

Organizations differ in their degree of control over their boundaries, including their control over technology flow and their degree of dependence on free professions. For example, interorganizational relations differ in their degree of reciprocity: "center" firms dominate subordinate firms in the periphery, which are often "backward satellites"[58] that have little choice but simply to react to external shocks. Firms' control over

---

[56] Michael Hannan and John Freeman, "The Population Ecology of Organizations," *American Journal of Sociology* 82 (March 1977): 929–64; Howard E. Aldrich, *Organizations and Environments* (Englewood Cliffs, N.J.: Prentice-Hall, 1979).

[57] See, for example, Alfred D. Chandler, *The Visible Hand* (Cambridge: Harvard University Press, 1977); and Alfred D. Chandler and Herman Daems, eds., *Managerial Hierarchies* (Cambridge: Harvard University Press, 1980).

[58] Robert T. Averitt, *The Dual Economy: The Dynamics of American Industry Structure* (New York: Norton, 1968).

suppliers also varies, with the Japanese *kanban* inventory system, for dealing with production needs for parts by frequent daily deliveries, an example of very high control; depending on how much control they exercise over their suppliers, firms will differ in their needs for higher or lower inventory levels.

As we have noted, the distinction between intraorganizational and interorganizational correlates becomes cloudy when we regard the organization as consisting of all people who are dependent upon a given company. In this broader definition of the firm, patterns of dependency among subunits, as in the case of "backward satellites," are not really interorganizational correlates, but instead relations *internal* to the organization.

For example, franchising could be considered both an intraorganizational and interorganizational correlate depending on which definition of organization is adopted. In the franchise system, people outside the firm in the payroll sense may be considered to be organizational members in that they are economically dependent on it.[59] Franchising alleviates problems that arise when permanent employees become fixed costs of production, since it serves management well to control people they do not have to pay. Through franchising, firms are able to get around collective bargaining obligations since suppliers are generally not unionized. Though the parent—General Motors, say—is organized, its franchised auto dealers' mechanics are not viewed by the courts as being part of the bargaining unit. And franchisees' operations are also often so small that they are not covered by minimum wage laws, an operating cost advantage that redounds to the supplier in economic negotiations with franchises.

The organizational correlates we have discussed in this section are intimately related to a firm's products and the nature of its technology. These are correlates of industries, to which we now turn.

CORRELATES OF INDUSTRIES

Industrial differences have been of considerable interest to social scientists, who have often sought to distinguish among preindustrial and industrial societies on the basis of their products and services. Lately, a full-fledged writers' cottage industry has grown up around the concept

[59] The extent of franchising has increased in recent years: for example, in 1975, there were a total of 434,538 franchises in the United States, accounting for over $182 million in sales; in 1982, there were 465,594 franchises, accounting for over $437 million in sales. See *Franchising in the Economy, 1975–1977* (Washington, D. C.: U. S. Department of Commerce, 1976); and *Franchising in the Economy, 1980–1982* (Washington, D. C.: U. S. Department of Commerce, 1982).

of "postindustrial society," referring to the emergence and growth of service sectors and the correlative decline in mass markets and mass production. Others have been interested in industrial differences because it is firms that produce these products or services. Studying industries thus reveals important things about how firms operate. Still others have found industries to be very convenient contexts for case studies of work processes.[60]

An industry implies the presence of more than one firm in a product line; in cases in which a single monopolistic firm fills nearly all of the economy's need for a product (as Bell Telephone long did for telephone services), it is the firm's market power that is the most important correlate of such industries. Firms within the same industry employ similar technologies and are similar in the centrality of their goods or services to the economy. It is useful to pay attention to these industrial correlates in efforts to design research investigations targeted on identifying the causes of a number of phenomena in our economy.

It should be noted, however, that because the products of firms *across* industries can be in direct competition—glass and brick, steel and aluminum—it becomes necessary to consider *market-specific* factors as well as *industry-specific* factors in designing research just as it is imperative to do so in applying laws to business corporations. Thus the jobs of workers in the building and construction trades are influenced by the ways and means of employers in the steel, cement, aluminum, lumber, and glass industries, each with almost unique industry-specific technologies and market structures.

Classifying Industries

Since millions of products are generated by firms in the United States economy alone, there are thousands of "theoretical industries." How one classifies these industries depends on one's research purposes. Sociologists have tended to use highly aggregated industry categories (such as agriculture, manufacturing, and services or primary, secondary, tertiary) when studying differences among societies. Economists, on the other hand, generally use detailed industry categories that more closely ap-

---

[60] See, for example, Andrew Zimbalist, ed., *Case Studies on the Labor Process* (New York: Monthly Review Press, 1979); Michael Wallace and Arne L. Kalleberg, "Industrial Transformation and the Decline of Craft: The Decomposition of Skill in the Printing Industry, 1931–1978," *American Sociological Review* 47 (June 1982): 307–24; and Katherine Stone, "The Origins of Job Structures in the Steel Industry," *Review of Radical Political Economics* 6 (1974): 113–73.

proximate specific product markets. Industrial classifications thus vary in detail and often diverge widely from notions of a theoretical industry. That is, when we aggregate we perforce introduce often frustrating degrees of heterogeneity among the firms assumed to represent the same industry; such heterogeneity is frustrating because it unsettles the Cartesian urge we have to see wholes in their homogeneous parts and thus the constituent causes of the wholes of which they are parts. Further, similarity of products is always a relative notion, and industry boundaries fluctuate as sellers shift from one group of buyers to another and vice versa, as apparently different products become substitutes for each other. American railroaders, for example, virtually forgot that they were in the transportation industry when competition confronted them from auto and truck drivers, bus companies, and airline operators.

Industrial categories are illustrated by those developed by the federal (United States Bureau of the Census—the Standard Industrial Classification or SIC) and international (International Labor Organization) agencies that collect such data. For example, SIC code 36 (electrical machinery, equipment, and supplies) is broken down into three-digit codes (361: electric transmission and distribution equipment, 362: electrical industrial apparatus, 363: household appliances, 364: electric lighting and wiring equipment, 365: radio and television receiving sets, 366: communication equipment, and so on). Each of these in turn is divided into four-digit codes (for example, SIC code 363 includes 3631: household cooking equipment, 3632: household refrigerators and home and farm freezers, 3633: household laundry equipment, 3635: household vacuum cleaners, 3636: sewing machines, and so on).

As we have already noted in several other contexts, the concept of industry has become an increasingly ragged one. Corporations in the basic product industries, for example—steel, autos, glass, rubber, and so on—have sought to reduce their vulnerabilities to cyclical economic swings by diversifying their product lines and expanding, within the legal limits applied to horizontal and vertical integration, through the formation of conglomerates by mergers and acquisitions. Since the election of 1980 the restrictions on integration have been eased and conglomeration has been much encouraged. Recent news stories, like those about U.S. Steel entering the oil industry and about the increasing tolerance of the FTC toward manufacturers who wish to dictate retailers' prices are cases in point. And within-industry boundaries have become increasingly differentiated as well. For example, in the steel industry, we now have "minimills" alongside giant steel plants. And, in the auto industry, there are many firms providing labor, parts, and even fairly complex "subassemblies" to the major auto manufacturers on a subcontracting basis.

Changes in Industrial Structure

In this century, there have been profound changes in the structure of industries in the United States. These changes are due to a number of factors: technological changes; variations, cyclical and otherwise, in the supply of and demand for different products; and changes in government spending in support of certain industries essentially at the expense of others (whether by policies or programs and whether intended or not). In Table 2, we present changes in the distributions of the American labor force employed in nine broadly defined industrial groups.

Some of these changes, the transformation of the economy from one based on agriculture to one based on the manufacture of goods most notably, are continuations of those that began before 1900. The percentage of the United States labor force employed in agriculture, for instance, went from 38 percent in 1900 to less than 4 percent in 1980. In contrast, the proportion of workers in service industries more than doubled during this period.

There are several conceptions among investigators as to what constitutes the service sector, ranging from the broadest definition that ex-

TABLE 2. Industrial Distributions, 1900–1980

Industry	1900[a]	1930[a]	1960[b]	1980[c]
Agriculture, forestry, fisheries	38.0%	22.6%	7.0%	3.6%
Mining	2.6	2.4	1.1	1.0
Construction	5.8	6.4	6.2	6.2
Manufacturing	22.1	23.1	28.2	22.2
Transportation, public utilities	7.3	10.2	7.2	6.6
Wholesale and retail trade	8.4	12.7	19.0	20.3
Finance, insurance, real estate	1.2	3.0	4.3	6.0
Services	13.4	17.3	21.8	28.8
Government (not elsewhere classified)	1.0	2.2	5.2	5.4
Total	99.8%	99.9%	100.0%	100.1%[d]
(N, in thousands)	(28,700)	(47,490)	(62,031)	(97,270)

[a] SOURCE: United States Bureau of the Census, *Historical Statistics of the United States, Colonial Times to 1970, Bicentennial Edition, Part I* (Washington, D.C.: U.S. Government Printing Office).
[b] SOURCE: United States Bureau of the Census, *U.S. Census of the Population, 1960: General Social and Economic Characteristics, United States Summary.* Final Report PC (1)-1C (Washington, D.C.: U.S. Government Printing Office).
[c] SOURCE: United States Department of Labor, Bureau of Labor Statistics, *Employment and Earnings* (Washington, D.C.: U.S. Government Printing Office).
[d] Difference from 100.0% due to rounding.

cludes all but extractive and goods-producing industries (e.g., agriculture, mining, construction, manufacturing) to the narrow one that includes only personal and business services. The service–goods distinction thus borrows some difficulties from those we discussed in conceptualizing industries *per se*.

In any event, Table 2 shows that employment in services, finance, government, and other non-goods-producing industries has increased markedly during the past century. These increases in services have occurred primarily at the expense, so to say, of the agricultural sector, however, not the manufacturing sector, since the percentage of workers employed in manufacturing has remained fairly stable during this century.

Industries and Product Markets

Industries overlap to some degree with product markets and a number of recent changes in the structure of industries are indeed associated with substantial changes in American product markets. As Piore[61] sees them, mass markets have taken on more and more of the characteristics of batch markets (that is, markets in which demand is easily and quickly sated) in that their products' suppliers increasingly use capital equipment that can be retooled for use in making different products. More refined tastes and quality consciousness on the part of consumers, coupled with the use of subcontractor firms and the decline of mass markets, have contributed to increases in the amount of Americans' discretionary income that is expended on the products of batch-producing firms. Modern advertisers' skills in promoting fads and fashions have aided in encouraging fickleness among consumers. At the core of the reputation of today's so-called Yuppies is, after all, their apparently insatiable demand for new and novel products; a small jar of mustard blended with honey(!), selling for $5.00, is in short supply in New York delicatessens serving young brokers and their occupational kin.

The operation of product markets is intimately related to many important correlates of industries. These correlates include: product market concentration; product differentiation; susceptibility to business cycles; degree of profitability; vertical and/or horizontal integration; vulnerability to foreign competition; the capacity and utilization of the industry's productive potential; the nature of barriers to entry of new firms; the growth

---

[61] Michael J. Piore, "American Labor and the Industrial Crisis," *Challenge* (March–April 1982): 5–11; see also Michael J. Piore and Charles F. Sabel, *The Second Industrial Divide: Possibilities for Prosperity* (New York: Basic Books, 1984).

rate of market demand; the short-run ratios of fixed to variable costs; the involvement of the government in the industry through purchases, taxes, tax expenditures, public subsidies, and regulation; the relations between buyers and sellers; economies of scale; and unionization patterns. Many of these correlates of industries are affected by the actions of the nation-state.

Nation-States and Industries. It is important to note that, although our economy has become more and more a service network, we are still living with the consequences of initiatives put forward by manufacturers even if they are less powerful than in their heydays. These include residual interests in protectionism and continuing resistance to publicly supported health care, clean air and safety regulations, restrictive zoning, conservation measures, and more. Recognizing that the corporate community's "Age of Aquarius" has allowed the topography of ownership to change and that competitive markets may allow for product substitutions does not mean that we can totally scrap older notions about establishments and firms that are in similar product lines, face similar regulatory challenges, compete for customers at least in the prices of some products, use similar capital equipment, often bargain with the same national and international unions, and share similar interests in selected public policies and programs.

To put it differently, we cannot dispense with industry structures in efforts to understand a fairly substantial number of the dependent variables of interest to students of work, economic development, income distribution, community welfare, and related issues.

Large steel-making establishments together with others of their kind, for example, still constitute formidable communities of interest whose policies, actions, dispositions, and practices in different markets raise questions that are more or less independent of questions of whether they are or are not the corporate children of integrated or conglomerated parents. Consequently, there are a number of industrial correlates that are still relevant to our concerns despite the changes that have taken place in the nature of industries. In all the clusters of these industrial correlates that survive in importance, despite the changes that have occurred in industrial organization, the hands of the nation-state are quite plainly visible. These include correlates

1. that relate to common production techniques;
2. that relate to joint (or competing) efforts to win federal, regional, or local support for makers of a product (e.g., tariffs, depreciation allowances, loan guarantees, and tax abatements);

3. that relate to credit requirements for the purchase of tools, equipment, and production inventory, for example, with implications for suppliers and their constituents;
4. that relate to industry-specific collective bargaining activities. These correlates are of special interest following the merger and acquisition boom: unions find it more difficult to deal with integrated and diversified corporations because these firms have risk-taking capacities in collective bargaining and related activities like plant relocations and plant shutdowns that are well beyond those of single-product firms;
5. that relate to industry-specific regulations—mine safety, tariffs, equal-time provisions, auto safety, environmental regulations, and so on. Among the most direct correlates are industry-wide managerial misgivings about the cost outlays that allegedly affect: (a) a product industry's prices in the national and international markets in competition with foreign exporters and (b) their wage and salary options;
6. that relate to the types of skill mixes (a) they require in their labor market searches or (b) they generate by their own investments in training and apprenticeship programs or (c) both. Since their skill-mix demands can change over time, with changes in capital equipment investments, for example, the correlates involved can be very telling in a given community or region. Thus, in one-industry or few-industry towns—Akron, Ohio: rubber; Butte, Montana: copper; Houston, Texas: drilling machinery; Silicon Valley, California: high-tech computers; Groton, Connecticut: defense—the changing fortunes of a few *personae fictae* and their owners—the latter of whom often, as in the case of institutional investors, are acting on short-term criteria in the service of pension funds, for example—spill over and profoundly affect the fates of employees, their families, and the fates as well, of the communities and regions in which they live.

Differences among Industries

Industrial Concentration. Concentration is a key correlate of industries and one that affects the behavior of firms in many important ways. For example, firms in highly concentrated product markets may have a high degree of market power enabling them to have great control over the sales of their products and to pass on many of their costs to consumers. In such circumstances they are able to reap higher "uncompetitive" profits with a minimum of risk. By theoretical implication, the quality of an industry's performance is strongly affected by its degree of competitiveness.[62]

Industrial concentration is generally measured by the proportion of the value of shipments controlled by the top four, eight, twenty, or fifty firms in that industry. (Of course, the degree of industrial concentration depends on one's definition of *industry*: the more detailed the definition, the more likely the industry is to be seen as concentrated.) Some industries are very highly concentrated, such as motor vehicles and car bodies (in 1977, the top four firms accounted for 93 percent of the value of shipments; the balance was attributable to four additional firms, as 99 percent were sold by the top eight), photographic equipment and supplies (72 percent by top four, 86 percent by top eight), and aircraft (59 percent by top four, 81 percent by top eight). Other industries are not very concentrated at all, such as commercial printing, lithography (6 percent by top four, 10 percent by top eight), and bottled and canned soft drinks (15 percent by top four, 22 percent by top eight).[63]

Technology. Blauner, among many determinists, argues that the single most important attribute distinguishing industries is their *technology*, that is, "the complex of physical objects and technical operations (both manual and machine) regularly employed in turning out the goods and services produced by an industry."[64] Since the nature of the product in large measure dictates the types of technology used to produce it, major variations among industries correspond to differences in production technology.

Many analysts view the degree of *standardization* of the product as the key dimension along which technologies vary. Product lines in which each unit is unique and made on order to a customer's specifications are the least standardized, and each order requires a distinct set of operations, work tasks, raw materials, parts, testing procedures, and production scheduling.

At the opposite extreme, "dimensional" products, to use Woodward's[65] term, have no unit character but are totally homogeneous substances such as liquids, powders, or sheets. Although the quantity sold of the latter may vary with a customer's order, its qualitative nature is always the same. The production of homogeneous goods involves such uniform

[62] See R. Caves's and F. M. Scherer's studies.
[63] Source: *Statistical Abstract of the United States, 1982–83*, 103rd ed. (U. S. Department of Commerce and Bureau of the Census).
[64] Blauner, 6.
[65] Joan Woodward, *Industrial Organization* (London: Oxford University Press, 1965).

operations that they can often be highly automated. Chemical refining, food processing, and the manufacture of building materials such as masonite or container materials (e.g., cardboard) allow for long runs of continuous operations in which the materials worked move in continuous flows or sheet forms.

As we indicated in the previous section, neo-Marxists maintain that the technology adopted by a firm is largely due to its needs for qualitative efficiency. A similar argument has been used to explain the type of technology used by particular industries. For example, Stone[66] argues that the Bessemer furnace was introduced in the steel industry not primarily for reasons of technical efficiency but to control a restive labor force that had been largely stripped of its craft skills in previous decades. Similarly, Edwards maintains that technical control systems are introduced in order to direct the activities of blue-collar as well as white-collar (e.g., clerical) workers.[67]

Relations among Industrial Correlates: A Dual Economy? A way of classifying industrial correlates is suggested by the "dual economy" model,[68] which assumes that the operation of product markets results in a bipolar industrial structure. Some product markets operate by competitive principles, and organizations in these competitive/periphery industrial sectors tend to be relatively small, having relatively low degrees of market power and low assets, sales, and capital intensity. In contrast, organizations in monopoly/core industrial sectors operate in relatively concentrated product markets and tend to be larger in size, and to have high degrees of market power and high assets, sales, and capital intensity.

Analyses of the consequences of economic segmentation have been conducted at both industry and organization levels, both of which have been shown to be important for understanding the nature and consequences of economic segmentation.[69] Unfortunately, the problem of determining which correlates are unique to each of these levels of analysis has not yet been resolved. For example, Hodson defined industry structure in terms of the *organizational* characteristics of capital and measured similar concepts at organizational and industry levels of analysis: concentration, size, capital intensity, profits, and corporate autonomy. This strategy is problematic since industries and organizations are distinct

---

[66] Stone.

[67] Edwards.

[68] For example, Randy Hodson and Robert L. Kaufman, "Economic Dualism: A Critical Review," *American Sociological Review* 43 (1982): 534–41.

[69] Randy Hodson, *Workers' Earnings and Corporate Economic Structure* (New York: Academic Press, 1983).

units of analysis. Moreover, different processes in connection with any of the attributes or properties on the list may be operative at each level.

Writers in the dual economy tradition often assume that the characteristics of firms and product markets have led to corresponding labor market conditions. For example, the mass production nature of core industries led to the development of industrial unionism, which shaped labor–management relations in these sectors in a number of important ways. In general, workers are able to obtain greater power when employers are strong as a result of their ability to be dominant in concentrated product markets; unions' demands are less likely either seriously to weaken employers in such industries or, even in extreme instances, to drive them out of business.

The idea that industrial correlates can be described by a two-sector model has been shown to be highly problematic by several empirical studies reporting that the structure of industries is much more complex.[70] For example, some concentrated industries are relatively nonunionized; and some unionized industries do not rely heavily on capital-intensive technologies. Moreover, there is considerable heterogeneity within industrial sectors produced by occupations, classes, organizations, unions, and jobs. As a result, there is less correspondence between industrial sectors and occupations than is often assumed by the dual economy model: good as well as bad jobs may be found in both sectors.

Indeed, blue-collar manufacturing, which comprises much of the core, has spawned a large white-collar army of service workers even as the service sector, much of it peripheral, has spawned a secondary blue-collar work force as we noted earlier in our discussion of occupations. This points to the need to consider exactly what accounts for differences among sectors in consequences such as earnings and career mobility (see Chapter 4) to a greater degree than in the past. There are two critical questions: Are the observed sectoral differences due to differences in the correlates associated with industries, occupations, classes, organizations, unions or jobs? And how do these differ across national borders?

Industry and Occupation Changes: A Postindustrial Society?

The increase in service sector employment has been interpreted by some[71] as representing a shift toward a "postindustrial" economy. Whereas

---

[70] Wallace and Kalleberg, "Economic Organization of Firms and Labor Force Consequences."

[71] Daniel Bell, *The Coming of Post-Industrial Society* (New York: Basic Books, 1973).

TABLE 3. Industry X Occupation Distributions, 1950 and 1980

Industry		Total (in thousands)	Professional, technical	Managers, proprietors	Clerical	Sales	Craft	Operatives	Nonfarm laborers	Service	Farm
Agriculture	1950[a]	(7,017)	.6	.3	.3	.1	.3	.8	2.0	.1	95.5
	1980[b]	(3,737)	2.1	1.1	2.7	.3	1.7	1.4	9.2	.5	81.1
Mining	1950	(928)	3.5	4.0	4.5	.2	17.2	69.5	.1	.7	—
	1980	(926)	12.0	7.7	10.8	.9	27.5	36.0	4.2	1.0	—
Construction	1950	(3,398)	3.7	8.4	3.2	.3	56.9	7.6	19.1	.5	—
	1980	(6,438)	3.0	12.7	7.9	.3	53.6	7.7	14.5	.4	—
Manufacturing	1950	(14,453)	4.8	4.8	11.0	3.0	19.5	45.8	8.8	1.9	—
	1980	(21,544)	11.3	8.2	12.6	2.5	19.4	39.7	4.5	1.9	—
Transportation, public utilities	1950	(4,347)	3.5	6.9	23.4	.5	21.2	27.9	12.8	3.4	—
	1980	(6,419)	10.3	10.1	23.3	1.1	21.0	23.9	7.7	2.7	—
Wholesale and retail trade	1950	(10,389)	2.0	23.0	11.5	27.6	6.1	12.7	3.2	13.7	—
	1980	(19,684)	2.3	19.1	17.3	20.3	7.2	8.4	6.3	19.1	—
Finance, insurance, real estate	1950	(1,883)	3.3	16.8	41.9	23.6	2.3	.7	1.8	9.2	—
	1980	(5,698)	5.8	18.8	47.4	20.5	1.5	.4	1.4	4.3	—
Services	1950	(10,119)	31.9	5.9	12.5	.9	9.2	8.1	2.2	32.0	—
	1980	(27,865)	35.6	7.4	18.4	.8	5.5	3.6	2.5	26.3	—
Public administration	1950	(2,491)	11.7	10.1	43.6	.2	8.3	4.7	4.7	16.0	—
	1980	(5,465)	19.7	12.0	36.8	.1	5.5	2.0	3.4	20.6	—

[a] SOURCE: U. S. Census of the Population: 1950. Vol. IV, Special Reports, Part 1, Chapter C. Occupation by Industry (Washington, D. C.: U. S. Government Printing Office).
[b] SOURCE: U. S. Department of Labor, Bureau of Labor Statistics, Employment and Earnings 27.7 (July 1980) (Washington, D. C.: U. S. Government Printing Office).

industrial society is organized around the production of goods and the dominance of machinery, the postindustrial society represents a transformation in the economy and occupational structure, such that knowledge emerges as a growing source of power. Postindustrial societies are assumed to be oriented primarily toward the production of services, not goods, and characterized by the preeminence of professional and technical occupations, the members of which possess valued theoretical knowledge.

Although profound industrial shifts have occurred in response to changes in the demands for particular goods and services and because of changes in national policies and social change more generally, it is unclear whether these signal the emergence of a qualitatively different or postindustrial environment. That is, it may not be true that there has been a qualitative break with the past, such that we are in a distinctive *phase* of postindustrial development. Rather, these changes, like those in all of our work structures, can be explained on the basis of correlates deriving from fundamental market structures and processes.

The simultaneous study of occupational and industrial changes sheds light on the debates about a postindustrial society. In Table 3, we present the proportions of people employed in nine broad occupations within each of nine broad industries for 1950 and 1980. Such analyses allow us to consider the kinds of issues raised by postindustrial theorists about the implications of industrial changes for the organization of work.

Taken as a whole, these trends suggest that industrial changes in the United States since 1950 have indeed been accompanied by marked changes in the proportions of workers employed in different occupations within these industries. Our overall observation, however, is that the patterns of occupational change within industries are very complex, belying simple explanations. The evolving trends, whereby white-collar and blue-collar workers are becoming more mixed in industries that were once more nearly one or the other, are intriguing but not easily explicable.

A few suggestive patterns, however, are notable. With only a few exceptions, industries have increased their employment of professional and technical, managerial, administrative, and clerical occupations; auto companies, after all, must design and sell cars (and manage the credit corporations to which their customers repair) as well as build cars. These developments reflect, among other things, changes in the organization of work toward a greater reliance on data and administration in all industries. Moreover, there is a general decline in the proportions of operatives, the semiskilled and unskilled occupations using machinery. This shift reflects changes in technology toward greater automation requiring fewer people to operate machines.

These industrial and occupational trends have had important consequences for our final work structure—unions—which we discuss in the last section of this chapter.

CORRELATES OF UNIONS

In our discussions of the other work structures, we have made frequent references to unions. As organizations designed to represent workers in their transactions with managers and employers, unions are intimately related to such matters as: the power of occupational groups; whether there is a unified working class; whether industries are high- or low-paying; and how firms organize the work of their employees. We now examine more systematically the correlates of unions themselves. We first discuss the ways in which nation-states affect unions and then consider the ways in which unions make a difference for work and workers.

Nation-States and Unions

As one might expect, the critical quality of the relationships of unions to firms and industries in Western-type democracies derives from the fact that the transactions occur between *property owners*, whose rights, privileges, and immunities have been sanctified by fundamental laws, on one side, and those who seek either to limit these claims or to make proprietary claims of their own, on the other.

The fact that individual property owners could form collectives, called corporations, and that these organizations became (sometimes very formidable) persons, led to social asymmetries that encouraged dependent nonowners, early on, to form their own organizations in order to temper imbalances and inequalities both in the marketplace and in the polity.

As we noted in Chapter 1, Andrew Hacker once described our very large corporations as "elephants dancing among chickens"; and the chickens' impulses, so to speak, were to protect themselves from the stompings, real and threatened, that were their lot. The relationships between workers and employers were more or less stormy at the outset, depending on whether unions thus formed were a link to class-based political parties, thereby exacerbating conflicts, or on whether political leaders saw benefits in encouraging the development of fairly inventive social technology like collective bargaining. By 1935 these leaders concluded that economically, politically, and socially disruptive conflicts could be substantially contained or reduced if not entirely eliminated by institutionalizing employers' obligations to recognize and bargain with unions.

In the United States, trade unions had their origins, in the late nineteenth century, in the craft segments of the laboring classes, whereas industrial unions were born of the substantially "deskilling" effects of mass production techniques, at first slowly and then more rapidly, after the First World War. Unions have enjoyed a legitimacy, in the legal sense of the term, in the United States since the 1870s, when they were finally judged to be legal corporate associations and not "conspiracies." It was not until the mid-1930s, however, with the passage of the National Labor Relations Act (NLRA), that organized workers enjoyed legally protected rights not only to organize but to reach binding agreements (nowadays more frequently called contracts) with employers who were obliged, under the rule of law, to bargain with workers' duly certified representatives "in good faith." Wartime wage and price controls in 1941, however, a scant six years after the NLRA was enacted, virtually froze the new relationships between organized labor and management.

The second test of the public's and Congress's intent regarding collective bargaining did not actually occur until there was a great rash of strikes after the Second World War. It turned out, only twelve years after NLRA, that the public was nearly as offended by union demands, pent up though they were during the war, as by managers' unyielding antiunionism before the war. The result, the passage of the Taft-Hartley Act in 1947, circumscribed some of the rights of unions that were rather vaguely formulated in the NLRA and circumscribed "irresponsible" union leaders, as well, by enforcing more union democracy and eliminating "closed shop" requirements prior to employment. Workers could be obliged to join a union in a given work site *after* they were employed (the union shop) but not before (the closed shop).

When cases of union corruption were uncovered during congressional hearings in 1958 and 1959, originally aimed at unions' political activism, the public's representative again took offense and ordered more union democracy and more reporting and disclosure requirements by parties to union agreements as ways of assuring leaders' responsiveness to their followers; the fond hope, not always realized, was that workers would not vote for corrupt leaders.

Less attention was given to the possibility that union leaders would be far less tractable negotiators in collective bargaining exchanges under conditions that made their positions, in increasingly democratic structures, insecure. And not a few managers, we now recognize, have become chary of efforts to engage in stable "trade-off" relationships with union leaders whose claims to their roles as union spokesmen are made fragile by union democracy. Since the presidential election of 1980, furthermore, Mr. Reagan's National Labor Relations Board (NLRB) has been avowedly far more scrupulous in its insistence on legally required disclosures by unions than on those required of employers under the law.

Among the leading correlates of the last two decades of national public policy intervention in labor–management relations we must consider as well:

1. Unions have realized that mergers, acquisitions, and divestitures, much encouraged by public policies, are seriously destabilizing in their effects on both international and local unions following plant shutdowns, reorganizations, divestitures, plant consolidations, and the use by employers of unions' long familiar "whipsaw" techniques (playing unions and unions' locals off against each other).

2. National policy, reflected in court decisions, has encouraged "right-to-work laws" forbidding union shop requirements. At first these laws had trivial effects on unions because they were passed only in the so-called Sunbelt which was industrialized much later. Long after the right-to-work movement first began, however, much industry has moved to or started up plants in the Sunbelt and these laws have given managers considerable "spine"—and heart—in the use of what are known as union avoidance measures. These measures include those long commended by well-intentioned social scientists determined to improve workplace relationships by the use of group dynamics techniques, "work restructuring," and work enlargement gambits. These techniques are designed, as their protagonists see it, to reduce workers' dissatisfactions, thereby diminishing their interests in collective bargaining. The results have been mixed, though employers have apparently done better than union organizers, at least over the short haul; union membership has skidded downhill to 20 percent of the work force.

3. Growing national concerns with productivity in the Western-type democracies (amid widespread beliefs that unions foster inefficiency, excessive pay, and restrict management initiatives otherwise) have put unions very much on the defensive, even as national policies have backed up managers' efforts to shore up their circumstances. In the process, bargaining agreements have become longer, the labor relations process more legalistic, and employers have recently been obtaining "get backs" and "give backs" where unions had previously secured a variety of gains in wages, workrules and benefits. In the most dramatic case, it was clear that the United Auto Workers' cautious program of demands and its benign response to managers regarding reforms of work processes, in recent years, impressed the public's servants, a development that helped Chrysler when it sought and won loan guarantees from Uncle Sam.

4. A significant narrowing of the differences in economic returns to union and nonunion workers has occurred since 1975. On one side, unions' bargaining strength has been thoroughly sapped by periodic recessions during which inflation was coupled with unemployment. Unions

were thus put—or helped put themselves, as some would have it—in economic double jeopardy.

In addition, unions have become obliged to negotiate with employers whose capacities to pass on the costs of attractive agreements have been tempered by the harsh discipline of foreign competition. American employers were relatively quicker to recognize their new competitors' lower wage scales than to apprehend or appreciate their technical or managerial skills in several of what for many post–World War II years were oligopolistic markets.

Theories of capitalism's advantage assume that rational entrepreneurs and managers would win out in the economic game, but the theory does not guarantee that *American* entrepreneurs and managers who finger that theoretical rosary are going to be the ones rewarded for their abiding faith alone, never mind whether or not they will live by the faith, in practice. The fact is that for many American employers the faith in their beliefs was not matched by their own deeds of economic derring-do, by quite a long shot. At the same time, the would-be competitors who later forced American employers into more efficient ways had been suffering for many years from the effects of World War II.

5. Japanese unions have been essentially limited in their capacity to have significant effects on their economy by a variety of Japanese management practices that add up to what many conceive to be paternalistic policies. But the situation is changing: the "career job" system now covers less than half the labor force, and "lifetime" job guarantees have been defined in demographic terms as ending at age 55 in a country in which life expectancy now exceeds age 70. And many Japanese firms are small suppliers who offer few of the benefits that the established larger companies accord to trade unionists.

6. Western European unions have a more clearly class-based character. One result of this is that much of what is collectively bargained at local and industry-wide levels in the United States lies well beyond the scope of company–union relations in that region. And most of what we think of as fringe benefits in the United States, health insurance, for example, are usefully beyond the realm of labor–management relationships because they are and have long been the subjects of national political will in Europe.

In the Scandinavian nations and in the United Kingdom, unionists for the most part belong to labor parties as well as to their trade or industry-based unions. In countries with national labor parties anxious to take national leadership, unions are fairly actively engaged in keeping rank-and-file members "cool," thereby preserving a public face of what we may call principled reasonableness. In these events, unions have come close to being instruments of labor parties' social control. When labor parties thus come to power, alone or as members of governing coalitions, the state apparatus comes to have almost as much influence over unions as unionists, through their unions and labor parties, have over the state!

What Do Unions Do?

The logic of the inclusion of unions in the conceptual apparatus of the type underlying this volume, as it applies to the United States at least, borrows a good deal more from the history of (some might even say nostalgia about) the period 1925 to 1975 than from the realities of the past decade.

The fact is that the current effects of unions—on the socioeconomic operations of contemporary nation-states, on social groups or classes, on occupations, or on organizations in the United States (and to an only slightly lesser degree in other Western-type democracies)—are essentially very much reduced versions of their earlier capacities to influence the course of industrial development.

From one point of view, American unions never had enormous power to affect any of our other structures. They could more or less temper governing officials who wanted their support in elections and in legislative battles, but it was a rare Democrat who could not take institutional union support and a significant rank-and-file vote pretty much for granted from 1932 to 1964. And, although unions could raise their members' wages in the so-called basic industries, the costs were passed on to the industries' customers or repaid by lower employee turnover and other trade-offs that enhanced one or another component of corporations' often modest programs aimed at increased productivity. It is not at all obvious how one would go about measuring either the marginal costs or marginal benefits to industries of their being organized by unions; measures of output per manhour and the dollar cost of output per manpower are influenced by many, many factors.

The least ambiguous effects of unions in the United States have had to do with the configurations and innumerable substantive developments internal to occupational structures within and across industries and organizations' productivity programs. In some instances, the effects have been to slow down appreciably changes desired by employers in these structures. In other instances, perhaps the majority of them, unions adapted to the automated processes and the resulting work structures that managers designed and redesigned. In particular, unionists accepted the job-centered (rather than craft-centered) organization of production. In the building trades, contractors were obliged to live very long with a division of labor that has only recently begun to change as a result of the development of new construction methods. In the printing industry, the typographers fought hard to preserve their craft jobs but eventually settled for substantial reductions in their numbers by attrition and/or nonreplacement and attractive retirement benefits, as waves of new printing methods succeeded older compositing methods using handset type. Much the same occurred, in the 1960s, to longshoremen on the West Coast docks. And, of course, loss of craft occupations' skills weakened the power of craft unions as well.[72]

It bears emphasis that the breakup of craft unions reflected the ability of employers to transform occupations into jobs and thus to make fairly general skills more firm-specific and less easily transferable to other employers' precincts; this is an ability that managers have sought to apply since the 1920s. The effect has been to heighten the possibilities, in the stretch, that unionized workers would be job-conscious in regard to security rather than class-conscious in regard to income distribution questions.[73] For example, auto workers, following the introduction of assembly line technology, were effectively regrouped from a multitude of crafts and trades into "the skilled trades," on one side, and assembly or "line workers," on the others. The tensions between the two groups have not aided the UAW's efforts to bargain coherently with employers.

The basic determinant of employers' responses to unions, historically, was the degree to which employers were either dependent upon different skills that had traditionally been performed by members of rather different skill and craft groups, or were in need of larger numbers of mass production workers in divisions of labor in which traditional skill hierarchies were needed hardly at all. This dependency, in turn, can be traced to market conditions: where there were mass markets that could support massive capital investments to mass-produce a product, trades and crafts gave way to fewer tiers of skills.

In the cases of trades and crafts, unions and their members sought to protect their jobs in specifically jurisdictional terms, either by special or blanket agreements covering all skilled crafts and trades in a given work setting or in the separate establishments of a multiplant firm. In mass production industries—autos, rubber, glass, and, to a somewhat lesser degree, steel—unionists were also very job-conscious, but with far

---

[72] See Zimbalist for further illustrations of how technological changes weakened the power of craft unions in a variety of industries.

[73] For a discussion, see Piore, "American Labor and the Industrial Crisis."

less regard to their skill components, *per se*. Both groups, skilled and unskilled, meanwhile, were concerned with negotiating limits on employers' unilateral rights regarding layoffs, discipline, and hosts of rules determining "how fair is fair," "how fast is fast," and "how reasonable is reasonable" (and, later, "how safe is safe"), with special reference to assembly line speeds, crew sizes and workloads, work procedures, and hazards in work settings.

In the comparatively low unemployment, "tight" labor markets of the early decade of the post–World War II era, unions of both craft and industrial stripes enjoyed many more successes than they have since the onset of the high unemployment–high inflation or "stagflation" period of the past ten years.

Some of the most socially significant gains of yesteryear, it turned out, were not really very much the result of unionists' single-minded efforts. Thus, about half of all Americans receive automatic pay increases as the Consumer Price Index increases. It was General Motors, not a union, however, that invented the so-called COLAs (cost-of-living allowances) in the early 1950s and offered them to the UAW (whose leaders had some fears that inflation might occur) in return for multiyear contracts that would make the companies' fixed expenses more stable over time. When inflation did set in during the 1970s, much later than managers had anticipated, unionists were blamed for (or credited with) these COLAs. Initiatives, overall, have changed hands since then as employers, faced with growing imports, more exacting customers, and what they aver are costly regulations sponsored by a variety of interest groups, have stiffened their backs vis-à-vis union demands; they are now anxious to undo the COLAs they had themselves used earlier to *counter* their antagonists' demands. If consistency is the "hobgoblin of little minds," then employers are, in that event, geniuses.

Labor markets in almost every region in the United States and the rest of the industrial world began to "loosen": (a) with the Great Recession of 1974 to 1975 and the failure thereafter for them to retighten to the lower unemployment rates of other days; (b) in the United States, with mounting foreign imports to this country and foreigners' lower-priced exports to America's erstwhile overseas customers; (c) in the United States, with mounting concern about runaway inflation and declining rates of increase in output per manhour (which may or may not have been workers' fault in given or even in most cases); (d) with unemployment running at annually high rates; and (e) with a popular, if simple-minded, view that unions were restricting productivity while they were making excessive demands for pay and fringe benefits and holding fast on the matters of work rules and cost-of-living allowances accorded to them in lower inflation periods.[74]

Unions, especially in the older industrial regions of the United States, thus have increasingly found themselves beleaguered and almost totally on the defensive. And when they have tried to replace lost jobs (and rank-and-file members) with organizing drives in the Sunbelt, they have been greeted with stiff opposition from employers ably assisted, as we have noted, by "union avoidance" experts. Whether, over the long run, employers (or the American people as a whole), will be well served by spokespersons, some social scientists among them, for work reforms and improved worker morale, eclipsed unionism, and modifications of industrial democracy remains to be seen.

In the meantime, most unions have been more than a little mindful both of employers' competitive problems and of the public's widespread misgivings about unions' ways and means. As a result, they have been more than just a little responsive to employers' demands, across organized American industry, to settle on "give backs" and "get backs." The result has been a slowing in the growth of the work force in manufacturing, more subcontracting of work, reduced wage demands, and joint labor–management productivity campaigns favoring fundamental changes in restrictive work rules. In the case of work rules, current workers' representatives have substantially overlooked the "quids" their predecessors and members paid, themselves, for the work rules "quos" that have been so often maligned; it is rare that a workrule's history does not describe an exchange, way back in time, from which both parties realized significant benefits![75]

In specific terms, we can say, following the recent appearance of econometric and statistical analyses by Freeman and Medoff,[76] that unions have probably helped to raise their members' wages relative to wages paid to unorganized Americans. It is not easy, however, to sort out how much of the difference is attributable to the favored market circumstances of the large firms in heavily organized industries compared to the putative economic power of unions therein. The fact is that wage and related settlements are bargains between self-interested economic agents with some shared values and interests, and bargained wages are not quite

[74] For a review of the cause of stagflation from a "democratic-centrist" point of view, but one informed by modern econometric analysis, see Eckstein.

[75] For an elaboration on the trade-off quality of work rules, see Sumner H. Slichter, James J. Healy, and Robert E. Livernash, *The Impact of Collective Bargaining on Managment* (Washington, D. C.: Brookings Institution, 1960), 466–81.

[76] Richard B. Freeman and James L. Medoff, *What Do Unions Do?* (New York: Basic Books, 1984).

equatable with prices set by markets. Nor is it by any means a simple task to "cost out" the benefits to a firm of: (a) the lower worker turnover of unionists observed by Freeman and Medoff; (b) the benefits of peaceful settlements, for example, to reasonable people who disagree over the best ways to serve themselves and each other; or (c) grievance machinery which often acts to temper union members. Grievance mechanisms, otherwise, function as lightning rods in that they drain off worker affect "before sore points become cancer sites," in a phrase commonly used by industrial relations practioners.

We can also say that unionists are progressively less inclined to follow their leaders' pleadings and urgings about national political, social, or economic issues.[77] Unions' successes in winning unemployment and fringe benefits during the period from 1946 to 1975 undoubtedly constricted the larger market, in American political terms, for extended public welfarelike programs. Moreover, divisions within unions along craft, industry, gender, age, and race lines have contributed to union leaders' difficulties in aspiring to speak for a broad-based working class, or labor movement. Union members' pension funds, finally, include significant quantities of corporate securities, giving organized workers some very considerable stakes in the institutional status quo. If one adds the problems union leaders have as a result of progressive efforts to assure that unions be increasingly democratic, one has another cluster of reasons for viewing unions with less apprehension than their most energetic management critics claim they are obliged to endure.

As we implied at the beginning of this section, unions have been included among our consequential work structures because, though presently eclipsed, their claims have not, by any means, been liquidated. It is also possible that unions will reemerge, after battling to hold some of the gains they have won and after adjusting to worldwide recessions and the restructuring of industries through mergers and other debilitating developments, to play more prominent roles in American society. Initially, unions engaged in desperate struggles to become recognized, while employers were aided in their resistance by the state in World War I. Later, the government became more of an adjudicating body rather than an adversary to unions, the PATCO strike and PATCO's collapse, under Reagan's leadership, notwithstanding.

[77] See Derek C. Bok and John T. Dunlop, *Labor and the American Community* (New York: Simon & Schuster, 1970). We may note that it has not been uncommon, where a few unions have worked hard to elect a president, that they have been essentially forgotten after the fact. Consider the treatment accorded the Airline Pilots Association, the Teamsters and the Air Traffic Controllers after they supported the Republican candidate in the 1980 election. Indeed, Mr. Reagan literally liquidated the tower controllers.

Unions in other Western-type democracies have played more significant roles, through labor parties, in national policy making, than they have in the United States. Often, in Scandinavia and Germany most notably, unionist parties' capacities are augmented by laws requiring worker representation on corporate boards.

Mention of grievance mechanisms, earlier, serves to flag several important aspects of the American version of collective bargaining that are far too often lost in studies of the subject, especially in the predominantly quantitative ones. These often neglected aspects of collective bargaining, like the more familiar ones, impact upon our work and industry structures and are made operative in several of our markets.

Consider first that, in the United States, collective bargaining is almost always a continuing process in all the days following a contract settlement. Strikes, like the use of formal grievances at the final step in arbitration proceedings, are to collective bargaining, properly understood, as punctuation marks are to long paragraphs; between the more celebrated or notorious and publicly noted developments—settlements, arbitration proceedings, strikes—are the daily transactions that are the flesh and blood of collective bargaining.

On one side, for example, the more active and engaged members of a union local participate about decisions of the quality of their representation, about managment decisions vis-à-vis the protections they claim, and about grievances filed and contemplated. On another side, union leaders engage in continuing dialogues with responsible managers (and among themselves) about interests that both overlap and conflict.

Much the same shop or office talk, including rumor mills, regularly takes place among unorganized workers, of course. But in organized settings the prospects of *concerted* action following from these multitudes of shop floor exchanges are always greater and the exchanges are therefore potentially more consequential, sometimes for productivity, but always for worker morale and management's control over its prerogatives.

The result has been that many managers (with the conceptual help of Chester Barnard's frequently reprinted work, *The Functions of the Executive*, and those of his contemporary in the academy, Elton Mayo) have come increasingly to see themselves as the administrators of social systems, rather than the types of entities contemplated in the theory of the firm. This managerialist demiurge has been translated into programmatic do's and don'ts in ubiquitous business school courses in human relations, group dynamics, and organizational behavior. Fairly antiunion in their intent, the applied versions of these pedagogic undertakings understandably appear with growing frequency in unorganized firms, as MBAs pour out of the academy's doors held open by business school mentors whose attitudes toward unions are not typically admiring ones. The microscopic perspective on firms as mini-social-systems is useful but would be more useful if one acknowledged that at least some of the happenings in firms are attributable to developments beyond their gates.

Despite the risks in accepting the oversimplifying diagnoses with which human relationists confront us, however, we urge that organized as well as unorganized firms be considered as social systems somewhat unto themselves; they are so considered among most students of organizations, because the *contents* of the day-to-day exchanges within organizations in and of themselves recapitulate well the operations of markets and the interactions among our wider-reaching structures. These contents, now this one, now that one, reflect all of the developments in each of the cells of our matrix: the pressures of business cycles, the operations of labor markets, the pressures of competition, the shifting ratios of capital to labor and their effects on jobs and occupational jurisdictions, and so on. Macroscopic economic forces, to front-line managers, union "reps" and rank-and-file workers in a work setting, are not abstract but palpable. Most actors in an organization thus recognize that extramural developments do indeed affect the transactions in their workplaces. The real mirrorlike character of transactions in a shop, mill, or forge are, by clear implication, not readily appreciated by social scientists if they are viewed, as they so regularly are, in entirely intraorganizational perspective.

The minute, for example, that the Supreme Court held, as it did in April 1984, that a company filing for bankruptcy may unilaterally abrogate an agreement with its union, it triggered reverberations among rank-and-file unionists that could be heard in every firm in the nation in which managers were in financial straits. And talk about protective tariffs, import quotas, and productivity problems is as rife on the floor of a steel mill or on an auto assembly line, where workers are otherwise contemplating their reactions to plant rules or a bargaining settlement, as they are in cognizant congressional committees, at specialists' desks in brokerage houses, or in law offices in which attorneys are planning to buy oil companies for U.S. Steel or computer hardware makers for General Motors.

A second neglected aspect of United States collective bargaining has to do with unions' intended *and* unintended contributions to capital investments in labor-saving machinery and to subcontracting and "outsourcing." Thus, the perceived costs of union agreements undoubtedly figure prominently in many managers' decisions regarding capital investments. And costs of fringe benefits encourage managers to use their machines for longer or shorter periods, over swings in the business cycle, by adjusting their labor needs with the help of layoffs and overtime requirements, as appropriate. Employers can thereby constrain their fixed costs: employers' costs would increase if workers were added in peak production periods because they would earn additional fringe benefits, as overtime workers would not. We may note that although overtime pay—"time and a half"—has not gone up, fringe benefit costs have soared. There will also be trade offs in the uses of personnel and machines, following OPEC, depending on the relative costs of labor compared to fuel.

On another side, critics of unions, especially, have given them virtually no credit either for their formal or informal contributions to the efficiency of employers' enterprises. Thus the Lithographers Union spends substantial sums of money on new methods of production, like silk-screening, in the design and packaging industry. John L. Lewis organized *and* modernized hundreds of smaller deep-shaft coal mines while holding voting stock in them as collateral for loans to Cyrus Eaton (from funds deposited in the Mineworkers' Bank!) at a cost of thousands of miners' jobs. The West Coast longshoremen, under the leadership of Harry Bridges, long persecuted as a communist, entered into a modernization and mechanization agreement with Paul St. Cyr, representing the West Coast stevedoring companies, that was designed to trade off early retirement for reduced port time (loading and unloading) for the companies, through the use of larger loading crane sling loads, fork lift trucks, and "containerized" cargo. Ironically, although all the companies had complained about earlier unions' restrictions on their right to modernize, only a few took advantage of the "M&M" agreement for, as it turned out, many employers, with stout-hearted resistance to technological change, wanted only to reduce their work force, *not* to make capital investments. Finally, firemen who tended no fires on diesel locomotive engines insisted on assurances about their seats on locomotives *not* in order to slow "dieselization" but as a quid pro quo for passing up a World War II pay increase at a time when managers, privately, did not expect that the railroads would ever "dieselize."

A final aspect of unions' efforts is at least as hard to assess as those noted in this section, for it relates to the quality of life in an industrial society in which workers have systematically forsworn interest in a labor party. Thus we cannot calculate the worth, to the approximately 20 percent of the work force that is presently unionized, for whatever sense of dignity and control over their circumstances that is born of the knowledge that they are not automatically and totally vulnerable to the unilateral authority of fellow citizens who, for whatever reasons, have come to lead the enterprises in which they earn their bread. Pride may well "goeth before a fall," but a decent quantum of that semiprecious commodity probably accrues to one who knows that the terms of trade between oneself and others, in a variety of markets in which unions have programmatic effects, can be influenced by all of the parties to these terms, not just employers.

INTRODUCTION TO CHAPTERS 4 AND 5

Consequences of Work Structures

In this chapter and the next, we discuss the *consequences* of work structures and their correlates: how they make a difference in explaining things that people care about. The dependent variables we consider selectively, and thus illustratively, are broad-ranging but prototypal areas of research in many subfields within sociology, economics, and related disciplines. The dependent variables include labor market outcomes such as income inequality, career paths, and mobility; and labor force outcomes such as work attitudes, unemployment, collective bargaining phenomena, labor force participation rates of different subsets of the population, and the distribution of skills.

Our conceptualization of work structures and their correlates has important methodological implications for the way one collects, analyzes, and interprets empirical data. We have argued that there are interrelations between markets and work structures as well as among the work structures themselves. These conceptualizations have the character of theoretical assumptions useful in guiding the design of research directed at studies of the consequences produced by work structures and their correlates. In this introductory section, we discuss some key implications of our conceptualization for research on these consequences. The issues we raise are sufficiently general so as to be common to many of our dependent variables and will reemerge in our discussions of them.

WORK STRUCTURES AS CAUSAL AGENTS

Causes and consequences must be understood within the context of a theoretically informed model that specifies the interrelations among structures, processes, and outcomes. We have argued that the operation of markets gives rise to the correlates of industries, classes, occupations, organizations, and unions. These markets and work structures are temporally and thus logically prior to the consequences we discuss in this chapter: they define the contexts of work to which people must adapt and react and over which they, as individuals, often have little control.

Our assumption that work structures are causal agents implies that their properties and related correlates produce certain consequences. Changes in our work structures, in short, will result in changes in outcomes. For instance, increasing an occupation's skill level should increase the earnings of its members with a variety of consequences for its members' and their families' welfare, their attitudes on a number of matters, and the plans of employers. At the same time, industrial relationists have long criticized microeconomists for neglecting to take systematic account of the large differences in the wages often accorded to members of the same occupations in different organizations even in the same localities.

To illustrate the causal relations among markets, work structures and consequences, we may comment further on labor markets. Many of the consequences we will discuss in this chapter and the next have been assumed to result directly from the operation of these markets. We have discussed how labor markets are segmented by industries, occupations, organizations, and classes and how they are affected by unions and national economic and political policies. Correlates of these work structures, in turn, explain what it is about labor markets at different levels of the economy that produce differences in the outcomes of these markets. For example, occupational (skills, licensing), organizational (job ladders), and industrial correlates (technology and concentration) help explain some of the differences in earnings among members in different labor markets.

A focus on these labor markets calls our attention to the connections between work structures and people because individuals are matched to jobs in such markets. It has been our aim, all along, to understand individual differences as a function of work structures, since we want to identify the correlates of structures that make a difference for labor force members. We should add, though, as John Dunlop has emphasized for a quarter of a century, that wages are generally constructed around job classifications and are administered in internal labor markets; wages are accorded to organizational positions, not, most commonly, to these positions' incumbents *per se*.

ALLOCATING PEOPLE TO JOBS

Many key differences among labor force members can be summarized by three basic ascribed demographic characteristics: gender, race and ethnicity, and age. These groups' attributes serve as proxies for a wide range of biological, psychological, and sociological factors, including familial and other nonwork social roles, that affect many of their labor market decisions and the importance people place on their work activities. For example, Duncan[1] has recently shown that family structure (specifically, being divorced) has a profound effect on whether women, in a given time period, are classified as poor. While we do not review the vast literature on gender, race, and age differences in work-related experiences and outcomes, we allude to these studies and, of course, our arguments have direct implications for the ways in which issues related thereto may be joined.

These ascribed characteristics, together with a host of attributes achieved by individuals such as education, training, and so on, have pervasive—even dispositive—effects on the kinds of work structures to which people are allocated. One of the many reasons why these characteristics sort people into particular jobs is that employers use them as screening mechanisms, that is, employers believe that they are indicators of potential work performance. However, although education and other "human capital" attributes may result in greater incomes, this does not necessarily mean that they are related to productivity,[2] a matter to which we will return in due course.

In a sense, the background attributes that people bring with them to the labor force are logically and temporally and therefore causally prior to work structures. Ascribed characteristics—especially race, age, and gender—are acquired by people before they enter the labor force and are not generally affected by the kind of work one does, though some jobs may age people more than others. These ascribed characteristics often reflect both different socialization experiences and opportunities that lead different people to choose particular kinds of work.

Moreover, leaders of work structures often use these ascribed attributes as bases of statistical discrimination for selecting certain kinds of people.[3] Hence, whether individuals are successful in getting the kinds of jobs they want depends on whether their attributes match job requirements, both actual and putative. Thus, particular firms, occupations, or unions will have preferences for men as opposed to women, blacks as opposed to whites, significantly well-educated or marginally educated workers, and so on.

---

[1] Greg J. Duncan, *Years of Poverty, Years of Plenty: The Changing Economic Fortunes of American Workers and Families* (Ann Arbor: Institute of Social Research, University of Michigan, 1984).

[2] Ivar Berg, *Education and Jobs: The Great Training Robbery* (New York: Praeger, 1970).

[3] Lester C. Thurow, *Generating Inequality* (New York: Basic Books, 1975).

In these ways, the work structure's selective policies of recruitment and selection cause it to have more or fewer people with certain attributes. This differential selection is illustrated in the case of the segregation of women or blacks into particular occupations, firms, or industries. Sex-typing of occupations, for example, results from socialization experiences and opportunities that influence the occupational choices made by men or women, on one hand, and lead employers—and many other Americans—to regard some occupations as "women's" work and others as "men's" work, on the other. Thus, the *New York Times*, citing a new National Academy of Sciences study, reported on 12 December 1985, that 275 of the 503 census occupations were greater than 80 percent male or female in 1980![4]

The complexity of the causal relations between correlates of work structures and attributes of people cautions us to be sensitive to characteristics of people when interpreting structural effects. For example, the low incomes earned by incumbents of many occupations may reflect the fact that their members are mostly young, black, and/or women as much as the fact that the occupational skills involved are minimal. That this is very likely so is evident in the aforementioned report by the National Academy of Sciences:

> In 1981 the median salary for women who worked full time . . . was $12,000, about 59 percent of the median male salary of $20,260. White women over 18 earned about 60 percent of the salary of white men, black women earned 76 percent of the salary of black men, and Hispanic women earned 73 percent of the salary of Hispanic men. Black women earned about 54 percent of the salary of white men.

Significant segments of such differences are race- and gender-linked by subtle (and not so subtle) discriminatory preferences of those who bid for labor and their agents.

TYPES OF DATA

As we have noted, the search for structural effects must always be conducted within the context of a model the causal assumptions of which can be defended on conceptual grounds. However, our interpretation of these structural effects often depends on the kinds of data that are used: whether cross-sectional or longitudinal, macroscopic or microscopic.

One way to classify types of data is by the *time period* involved. Data

---

[4] *New York Times*, 12 December 1985, A20.

may be collected at one point in time, or be *cross-sectional*, so-called because they provide a "snapshot" of a population's cross section.

Alternatively, data may be collected on the same population for a number of periods; that is, they may be *longitudinal*. Such data may be collected for many (20 or 30 or more) periods, and we refer to them as *time series* data. For example, data on the sequences and timing of, say, the jobs held by individuals at various points in their careers are especially useful in answering questions related to mobility and careers. If the longitudinal data are collected in several discrete waves, we refer to them as *panel* data. Panel data may be ecological (for example, the U.S. Census or Current Population Surveys), which consist of different samples of individuals drawn from the same population (the national labor force) over time. Or, panel data may be collected from the same individuals at different points in time.

Causal processes are best studied using longitudinal data, as one can directly observe how changes in independent variables produce changes in specific dependent variables. But even with longitudinal data, the assessment of relative effects of variables requires us to make certain assumptions about the nature of causality among them. And if the data are longitudinal cross-sectional, not longitudinal panel, we must worry about committing the "ecological fallacy."

The data used to study issues related to work and industry can also be classified according to whether they are *aggregated* or *disaggregated*. Aggregated data are collected on macroscopic units of analysis such as nations. Such data permit the investigation of broad cleavages among actors in the economy and are useful for understanding macroscopic differences. However, if other work structures produce substantial variation in these processes within sectors or segments of the economy, then analyses of aggregate data may simply average these divergent trends. More precise data are collected by those using the disaggregated approach, which sacrifices generality in order to learn a great deal about a specific work setting. Intensive examinations of specific work structures and their consequences, whether observational or historical, are often more informative than large-scale surveys about the nature and consequences of work structures.

RESEARCH DESIGNS

What kinds of research designs are consistent with a multivariate structural approach? Such designs could be very diverse in their methods of data collection, in the particular work structures examined, and so on.

However, in order to be useful for advancing our understanding of the interrelations among work structures, research designs must conform to certain requirements.

First, the research design must permit inferences to be made about the consequences of *multiple* work structures. Highly aggregated data, such as for entire societies or even industries, allow the analyst to make intramural comparisons among countries or industries. However, such data do not often allow extramural comparisons among *different* kinds of work structures. Therefore, studies of industries must also be capable of examining occupational and organizational differences within industries; studies of occupations must pay close attention to how these activities are structured within particular firms; and organizational studies must consider their occupational and industrial contexts.

Of course, not all studies can or should incorporate all of our work structures. Large comparable data sets containing information on all of these structures are generally not available for many countries.[5] Indeed, it is not clear whether studies should consider all of the work structures simultaneously: in many cases, it is as necessary as it is useful to hold one or more of these structures constant in order to study others. For example, studies of industries are able to control for the impacts of concentration, profit levels, technology and so on while investigating differences produced by correlates of occupations and firms. Similarly, studies of occupations hold workers' power and skill levels relatively constant and thereby permit one to study differences in how different firms organize similar occupational activities. The key point is not how *many* work structures are studied in a given research enterprise, but whether the design enables the analyst to consider the impacts of other structures in addition to the one(s) under scrutiny by taking account of others' relevant findings in the construction of the project in question.

Studies of work structures can be either quantitative or qualitative. Regardless of the method used to collect and analyze data, our logical

[5] Several cross-national projects currently in progress may help to alleviate this situation. For example, the Comparative Project on Class Structure and Class Consciousness headed by Erik Olin Wright has produced comparable data on the labor forces of five nations (the United States, Canada, Norway, Sweden, and Finland), and information on five more (West Germany, Britain, Denmark, New Zealand, and Australia) will be available shortly; additional surveys are planned in socialist countries such as Hungary. Moreover, the National Opinion Research Center's General Social Survey is participating in the International Social Survey Program (ISSP), a project that was started in 1985 and that will produce comparable data annually on selected topics (in addition to the United States, the participating countries are Germany, England, Australia, Austria, Italy, Ireland, the Netherlands, and Hungary).

assumptions about work structures and their causal relations are the same. Indeed, the disaggregated and aggregated approaches are *complementary*. On the one hand, case studies of specific work and industry contexts are necessary for understanding precisely how specific correlates influence particular outcomes. The most widely cited studies of internal labor markets were case studies by Doeringer and Piore. On the other hand, comparative research is needed to address basic questions with sufficient generality to permit the construction and testing of theories.

CHAPTER 4

CONSEQUENCES OF WORK STRUCTURES I

Labor Market Outcomes

INCOME INEQUALITY

Inequality of income or earnings[1] is perhaps both the most widely studied of the labor market outcomes of interest to our reader community and the subject of the greatest amount of interdisciplinary research by this community's major investigators. The importance of income derives, understandably, from its centrality to life chances, power, and motivation in highly consumption-oriented societies and societies in which incomes measure personal worthiness, such as the United States.

Income has also proved to be a useful dependent variable for the beginnings of efforts to integrate economic and sociological theories, since it provides a good yardstick against which to measure the power of different groups in the economy. Researchers on these issues have been preoccupied mainly with questions about *inequalities* in income, especially its *distribution* and *redistribution* among individuals, organizations, occupations, and other units within and among societies.

Recent structural explanations of income inequality have turned to theories of economic segmentation in an effort to illustrate the organi-

---

[1] Income is more inclusive than related concepts such as earnings, salaries, and wages or wage rates, since it includes all kinds of unearned income. Most studies use one of the latter measures (often logged) instead of income, avoiding complications produced by income returns to capital investments such as dividends and interest as well as transfer payments.

zational bases of stratification and to underscore the belief that the socioeconomic achievements of individuals are conditioned by differences
in the social and economic organization of different types of production.

These structural approaches—structural because they stress socioeconomic *contexts*—evolved earlier, lay long neglected but reappeared
recently largely in reaction to studies in the status attainment and human
capital traditions dating from the early 1960s. Both of these aspire to
explain income inequality on the basis of an individualistic model in
which the only structural element is a putatively competitive market for
labor: people with the same ascribed and achieved characteristics are
assumed, over the long run, to have the same earnings. This research
has provided many useful insights into the income determination process,
documenting the importance of social background, such social-psycho-
logical factors as motivation, and of investments in training and education. However, by their emphasis on the supply side of the income determination process, these studies tend to oversimplify (as in the case of
the status attainment tradition's reliance on occupational status) or to
assign only marginal significance (as in the human capital tradition) to
the demand side of the story—the structure of jobs and the matching
processes that bring jobs and people together in labor markets.[2] When
they do attend to demand they do so in terms of the attributes of available
supply: youths suffer in the labor market because it would be inflationary
to hire additional inexperienced workers or to pay them attractive wages.
As we will shortly see, the same tendencies occur in a number of studies
of unemployment that parallel those of income distribution.

The insights from the status attainment and human capital traditions
must be integrated with explanations based on work structures and their
correlates, a need not easily met by "straight" economic research because
it generally overlooks the strategic roles of firm and occupational internal
markets; the role of bargaining (over "implicit contracts" between employers and individuals); and the roles of differences in product markets'
treatments of almost any given occupation's incumbents.[3]

A focus on structural determinants of income inequality in no way
implies that individual differences in ability or disability are unimportant
to explanations of inequality. Rather, structuralists, industrial relationists,

[2] For a discussion, see Mark Granovetter, "Toward a Sociological Theory of Income Differences," in *Sociological Perspectives on Labor Markets*, ed. Ivar Berg (New York: Academic Press, 1981), 11–48.
[3] For an updated version of his long-time critique of conventional microeconomists' treatment of wage determination by John Dunlop, see "Industrial Relations and Economics:
The Common Frontier of Wage Determination" (Privately circulated manuscript, Harvard
University, December 28, 1984).

and institutionalists attempt to correct the overemphasis on individual-istic, "marginalist" models by focusing on jobs and work structures as key explanations of income differences. This attempt has been a prom-ising one, but structuralists have not yet proposed a model of income inequality that is as comprehensive as the one advanced by human capital and status attainment researchers.

Sørensen[4] identifies a number of limitations in the research by the new structuralists in stratification research. This research seeks to find structural effects on earnings or income, and there have been studies of income differences using each of our work structures. One problem is their failure to specify the underlying mechanisms that sug-gest a neat theoretical explanation for why a correlate shapes a conse-quence. Indeed, their conclusions are often consistent with many theo-retical interpretations.

Another difficulty involves the study of causal processes using cross-sectional data. Differences observed in such data may appear big, but theoretical questions often do not involve the size of effects but the extent to which they are transient or stable in the long run. With cross-sectional data, one must assume that big effects are persistent effects. Moreover, these analysts often assume that correlates affect consequences *addi-tively*; that is, work structures are associated with more or less of some consequence (income, power). Studies have documented the existence of such additive effects for many structures and consequences, but these findings are consistent with many theoretical interpretations. For ex-ample, although these studies demonstrate that labor markets are not homogeneous, their authors do not spell out the character of their het-erogeneity nor do they tell us why they are heterogeneous. A more fruitful approach to identifying structural effects is to specify particular inter-action effects between structures and consequences: structural variables do not simply add to a person's level of income; they determine the economic value of education, experience, and other investments made by individuals.

In addition, many of the studies by the new structuralists compare the amount of variance in one or more dependent variables that is ex-plained by work structures and by characteristics of individuals in an attempt to underscore the importance of structural correlates. But the use of explained variance as a criterion to assess the relative importance of variables can be very misleading, since this statistic is highly dependent on population variances themselves, the kinds of data used, and the

[4] Aage B. Sørensen, "Sociological Research on the Labor Market: Conceptual and Meth-odological Issues," *Work and Occupations* 10 (August 1983): 261–87.

measurement strategies investigators employ: some variables may explain a lot of observed variance in a dependent variable without having any theoretical significance. For example, amount of time worked explains much of the variance in income but this relationship is primarily an accounting one—the more hours one works, *ceteris paribus*, the more money one receives. This explanation simply pushes the question back one step: one must explain differences in hours worked, not differences in the incomes thus accorded to a population group. Conversely, an independent variable may explain only a little variance but may nevertheless be theoretically important in accounting for differences in the dependent variable. For example, one's earnings are undoubtedly a key cause of how one feels about a given job, but if people receive relatively equal earnings, then economic rewards as such will not explain much of the variation in the attitudes of research subjects about their jobs. (As we note later, though, peoples' feelings about the fairness of the same amounts of economic rewards can differ quite widely.)

Types of Work Structures and Income Inequality

Class. Studies by Wright and his associates[5] have analyzed income differences using the Marxian conception of class. They have documented empirically what Marxists have always assumed: employers obtain higher incomes than managers who, in turn, are paid higher incomes than workers. Importantly, Wright also finds that the income *returns* to their investments in education are greater for managers than workers. These education–income interactions are assumed by Wright and others to reflect different processes of income determination due to structural properties of the classes as structures unto themselves. His answer to the question of why education is worth more economically for managers than for workers is consistent with the univariate class approach: these advantages for managers are part of the incentive system used to control them in the labor process and thus reflect the *exploitation* of managers by capitalists.

However, Wright's results are consistent with a number of alternative explanations. For example, as Sørensen has pointed out (see footnote 4), interpretations based on the "need to control the labor process" are equally

[5] See especially Wright, *Class Structure and Income Determination*; Erik O. Wright and Luca Perrone, "Marxist Class Categories and Income Inequality," *American Sociological Review* 42 (February 1977): 32–55; see also Kalleberg and Griffin, "Class, Occupation and Inequality in Job Rewards"; and Tom Colbjørnsen, *Dividers in the Labor Market* (Oslo: Norwegian University Press; and Oxford: Oxford University Press, 1986).

consistent with explanations that take account of the workings of internal labor markets as well as the gains in technical efficiency that result from the incentives provided by promotion systems in such markets. Attributing effects to class that are unique from those produced by internal labor markets, then, requires the analyst to show that internal markets are introduced and/or maintained in order to *avoid class action* even when this leads to additional costs of production. In any event, it is very difficult, if not impossible, to adjudicate, on empirical grounds, between these contrasting theoretical explanations.

Occupations. Researchers using the status attainment approach have shown that people who work in higher *status* occupations earn more money.[6] However, the theoretical interpretations of the relationship between occupational prestige or status and income are subjects of considerable controversy. Max Weber's discussion of prestige (on which much of the status attainment work of recent years is based) provides little justification for the assumption that prestige somehow causes income; in fact, it is more reasonable to assume that workers who command high incomes do, for that reason, acquire high prestige! Interpretations based on the functional theory of stratification—that earnings inequalities reflect differences in the contributions of high and low earners to the effective functioning of a given social system—are also dubious, given evidence suggesting that neither prestige nor status is a pervasive indicator of "functional importance."[7]

Some researchers have tried to specify why occupational differences generate income inequalities by dividing occupations into discrete labor market segments, which are assumed to differ in the processes by which a given income level is determined. In support of this assumption, occupational labor markets' attributes have been shown to *interact* with such variables as experience or education in the prediction of income.[8] For example, education and experience are more strongly related to income in occupational internal labor markets than in labor markets in which occupational incumbents have relatively little control over their activities.

Joined by critics of status attainment and human capital studies described earlier, institutional economists[9] have stressed the significant

---

[6] Sewell and Hauser.

[7] For discussions of these points see Goldthorpe and Hope; and Fligstein *et al.*

[8] See Osterman; Stolzenberg.

[9] See, for example, John T. Dunlop, "The Task of Contemporary Wage Theory," in *New Concepts in Wage Determination*, ed. G. W. Taylor and F. C. Pierson (New York: McGraw-Hill, 1957), 3–30, and his updated critique in "Industrial Relations and Economics: The Common Frontier of Wage Determination."

degree to which wages in different contexts—occupations, industries, and across organizations in different product markets, for example—are clustered together as a result of their members making selectively coercive or invidious comparisons of each others' economic gains. The members of these relatively insular groups are thus conceived to be at work in distinctive subsets of the larger labor market that are noncompeting. The results, these writers argue, describe identifiable wage contours that are given their particular shapes through separately *bargained* packages, not through the equilibrations of an overarching competitive market system in which labor costs reflect the interactions, in national terms, among factor costs. The distinction is thus between an agreement (or contract, as it is increasingly called) informed by a number of both economic and noneconomic considerations of importance to the parties, on one side, and a straightforward consideration of prices in an auction market, on the other.

These critics are especially skeptical of marginalists' explanation of earnings in productivity terms. Readers in large cities will recall that when one uniformed service—a police, fire, or sanitation department—wins new gains for its members, the other services' bargaining programs are aimed at achieving the same ends. As sociologists put it, groups assess their circumstances, in a wide variety of social, political, and economic contexts, to those of selected other groups such that they have a sense of *relative* deprivation or relative satisfaction, as the case may be. Wage markets are thus very clearly segmented, in the minds of their members at least, in accord with logic that is not less persuasive to them for appearing to be more than a little idiosyncratic to unfeeling taxpayers or consumers otherwise. We might pause to suggest, by implication, that failures of social scientists who have sought to differentiate among worker segments *to identify* their attributes in ways that are in fact consequential relate to the fact that these investigators often construct their prototypal segments without seeking to divine workers' own views of their reference groups.

A key correlate of occupations underlying the creation of these labor market segments is, as we noted in the last chapter, their power. Thus, some occupations have sufficient resources to control entry and training, while the activities of other occupations' members are learned in work structures such as firms. Further, occupations the members of which are able to establish occupational internal labor markets generally enable their members to earn higher salaries than they would otherwise.

Organizations. Studies of income differences among business organizations of different *sizes* have generally found that workers in larger establishments and enterprises earn more than workers in smaller ones.[10] However, why size affects income inequality is less well understood. Baron,[11] in a review of organizational perspectives on income inequality, notes that neoclassical economics and its neo-Marxist variant offer different explanations of this relationship: large bureaucracies may pay and promote more because scale economies increase worker productivity, and/or large organizations are more vulnerable to worker unrest and hence rewards are higher so as to reduce labor–management conflict. Therefore, the size–income link may be forged, alternatively, by: the greater power of large firms, organizational growth and development, demographic characteristics of organizations such as age and tenure distributions, the nature of technology, and so on. In addition, since unions are more likely to organize and be more militant in big firms, the size–earnings relationship may in part be accounted for by a "union effect," real or threatened.

In addition to size differences are inequalities in wages across organizations in a locality attributable to differences in the degree of competitiveness in different organizations' product markets.[12]

Sørensen[13] identifies two major correlates of firm internal labor markets that are related to the income determination process: wages in general are a function of jobs, not people (exceptions are entrepreneurs, where the two are the same); and promotion systems or job ladders are used by organizational leaders essentially as incentive systems (exceptions occur when job ladders are used to co-opt or otherwise divide workers by separating them from each other or, during periods of wage controls, to exceed legal limitations). These two correlates are linked, because individual bargaining over wages in unorganized not less than in organized settings would decrease the incentive qualities of promotion ladders. Within internal labor markets, then, income inequality results from a promotion process and should be studied through analyses of mobility within firms (see the section on careers and mobility below). Individual characteristics are still important in internal labor markets, but, more

---

[10] See, for example, Richard Lester, "Pay Differentials by Size of Establishment," *Industrial Relations* 8 (October 1967): 62–5.

[11] Baron, "Organizational Perspectives on Inequality."

[12] *Brookings Papers on Economic Activity* (Washington, D.C.: Brookings Institution, 1984), p. 220; William Brown *et al.*, "Product and Labour Markets in Wage Determination: Some Australian Evidence," *British Journal of Industrial Relations* 22 (July 1984): 169–76; and John Dunlop, "Industrial Relations and Economics."

[13] Sørensen.

generally, because they define an individual's mobility potential rather than because they increase one's productivity.

Unfortunately, the absence of uncontroversial measures of firms' internal labor markets has precluded a comprehensive assessment of their consequences for earnings and other important outcomes. Direct measures of firm internal labor markets are needed that are useful for both (a) differentiating job ladders within firms and (b) comparing job ladders across firms. The absence of such data is balanced by the hands-on lifetime experiences of a legion of industrial relationists—led by John Dunlop—who regularly testify to the extraordinary potency of internal labor market rule making.

Industries. Much recent sociological research on income inequality has focused on differences between core and periphery industrial sectors: workers in the so-called monopoly sector have been shown to earn more than their counterparts in the competitive sector.[14] However, it is not clear what these observed differences actually mean. For example, neoclassical economists interpret these differences as simply reflecting variations in some aspects of demand, and believe that they can be explained, additionally, by differences in the marginal productivities of workers in different industries, such that workers in some industries are made more productive because they have better training or because they operate better machines.

In contrast, dual economy researchers typically interpret these industrial differences as reflecting differences in the sectors' bigness, and generally assume that bigness is better with respect to earnings, since big firms have more power over other firms and the state, have more money to distribute to workers, and so on. The demand hypothesis gains some support when product markets are taken into account, as we noted above. The productivity hypothesis is far more difficult to test given difficulties in measuring the contributions of research and development, capital investments, raw materials, and managers-as-a-work-force to productivity.

The bigness of an industry, meanwhile, will not automatically result in higher incomes for workers unless employers are beneficent, an unrealistic assumption. This implies that a focus on the characteristics of employers needs to be supplemented by a consideration of the power of workers in different industrial contexts in order to account for income inequality. In any event, the key question regarding industrial income

---

[14] Beck, Horan, and Tolbert; Robert Bibb and William H. Form, "The Effects of Industrial, Occupational and Sex Stratification on Wages in Blue-Collar Markets," *Social Forces* 55 (June 1977): 974–96.

differentials is not so much how big they are but how permanent and stable they are. For example, industry differences in income must persist over time before they pose a challenge to neoclassical economic theories of inequality. If they are transitory, they can be reconciled within the neoclassical economic framework by regarding them simply as short-term imperfections—all things not being equal—in the labor market.

If there are different mechanisms underlying income inequality in the two industrial sectors, then not only should individuals in these sectors differ in their levels of earnings, but there should also be *interactions* by sector. Recent research has found differences among product markets but little evidence that such interactions exist within sectoral contexts.[15] However, a number of studies have found evidence of a negative interaction effect between concentration and unionization in the prediction of income.[16] This suggests the possibility that the high market power of firms in some industries hampers the ability of unions to obtain high wages for their members; it also points to the importance of considering the interplay between the power of employers and workers in explaining the generation of inequality. To the extent that unions have generated income gains for their members, these gains are balanced, from employers' perspectives, by displacing workers in favor of capital investments or by subcontracting work, as has occurred in autos.

Unions. As dual economy researchers often neglect unions, so sociologists who study unions often view their properties merely as attributes of economic organizations, not as social actors confronting employers. And in a large number of studies of the relations between unions and wages by economists, there is considerable controversy about the nature of union effects and how these are produced. Lewis,[17] in a pioneering work, found the issue too complex to resolve dispositively. Much earlier, Mathewson[18] analyzed workers in organized and unorganized firms in several industries *and their employers* and found that all the

---

[15] Compare, for example, Beck, Horan, and Tolbert, with Robert Hauser, "On 'Stratification in a Dual Economy'," *American Sociological Review* 45 (August 1980): 702–12. See also Hodson, *Workers' Earnings and Corporate Economic Structure*; Kalleberg, Wallace, and Althauser; and Colbjørnsen.

[16] See Leonard Weiss, "Concentration and Labor Earnings," *American Economic Review* 56 (March 1966): 96–117; James Dalton and E. J. Ford, "Concentration and Labor Earnings in Manufacturing and Utilities," *Industrial and Labor Relations Review* 31 (October 1977): 45–60.

[17] H. Gregg Lewis, *Unionism and Relative Wages in the United States* (Chicago: University of Chicago Press, 1963).

[18] Stanley B. Mathewson, *Restriction of Output Among Unorganized Workers* (Carbondale, Ill.: Southern Illinois University Press, 1969). The first edition was published by Viking Press in 1931.

actors "restricted output." Still earlier, in 1904, Wright[19] of the old Commission on Labor (now the Labor Department) reported the same results in a detailed analysis of twelve United States industries and of four industries in the United Kingdom.

In a very recent analysis, Freeman and Medoff[20] review a large number of studies of union wage effects and, on the basis of their own analyses and those of others, conclude that union members earn more than otherwise comparable but nonunionized blue-collar workers. They also report that unions tend to reduce wage inequality by raising the wages of relatively low paid workers such as women and unskilled blue-collar workers. In either event, they found it difficult to test hypotheses about the gains—loyalty, productivity—that unions may afford employers in return for the wage gains unions win for their members.

Income differences between core and periphery industries are no doubt due in part to the differential ability of unions to extract higher wages from employers. Industrial unions tended, in their halcyon days, to locate and acquire power in contexts where employers are big and have high resources. Moreover, unions often collaborate with employers in core industries to create higher entry barriers for nonunion sources of competition. This suggests that unions will help their members to get higher earnings at the expense of nonunion members. Unions also often act, in *de facto* ways, as agents of management by quieting, "cooling out," and by not processing grievances, as well as by maintaining discipline and other management-serving functions. However, unions are also important mechanisms, both symbolically and realistically, for ensuring that workers benefit economically from increases in productivity due to more capital-intensive forms of production. Indeed, some have blamed unions for inflation, arguing that they have pushed up wages, thereby contributing to high prices as employers try to pass on these costs to consumers. It is equally possible that unions' arguments contribute to managers' interests in labor-saving machinery, as in the West Coast longshore case, the modernization and mechanization agreement noted in Chapter 3, or when managers simply seek to reduce the labor factor in their cost structures by modernizing their plants without unions' encouragement.

Nation-States. There have been relatively few studies of cross-national patterns of income inequality.[21] Some analysts have focused on the

---

[19] Carroll D. Wright, *Regulations and Restrictions of Output* (Washington, D. C.: U. S. Government Printing Office, 1904).

[20] Freeman and Medoff.

[21] See the review by Larry Isaac, "Comparative Economic Inequality," *International Journal of Comparative Sociology* 22 (1981):62–85.

historically variable structural links between capital and labor in a capitalist world economy; this is especially true of those using the so-called world-system perspective.[22] However, these investigations are limited by: the extremely aggregated nature of the data, the historically and culturally free causal reasoning often characteristic of quantitative cross-national studies, and the potentially serious statistical divergence between results obtained from analyses of cross-sectional and time series data. All of these militate against an adequate assessment of the dynamic interplay among macroeconomic processes, the organization of production, and income inequality within particular nations.

A key question in the study of income inequality, and one that takes on special significance in research on cross-national differences, is that of *redistribution*.[23] This is the process by which societies alter patterns of economic inequality by redistributing income and wealth away from some in favor of others. Producer incomes can thereby be transformed into user incomes. There are a large number of potentially income redistributive mechanisms, including direct income transfers, income maintenance programs, and negative income tax programs. Many public and private sector institutions, meanwhile, are involved in redistribution, including government agencies, insurance companies, philanthropic agencies, the educational establishment (with its massive student assistance programs), and the family. Thoughts about these and other redistributive mechanisms highlight the importance of nonwork institutions for explaining economic inequality.

Unfortunately, the issue of income redistribution has been less well researched than its distribution. As Lampman[24] has noted:

> Economists have more to do before we fully understand the set of changing institutions by which we can and do modify the pre-redistribution of income, the goals of redistribution (of which poverty reduction is only one) and the consequences, costs, and benefits of such redistribution.

Most readers would likely expect that at least *governments'* roles in collecting revenue and making expenditures have been progressive—that the net effects of interventions by governments (state, local, and national), in the United States is to take money from upper income groups

---

[22] For example, Richard Rubinson, "The World-Economy and the Distribution of Income Within States: A Cross-National Study," *American Sociological Review* 10 (1976): 638–59.

[23] See, for example, Paul Taubman, *Income Distribution and Redistribution* (Reading, Mass.: Addison-Wesley, 1978); and Morgan Reynolds and Eugene Smolensky, *Public Expenditures, Taxes and the Distribution of Income: The United States, 1950, 1961, 1970* (New York: Academic Press, 1977).

[24] Robert J. Lampman, "Transfer Approaches to Distribution Policy," *Papers and Proceedings of the American Economic Association* (May 1970): 270–79.

and redistribute it to low income groups. However, the two most recent and formidably rigorous studies, by Pechman and Minarik[25] for 1970 and by Reynolds and Smolensky for 1950 to 1972, do not support such a judgment.

Space does not permit a review of these investigators' detailed efforts to take account of the staggering number of measurement and estimation problems that must be confronted, but one comes away from Reynolds' and Smolensky's discussion of their and the Pechman–Minarik labors fairly well persuaded that "the net effect of government upon the final distribution [of income among different classes of earners] is substantial *in any year*" (emphases added). They go on to say:

> That distribution of income which includes the benefits of government expenditures and the burdens of taxation is significantly closer to equality than the distributions of factor or money income in each year. However, the difference between the initial and final distributions arithmetically attributable to government in each year has not grown significantly over two decades despite the rapid growth in government. That is, the distributive impact of each dollar spent by government or taxed by government has declined, but the overall distributive effect remained at least as large because government spent and taxed on a much larger scale.
>
> Disaggregation revealed that the overall tax system has drifted from progressive to proportional or perhaps even to slightly regressive by 1970. The rapid rise in government spending, however, preserved or slightly increased the difference between initial and final distributions.[26]

We must emphasize that conclusive judgments are hard to come by for many methodologically related reasons, among them the fact that a very substantial number of presumably redistributive expenditures are not carried on the books as expenditures as, for example, in the cases of tax expenditures (applicable but uncollected taxes like those waived on once in a lifetime windfall gains from house sales and loan guarantees in which loan repayments by college students appear to offset the dollars borrowed). Nor is it easy to determine what shares of corporate income taxes are passed on to consumers. The most reasonable statement is likely to be the one cited from the study by Reynolds and Smolensky: the dollars of income accruing to each income decile in the population appear to change within a given year but change very little year in and year out. Such data do not include transfers to the poor, like food stamps, nor tax expenditures for the not-so-poor such as the right to deduct interest

---

[25] Pechman and Minarik's work is described in Reynolds and Smolensky (pp. 92–94) and earlier in J. A. Pechman and B. A. Okner, *Who Bears the Tax Burden?* (Washington, D. C.: Brookings Institute, 1974).

[26] Reynolds and Smolensky, 92.

payments on mortgages on second homes at beach or ski resorts. But the final data on income deciles look remarkably like those offered by the investigations cited in which the authors traced the disaggregated flows and transactions within the limits of evenhanded and sophisticated analysis.

One might well ask: Why has the bottom 51 percent of earners, in a democratic system, not insisted on far more tax progressivity than longitudinal data series suggest has emerged, say, since the advent of the New Deal? The answer to that question is almost as difficult to apprehend as the answers to questions about the degree of re- or progressivity. We must recall that even a very steeply progressive tax system does not assure that income earners, loopholes aside, either will or can assess their earned incomes in quite the same way. Low-income people can not avoid the effects of inflation on necessities, and a high proportion of their annual wage and salary earnings is so spent, whereas higher earners have some degree of option in the disposition of their earnings, for example, to save and invest and thus to earn from their earnings. While the facts are not elusive, they are subtle because low-income earners can not readily gainsay the significance of savings to capital formation.

Moreover, low-income home owners, from their perspective, have as much interest in the tax deductibility of interest on mortgage payments, for example, as a steel corporation that borrows money to purchase oil-refining equipment as part of a leveraged takeover. There is understandably little, in such shared interests, to lead 51 percent of the taxed population to act, in class terms, in support of increasingly progressive taxes. Discussions in both of the United States Congress's houses over tax reform, as of July 1986, do not suggest that the tax deductibility of interest payments for either homebuyers or corporate raiders is in any danger.

Multivariate Structural Explanations of Income Inequality

Several recent studies illustrate a multivariate structural approach to explaining income inequality. For example, Kalleberg *et al.* posit two main types of structural correlates that generate differences in income: (1) employers with large amounts of resources are able, and often find it in their interest for a variety of reasons, to pay their workers higher wages; and (2) some workers have more ample resources and are better able to acquire power against their employers and other workers, thereby extracting higher earnings. The authors argue further that

> the structure of economic segmentation is multidimensional and reflects such distinct concepts as concentration, economic scale, state intervention in the market, capital intensity and organization size. Workers' power also is derived

TABLE 4. Unstandardized (Standardized) Coefficients Obtained from Regressions of (Log) Earnings on Determinants

Independent variables	United States			Japan		
	Male managers	Male workers	Female workers	Male managers	Male workers	Female workers
Age	.007(.108)†	.003(.069)*	.001(.015)	.014(.303)**	.013(.302)**	.003(.098)[a]
Education	.023(.044)	.050(.092)**	.040(.070)*	.032(.111)*	.027(.062)*	.073(.132)*
Married	.032(.019)	.111(.105)**	-.051(-.054)†[a]	.130(.122)**	.142(.172)**	-.059(-.083)[a]
Supervisor	-.700(-.569)**	—	—	-.107(-.142)**	—	—
Tenure	.004(.075)	.008(.156)**	.015(.275)**[a]	.011(.251)**	.018(.313)**	.033(.478)**[a]
Promote	-.002(-.002)	.005(.005)	-.053(-.045)	.059(.090)*	.084(.091)**	-.117(-.061)[a]
Firm on-the-job training	-.049(-.070)†	-.004(-.008)	-.026(-.046)	.032(.112)**	.018(.059)*	.029(.114)*
Number of ranks	.158(.282)**	-.061(-.136)**	-.053(-.094)†	.019(.091)†	-.009(-.033)	-.016(-.061)
Substantive complexity	.011(.012)	.082(.184)**	.076(.141)**	.019(.042)	.017(.037)	.045(.103)†
Autonomy	.059(.071)†	.031(.057)*	.027(.057)	.005(.011)	.003(.005)	.019(.046)

Union	−.090(−.070)	.166(.157)**	.294(.306)**[a]	−.213(−.263)**	−.132(−.135)**	−.154(−.208)†
Automation	.011(.044)	−.025(−.127)**	.047(.180)**[a]	.032(.174)**	.030(.122)**	−.003(−.014)[a]
Size	.114(.258)**	.081(.202)**	.051(.143)†	.036(.099)*	.053(.142)**	.087(.194)*
Independent company	−.127(−.093)†	−.000(−.000)	−.018(−.016)	.017(.023)	−.099(−.119)**	−.047(−.061)
Age of plant	−.002(−.100)†	−.003(−.169)**	−.003(−.174)**	−.000(−.014)	−.000(.013)	.003(.130)†
Reviews	.062(.071)	.121(.159)**	.053(.070)†[a]	−.072(−.140)**	−.102(−.149)**	−.129(−.368)**
Transportation equipment	−.152(−.159)*	.065(.088)*	.167(.183)**[a]	.038(.057)	.033(.034)	.146(.130)†
Electrical	−.003(−.003)	−.026(−.026)	−.046(−.068)	−.113(−.144)**	−.053(−.065)*	−.144(−.214)*
Chemicals	.005(.004)	−.042(−.040)	−.018(−.019)	.170(.225)**	.086(.079)*	.071(.097)
Metals	.047(.034)	.072(.051)	.234(.187)†	.101(.132)**	.039(.039)	.078(.081)
Machinery	.141(.116)*	−.054(−.058)*	.040(.041)	−.026(−.032)	.112(.120)**	.004(.003)
Food processing	−.193(−.171)**	.033(.034)	−.048(−.054)	.141(.177)**	−.007(−.006)	.098(.139)†
Printing	.155(.162)†	−.050(−.067)	−.329(−.362)**[a]	−.311(−.463)**	−.209(−.215)**	−.253(−.226)**
Constant (adjusted)	10.329	9.796	9.606	9.582	9.406	9.067
R^2 (adjusted)	.527	.400	.421	.500	.538	.349
(N)	(443)	(2063)	(730)	(567)	(1148)	(346)

SOURCE: Arne L. Kalleberg and James R. Lincoln, "The Structure of Earnings Inequality in the U.S. and Japan."

[a] Male-female worker difference significant at $p \leq .05$. Underlined coefficients are significantly different between the U.S. and Japan for that group at $p \leq .05$.

* $p \leq .01$; ** $p \leq .001$; † $p \leq .05$.

from diverse sources, such as union membership, occupational skill and licensing, class position, and tenure with an employer.[27]

Their analyses of data from two national samples of the United States
labor force provide considerable support for a multivariate structural explanation of income differences: all industry correlates with the exception
of economic scale were found to have independent effects on income, as
did all measures of worker power (occupational skill and licensing, union
membership, class position, and tenure with an employer). Finally, their
analyses showed both (1) that the effects of education on income differed
across firm and industrial contexts and (2) that income determination
processes differed for men and women.

This research was extended by a comparative study of American and
Japanese employees.[28] In this project the investigators collected data from
key informants in over 100 manufacturing plants and from over 8,300
managers, supervisors, and workers in the two countries. These data
enabled the researchers to examine the relative effects on earnings and
other work-related outcomes of country, skills, classes, unions, organizations, and industries. Their major results, summarized in Table 4,
suggest several important conclusions.

First, the effects on earnings of diverse work structures— correlates
of firms, industries, skills, unions, classes—are not reducible to one another, which is to say that they have independent effects on earnings.
Second, work structures affect earnings differently in different countries.
For example, because of the greater salience of one's organizational attachment in Japan, whether or not one is a member of a firm internal
labor market has a stronger impact on earnings in that country than in
the United States. Moreover, due to the *nenko* system of reward distribution, age and seniority are more strongly related to earnings in Japan.
By contrast, in the United States job skills are more strongly related to
earnings, the gaps in earnings between managers and workers are greater,
and the differences in earnings between union and nonunion members
are greater.

This research illustrates the utility of collecting data from organizations and their employees in order to examine the consequences of
multiple work structures for earnings. Such organization-based but multilevel research designs are necessary to isolate the relative effects of
diverse work structures on earnings. These results also demonstrate that

[27] Kalleberg, Wallace, and Althauser, 651.
[28] Arne L. Kalleberg and James R. Lincoln, "The Structure of Earnings Inequality in the
U.S. and Japan," *American Journal of Sociology,* Supplement on "Sociology and Economics," ed. Sherwin Rosen and Christopher Winship (1987): in press.

work structures affect labor market outcomes in different ways in different countries. Hence, comparative research is highly useful in efforts to understand the consequences of work structures. Only by examining these issues in a wide range of cultural and societal contexts will we be able to appreciate the cross-national diversity in the structure of earnings inequality.

CAREERS AND MOBILITY

Career is a central concept that links structural features of the economy to inequalities in the benefits and costs associated with employment. Careers are peoples' work histories and consist of the sequence of jobs they hold over their working lives. Careers differ in their *levels* of rewards (both economic and noneconomic) and in their reward *trajectories*, or *rates of change* in rewards. These aspects of careers vary systematically among diverse work structures, and an understanding of why some structural contexts are advantaged and some are not is necessary to account for the processes that generate inequality over the life course. Careers are also distinguished by the incidence and types of *job mobility* between and within particular organizations and occupations. Despite the considerable job mobility that characterizes the American economy, it is well known that there are barriers limiting mobility between certain sets of jobs (for example, from bad to good jobs, from one employer to another). The investigation of these mobility channels or pathways between jobs is a necessary condition for understanding the differential opportunities for advancement associated with diverse work structures.

Recent studies of the relations between work structures and careers have generally followed one of two approaches. The first, the *disaggregated,* approach, examines determinants of rewards and/or mobility within specific firms[29] or within bounded organizational units.[30] The focus on specific organizations permits the collection and analysis of precise data on jobs and on patterns of mobility; these efforts are essential for theory construction and hypothesis testing.

[29] James Rosenbaum, "Tournament Mobility: Career Patterns in a Corporation," *Administrative Science Quarterly* 24 (1979): 220–41.

[30] For example, the police: Shelby Stewman, "Two Market Models of Open System Occupational Mobility: Underlying Conceptualizations and Empirical Tests," *American Sociological Review* 40 (1975): 298–321; and the military: John Butler, "Inequality in the Military: An Examination of Promotion Time for Black and White Enlisted Men," *American Sociological Review* 41 (1976): 807–18.

The second, the *aggregated* approach, investigates the impact of work structures on careers for the labor force as a whole and attempts to discern reward trajectories and mobility channels that characterize sizable numbers of workers.[31] Although lacking the precision of the former, this approach permits the study of broad patterns of cleavage among workers in the economy. The approach is useful for understanding inequalities both in rewards and in opportunities for advancement among labor force participants in general as well as for assessing macroscopic explanations of career patterns. Unfortunately, this perspective is not well developed and, despite its potential, is characterized by considerable confusion regarding key concepts and how they are related. Our discussion of the *interrelations* among work structures will help to clarify these issues.

How Work Structures Affect Careers

Some of our work structures are more important for understanding reward trajectories and mobility than others. Occupations, organizations, and, to a lesser extent, industries most directly define the job ladders that form the contexts within which careers unfold and people move and are rewarded.

Organizations. The *size* of the organization affects people's chances for mobility and hence their careers. Persons who work in larger firms are less likely to change employers, reflecting in part the greater job security enjoyed by workers in big firms and their greater ability to obtain progressively higher-level jobs within the organization. Mobility differences between large and small firms are often explained on the basis of firm internal labor markets. Persons in FILMs have relatively greater probability of changing jobs with a given employer than non-FILM incumbents but are less likely to change employers. Moreover, since FILMs are associated wth greater potentials for upward movement, reward trajectories for FILM incumbents should be steeper than those for persons not in such internal markets.

Some of the most illuminating studies of the impact of internal labor markets on careers have been conducted by those in the disaggregated tradition who have focused on specific organizations, industries, and/or occupations. In a unique study, Gitelman[32] examined mobility over a

---

[31] Seymour Spilerman, "Careers, Labor Market Structure, and Socioeconomic Achievement," *American Journal of Sociology* 83 (1977): 551–93; Kenneth Spenner, Luther Otto, and Vaughn Call, *Career Lines and Careers* (Lexington, Mass.: D.C. Heath, 1982).

[32] H. M. Gitelman, "Occupational Mobility Within the Firm," *Industrial and Labor Relations Review* 20 (1966): 50–65.

thirty-year period (1860–1890) within the Waltham Watch Company. He found that intrafirm mobility is influenced by factors such as the technology employed, external labor market conditions, and changes in the composition of output. Beattie and Spencer[33] tested several hypotheses concerning the influence of age, seniority, and education on the salary attainment of men in bureaucratic careers in the Canadian federal administration. They argued that career discrimination is the primary factor accounting for salary differentials between Francophones and Anglophones in a Canadian context. In a study of British managers and technical specialists, Sofer[34] investigated the sources of mobility blockage in organizations. Another study of internal labor markets examined the impact of organizational contraction and growth on organizational careers.[35] Finally, Berg, in a 1970 study of a 5 percent sample of the entire civil service, reports that the single most important factor in the movement of federal workers from GS-4 to GS-14 level jobs was the number of subjects' interagency movements. These transfers counted more than any of the subjects' personal attributes, including their educational achievements,[36] in predicting their upward mobility over long career-type periods.

Occupations. The status attainment approach to careers is represented by the studies of Featherman and Kelley,[37] who examined patterns of mobility and stability among occupational status levels. A key question here is the degree to which careers have a "history": whether education and occupational status of first job continue to affect subsequent attainments. These studies show that education continues to have an impact on the kinds of occupations that people attain during the course of their careers, but its effects become attenuated as time passes.

As we have noted, the status attainment approach implicitly assumes that careers unfold within a homogeneous national labor market. It also assumes that continuous measures of occupational status capture the important occupational correlates related to careers. These assumptions are questioned by the labor market segmentation approach to mobility

---

[33] C. Beattie and B. Spencer, "Career Attainment in Canadian Bureaucracies: Unscrambling the Effects of Age, Seniority, Education, and Ethnolinguistic Factors on Salary," *American Journal of Sociology* 77 (1971): 472–90.

[34] C. Sofer, *Men in Mid-Career: A Study of British Managers and Technical Specialists* (Cambridge: Cambridge University Press, 1970).

[35] Rosenbaum.

[36] Ivar Berg, *Education and Jobs: The Great Training Robbery*, Chapter 8.

[37] David L. Featherman, "A Social Structural Model for the Socioeconomic Career," *American Journal of Sociology* 77 (1971): 293–304; Jonathan Kelley, "Causal Chain Models for the Socioeconomic Career," *American Sociological Review* 38 (1973): 481–93.

and careers, the followers of which divide the occupational structure into qualitatively distinct labor market segments. Thus, dual labor market theorists argue that a worker's location in one or another occupational segment is important for understanding features of his or her career such as the economic value of one's education, the kinds of mobility experienced, and the amount one earns.[38]

The dual labor market theory argues that the important distinction for analyzing the economy is that between good and bad *jobs*, rather than (as in much of neoclassical economic theory) between skilled and unskilled workers. However, investigators seeking to explain why mobility patterns differ among occupations must go beyond their distinction between good and bad jobs. Other theories of labor market segmentation are more useful in this regard.

For example, the links between occupational segments and mobility patterns can be viewed in terms of occupational internal labor markets.[39] As we have discussed previously, these are job ladders created by occupations, and movement up these ladders is associated with increasing levels of skill and knowledge. Unlike FILMs, OILMs span organizations and perhaps industries. Labor market segments overlap with these kinds of internal labor markets: upper primary occupations are most likely to constitute OILMs; subordinate primary occupations are more likely to be found in FILMs; and secondary market occupations are not associated with either type of internal labor market.

This reasoning helps explain differences in patterns of mobility among occupational segments. Secondary occupations, because they are characterized by relatively low skill levels and few opportunities for training and advancement, are characterized by higher rates of employer changes than subordinate primary occupations, which are more often located within FILMs. Employer changes within secondary labor markets are not likely to result in increases in rewards, since these changes may be chaotic and job rewards do not rise much with experience.[40] Workers in subordinate primary occupations are more likely to change jobs within firms, on the one hand, since they are more likely to be members of FILMs. On the other hand, members of upper primary occupations change em-

[38] For example, Duane Leigh, "Occupational Achievement in the Late 1960s: An Indirect Test of the Dual Labor Market Hypothesis," *Journal of Human Resources* 11 (1976): 155–71; Michael Piore, "Notes for a Theory of Labor Market Stratification," in *Labor Market Segmentation*, ed. Richard Edwards, Michael Reich, and David Gordon (Lexington, Mass.: D. C. Heath, 1975), pp. 125–50.

[39] Althauser and Kalleberg; Doeringer and Piore.

[40] See, for example, Osterman.

ployers more often than workers in subordinate primary occupations because of the presence of OILMs.

A study by Kalleberg and Hudis[41] examined the consequences of different patterns of occupational and organizational mobility. They investigated four types of mobility patterns defined by cross-classifying patterns of occupational and employer change and stability over a five-year interval. They found that the determinants of career advancement (measured as changes in wages) differed among these groups; that differences between black and white men exist only in certain contexts (among those changing their occupations but not their employers and those changing both occupations and employers); and that workers (especially blacks) who change both occupations and employers exhibit many features of disorderly career lines such as small wage changes.

Industries. A discrete classification of industries into sectors is generally useful for studying industrial differences in careers, since it simplifies the investigation of differences in organizational and occupational mobility. We would expect there to be relatively more upward movement in monopoly industrial sectors, because of the more common presence of job ladders therein, than in the competitive sector. Wanner and Lewis[42] find that many of the advantages of core sector employment occur early in the career when there is considerable intersector mobility (especially from the periphery to the core sectors). Using data for a cohort of older United States men, they find that education and training have greater effects on status movements at both early and mid-career stages in the core sector. This parallels the findings of Tolbert,[43] who reports that the careers of American men in the core sector are more orderly than those in other sectors. Employer changes are also rarer in monopoly sectors than in competitive industries. Further, job sequences are more chaotic in competitive industries than in other sectors, and hence reward trajectories are less hyperbolic. On the basis of these differences, Wanner and Lewis conclude that "any model of the occupational career that excludes some indicator of location in the industry structure will likely be misspecified."[44]

Other classifications of industries have been used to examine dif-

[41] Arne L. Kalleberg and Paula M. Hudis, "Wage Change in the Late Career: A Model for the Outcomes of Job Sequences," *Social Science Research* 8 (1979): 16–40.

[42] Richard Wanner and Lionel Lewis, "Economic Segmentation and the Course of the Occupational Career," *Work and Occupations* 10 (August 1983): 307–24.

[43] Charles Tolbert, "Industrial Segmentation and Men's Career Mobility," *American Sociological Review* 47 (1982): 457–77.

[44] Wanner and Lewis, 321.

ferences in mobility patterns. Stinchcombe[45] arranged Norwegian industries along a historical continuum from craft and professional to bureaucratic forms of organization. He found that wages were more age-graded in bureaucratic industries where FILMs operate. In addition, Steinberg[46] defined internal labor markets by whether the worker remained with the same employer in the same industry over a five-year period. He found that there was greater attachment to the internal labor market for women than men, even though men experienced greater upward mobility.

---

[45] Arthur L. Stinchcombe, "Social Mobility in Industrial Labor Markets," *Acta Sociologica* 22 (1979): 217–45.

[46] E. Steinberg, "Upward Mobility in the Internal Labor Market," *Industrial Relations* 14 (1975): 259–65.

CHAPTER 5

CONSEQUENCES OF WORK STRUCTURES II

Labor Force Outcomes

WORK ATTITUDES

Work attitudes refer to a wide range of people's feelings about their work. These include their satisfaction with and their commitment to work and to different work structures: jobs, organizations, occupations, unions, and classes. The literature on work attitudes is immense, and we make no attempt here to review this vast array of studies in any but the grossest sense of the word. Rather, we provide a broad overview of the prototypal kinds of studies that have been done in connection with each of our types of work structures.

Why Study Work Attitudes?

As the above observation suggests, work attitudes have been topics of enormous interest to social scientists and practitioners alike. The importance of studying work attitudes is rooted in several perspectives. Many have been interested in work attitudes in order to improve the work experiences of workers. These researchers generally adhere to a value system in which it is assumed that work allowing the satisfaction of one's needs furthers the dignity of the individual, whereas work without such prospects limits the development of personal potential and is to be avoided. Much of the research on work attitudes in the Marxist tradition falls into

157

this category, as well as research by many non-Marxist social psychologists.

Others have been interested in work attitudes because of evidence linking them to attitudes outside of the work setting. For example, there is considerable evidence that the degree of satisfaction with work affects the quality of one's life outside the work role. Thus, the HEW report, *Work in America*,[1] recommended that the best way to increase the physical and mental health of Americans was to improve the quality of their jobs and working conditions. Although health-related outcomes are related to work structures in ways similar to work attitudes, the issue of causality between work attitudes and mental or physical health is as yet unresolved.[2]

Still others have been motivated to study work attitudes because they want to improve productivity and organizational effectiveness by increasing employees' organizational commitment. This assumes that one way to improve the productivity of workers is by tying their interest to the fate of the company, a rationale behind the institution of employee stock ownership plans (ESOPs), "quality circles," and "participatory management." This concern underlies much of the research on work attitudes conducted by industrial psychologists and by a host of management consultants.

Data on work attitudes provide useful information on the correlates and consequences of work structures and enable us to draw informed inferences about their performance as causal agents. Indeed, the very reality of certain structures (e.g., class) often depends on whether incumbents of the work structure have common attitudinal responses that add up to class commitment or consciousness.

The study of work attitudes confronts a host of measurement and other methodological problems. Perceptual data obtained from interviews or questionnaires must be carefully scrutinized for the possibility that the results are contaminated by "response sets," socially desirable answers, and so on. Further, different versions of particular questions may elicit different kinds of responses, as often occurs in the case of inquiries into matters that are quite evidently linked to job satisfaction.[3]

---

[1] United States Department of Health, Education and Welfare, *Work in America* (Cambridge, Mass.: M.I.T. Press, 1972).

[2] For example, see the papers in *Mental Health in the Economy*, edited by Louis A. Ferman and Jeanne P. Gordus (Kalamazoo, Mich.: W. E. Upjohn Institute for Employment Research, 1979).

[3] Arne L. Kalleberg, "A Causal Approach to the Measurement of Job Satisfaction," *Social Science Research* 3 (1974): 299–322.

Types of Work Attitudes

Since people impute a variety of meanings to their work activity, there are many types of work attitudes. We focus here on two generic kinds of work attitudes that are outcomes of both the organization of work and individual differences in work-related expectations, values, and needs: *satisfaction* and *commitment*.

Satisfaction is an overall "affective orientation," as some writers describe feelings, on the part of individuals toward particular work structures. The most commonly studied is *job satisfaction*, a person's overall evaluation of his or her present work role. Since jobs are affected by all of our work structures, job satisfaction is an overall indicator of the quality of one's experiences with them. However, we can also study satisfaction with the other structures, for example, satisfaction with the company, union, or occupation and, of course, the relationships among these satisfactions.

Unlike satisfaction, commitment refers to the degree to which the worker is *involved* with a work structure, the degree to which there is *value congruence* between the worker and other members of the work structure, and the extent to which the worker is willing to exert *effort* on behalf of a work structure and its principals. Thus, the concept of commitment has both attitudinal and behavioral components. In contrast, satisfaction does not necessarily imply particular actions, since happy workers may not, on that account, be willing, say, to exert effort to help the organization to succeed. Neither perfect satisfaction nor commitment is necessarily desirable: satisfaction may breed complacency and commitment to some organizations (e.g., the Nazi party) may be morally reprehensible. Organizations also differ in the amount of loyalty they want from their members, since one's most loyal employees may indeed not be one's ablest. Moreover, Piore[4] argues that turnover in the periphery sector is an advantage for core firms since it helps them subcontract jobs to dependent suppliers whose "disloyal" workers, who are often not very skilled, can be turned over before wage increases accumulate and raise suppliers' costs and thus their prices.

There are at least as many different kinds of commitment (including some types that are conflicting and some overlapping) as there are work structures. Perhaps the most widely studied is *organizational commitment*, or the degree to which the worker identifies with the goals of the company and is willing to exert effort to help it succeed. Workers who are highly committed to their organization are less likely to exhibit neg-

---

[4] Piore, "American Labor and the Industrial Crisis."

ative behavior (from the organization's point of view) such as being absent, being late, or quitting.

Alternatively, workers such as professionals and craftspersons, with their highly organized occupational associations, are more likely to see their occupations rather than their employers' companies as their reference group and may be said to have a high degree of *occupational commitment*. Such workers may be very willing to leave an organization and to practice their occupational activity in another firm; indeed, this is a common form of advancement in many occupational internal labor markets, whose members tend to exhibit high levels of commitment. Among nonprofessionals, such worker communities as loggers, longshoremen, teamsters (real ones) and typographers (before the advent of word processors) were celebrated by scholars interested, for example, in interindustry propensities to strike.

Workers may also be committed to what they perceive to be their class and its interests. *Class commitment* is equivalent to *class consciousness,* a subject of considerable research in the sociological literature, as we noted in our earlier discussion of class as a work structure. Members of the capitalist class are generally more cohesive, having higher levels of class commitment, than are managers or workers. Indeed, one of the sharpest versions of class conflict in the United States, a product of corporate takeovers, is that between merger-bent and self-appointed spokesmen for stockholders and managers who seek to resist raiders by ESOPs, alliances with White Knights, and lobbying efforts aimed at winning legislators' support of restrictions on "takeover artists."

Finally, people differ in the extent to which they are committed to *work* itself. Work commitment refers to the importance of work in people's lives and is often conceptualized as workers' "central life interests."[5] Workers who are highly committed to work are likely to express this through strong attachments to particular work structures, such as their class, occupation, work organization, and/or union and through criticisms of welfare recipients.

The various forms of commitment are akin, to some extent, to a multifaceted "zero sum" game. Since different work structures may be associated with conflicting goals and demands, workers must often choose one over others. For example, professionals in organizations (such as lawyers) must often decide whether they owe their loyalty to their occupation or to their employers' organizations or their organizations' client firms. Further, class and occupation may compete as bases of worker

---

[5] Robert Dubin, "Industrial Workers' Worlds: A Study of the Central Life Interests of Industrial Workers," *Social Problems* 3 (1956): 131–42.

organization: often, class interests (solidarity among all workers) conflict with occupational interests (excluding nonskilled workers from collective bargaining); this is illustrated by the longstanding conflict between AFL craft and industrial unions during the years before (and for a time after) the formation of the CIO.

Determinants of Work Attitudes

Despite differences among work attitudes, they can be explained by a similar theoretical framework. Satisfactions and commitments are both, to a significant degree, outcomes of the convergence between what people want from work structures and their assessments of what they receive. This congruence or discrepancy framework has been developed most clearly with regard to satisfaction, as many authors have argued that satisfaction represents an outcome of the fit between what people want from their jobs (their values about which components of work are most important to them) and the kinds of rewards and benefits they actually receive (e.g., earnings, challenge, security).[6]

Similarly, people are unlikely to become committed to a work structure if they feel that the structure cannot provide them with what they want.[7] For example, workers may not become committed to their unions or class organizations if they perceive that these groups are less well able to provide them with valued benefits such as money or a sense of purpose than are their companies or occupations. This may help account for the relatively low degree of class commitment among American workers: they often perceive that, in the absence of well-developed organizations to promote their class interests, such groups are unlikely to do them much good. This is, of course, a "catch 22" situation: if workers do not become committed to class groups, these groups are unlikely to be effective; and if class groups' organizers and their emergent organizations are ineffectual, people are not likely to join them. The same is true for commitments to unions: since more and more workers apparently feel that their unions are progressively less well able to meet their needs, their commitments to and satisfaction with unions are likely to be low.

Explaining differences in work attitudes, then, requires us to account

---

[6] Edwin A. Locke, "What Is Job Satisfaction?," *Organizational Behavior and Human Performance* 4 (1969): 309–36; Arne L. Kalleberg, "Work Values and Job Rewards: A Theory of Job Satisfaction," *American Sociological Review* 42 (February 1977): 124–43.

[7] James G. March and Herbert A. Simon, *Organizations* (New York: Wiley, 1958); and Howard S. Becker, "Notes on the Concept of Commitment," *American Journal of Sociology* 22 (1960): 32–40.

for both: (1) the values that people have toward work and work structures and (2) differences in the rewards that people receive from their work-related activities.

Class. A modest body of research assesses the impact of class (variously defined) on a variety of work-related attitudes. Class affects both the distribution of job rewards and work values. For example, jobs in the employing and managing classes provide greater economic and intrinsic rewards than do working-class jobs.[8] Research on class differences in values is scarcer, though available evidence suggests that there may be putative class (e.g., collar color) differences in work and related values.[9] Consistent with these class differences in values and rewards, there are class inequalities in attitudes such as job satisfaction: Kalleberg and Griffin, for example, found that incumbents of working-class jobs are, perhaps understandably, less well satisfied than those in the managerial and/or employer classes.[10]

Occupations. The overwhelming majority of empirical studies of occupational differences in work attitudes has relied on some measure of occupational status or prestige.[11] Not surprisingly, these studies have found workers in higher status occupations to be better satisfied than workers in lower status ones, as well as to be more committed to their occupations (as are professionals and craftspersons).

Moreover, workers in higher-status occupations often place greater importance on intrinsic work features, perhaps because these are more attainable in such occupations, whereas those in lower-status occupations are more likely to emphasize earnings and security. However, the associations between occupational status and satisfaction and commitment are generally rather weak in these studies. This could be rooted in a sense of relative deprivation: people do not compare themselves to those in all other occupations but to workers in similar structural locations, as so often happens when employed Americans are questioned about their attitudes toward their wages and salaries, a fact we noted in our earlier discussions of wage contours.[12]

---

[8] Kalleberg and Griffin, "Class, Occupation and Inequality in Job Rewards."

[9] Herbert Hyman, "The Value Systems of Different Classes," in *Class, Status and Power: Social Stratification in Comparative Perspective*, ed. Reinhard Bendix and Seymour Martin Lipset (New York: Free Press, 1966), 488–99.

[10] Kalleberg and Griffin, "Positional Sources of Inequality in Job Satisfaction."

[11] For example, Robert Blauner, "Work Satisfaction and Industrial Trends in Modern Society," in *Labor and Trade Unionism*, ed. Walter Galenson and Seymour Martin Lipset (New York: John Wiley, 1960), 339–60; Christopher Jencks *et al.*, *Inequality* (New York: Basic Books, 1972).

[12] Bernard Strumpel, "Inflation, Discontent and Distributive Justice," *Economic Outlook USA* 1 (Summer 1974).

Differences in work attitudes produced by occupational correlates other than prestige have been extensively studied by Melvin Kohn and his associates.[13] Using both cross-sectional and panel data, their research focuses on the links between occupational characteristics and the psychological functioning of individuals, including their job satisfaction and occupational commitment. Their main conclusion is that *occupational self-direction* is the central correlate of occupations that is associated with differences in workers' attitudes and well-being.

Organizations. Many studies have investigated the links between organizational structures and work attitudes, particularly job satisfaction and organizational commitment.[14] A common finding is that job satisfaction is inversely related to organizational *size*, presumably because of the fewer opportunities for intrinsic rewards available in larger organizations. On the other hand, large organizational size may promote greater commitment to the firm, due to the greater prevalence of informal groups and opportunities for advancement in big organizations.

Industries. Several studies have examined differences in work attitudes among industries. Blauner[15] investigated differences in alienation and related attitudes across four industries he assumed reflected distinct stages of industrial development: printing (craft), textiles (machine tending), autos (mass production), and chemicals (continuous process). He found the least alienation and greatest satisfaction among workers in the printing and chemical industries. In contrast, alienation was highest in the auto industry. Moreover, textile workers had relatively low levels of job rewards but, because of the "culture" of this industry, based heavily on nonwork factors such as integrated communities, they had more positive work attitudes than would be expected on the basis of their rewards alone.[16] Unfortunately, Blauner's own evidence, fully exploited, does not unambiguously support his conclusion; indeed, many of his survey data, which he used selectively, do not fit this pattern at all.[17]

---

[13] Kohn and Schooler.

[14] See, for example, Lyman W. Porter and Edward E. Lawler III, "Properties of Organization Structure in Relation to Job Attitudes and Behavior," *Psychological Bulletin* 64 (July 1965): 23–51; and Richard T. Mowday, Lyman W. Porter, and Richard M. Steers, *Employee–Organization Linkages: The Psychology of Commitment, Absenteeism and Turnover* (New York: Academic Press, 1982).

[15] Blauner, *Alienation and Freedom.*

[16] See also Tamara K. Haraven, *Family Time and Industrial Time* (New York: Cambridge, 1982); Frank Hull, Nathalie Friedman, and Theresa Rogers, "The Effect of Technology on Alienation From Work: Testing Blauner's Inverted U-Curve Hypothesis for 110 Industrial Organizations and 245 Retrained Printers," *Work and Occupations* 9 (1982): 31–57.

[17] For a detailed critique, see Berg, Freedman, and Freeman, *Managers and Work Reform* (New York: Free Press), 44–46.

Unions. Freeman and Medoff[18] find that union members are less well satisfied with their jobs than nonunion members. Their responses, coupled with the lower turnover of union members, suggest that their lower job satisfaction reflects their sense of needs to exercise collective voices that alert managers to their work-related requests or gripes.

Other evidence suggests that both job satisfaction and organizational commitment are positively related to union satisfaction. The links between these attitudes may be explained in terms of a dual allegiance. That is, if union members are satisfied with their wages, working conditions, and job security, they will have favorable opinions of both the company and the union; conversely, if union members are dissatisfied with their job rewards, they will be dissatisfied with both of these work structures.[19] For example, Berg, Freedman, and Freeman[20] found that organized workers expressed more dissatisfaction with their unions in 1973 than in 1969. This is consistent with evidence that workers who are dissatisfied with their unions also participate less in their activities, since participation rates in a variety of union activities are apparently decreasing.[21] Moreover, union participation is positively related to commitment to the union movement in general, and workers who are highly committed to the union movement are more likely to be satisfied with their particular union.[22]

The evidence is less clear on what it is about unions that affects satisfaction and commitment. For example, studies of the impact of union size on union attitudes have produced mixed results. Marcus found that union size is negatively related to union democracy, which in turn is positively related to union satisfaction. On the other hand, Raphael found that larger and more bureaucratized unions are more democratic.[23]

Nation-States. Cross-cultural studies of work attitudes, as such, are as yet relatively scarce though studies of modernity often include work-related questions in their survey instruments.[24] Nations differ both in the

---

[18] Freeman and Medoff.

[19] Leonard R. Sayles and George Strauss, *The Local Union* (New York: Harcourt, Brace & World 1967).

[20] Berg, Freedman, and Freeman.

[21] Russell L. Smith and Anne H. Hopkins, "Public Employee Attitudes Toward Unions," *Industrial and Labor Relations Review* 32 (1979): 484–95.

[22] Daisy L. Tagliacozzo and Joel Siedman, "A Typology of Rank-and-File Union Members," *American Journal of Sociology* 61 (1956): 546–53.

[23] Phillip M. Marcus, "Unions' Conventions and Executive Boards: A Formal Analysis of Organizational Structure," *American Sociological Review* 31 (1966): 61–70; Edna E. Raphael, "Power Structure and Membership Dispersion in Unions," *American Journal of Sociology* 71 (1965): 274–83.

[24] But see, for example, Form, "The Internal Stratification of the Working Class."

rewards they make available to their work forces and in their members' cultural values as to what is desirable and important with respect to work. For example, a cross-national survey of work attitudes found that in Western European countries the majority of young people (18–24) agreed that "man works to make money"; in contrast, a higher proportion of young workers in socialist Yugoslavia agreed with the statement that "man works to do his duty to the state."[25]

Multiple Work Structures and Work Attitudes

Some studies have focused on differences in work attitudes produced by *multiple* work structures. For example, Berg *et al.* examined both intraorganizational and extraorganizational (occupational) determinants of job satisfaction. They found that each of these work structures has independent effects on satisfaction. In particular, workers were more often dissatisfied by pay inequities among occupations than by the earnings accorded them by their own employers. They conclude that "untouched by the workplace changes favored by work reformers are the mezzoscopic and macroscopic forces that collectively appear to account for more of workers' overall discontents than do those in the workplace itself."[26]

The interplay between occupational and organizational commitment has been studied in the case of professionals in bureaucracies. This was the subject of considerable research attention in the 1960s, as increasing numbers of professionals—scientists, lawyers, and doctors—were becoming employed by profit-making firms. A central problem addressed by these studies was the conditions under which professionals become committed to the organization as opposed to the occupation. In particular, it was feared that professionals would act in "unprofessional" ways when faced with conflicting demands from occupational and organizational leaders concerning how work is to be done and evaluated. Several researchers found that bureaucratic ways of organizing work often conflicted with professional norms. Consequently, companies often adopted new organizational forms to deal with this conflict, such as professional departments and dual promotion ladders and project teams.[27] A few celebrated cases in which professionals have sought to stop the introduction

---

[25] Connie DeBoer, "The Polls: Attitudes Toward Work," *Public Opinion Quarterly* (1978): 414–23.

[26] Berg, Freedman, and Freeman, 250.

[27] See, for example, Richard H. Hall, "Professionalization and Bureaucratization," *American Sociological Review* 33 (February 1968): 92–104.

of new and allegedly dangerous aircraft into passenger service and new sweetening agents into food markets, for example, have been the subjects of studies of "whistle-blowers."

The study by Lincoln and Kalleberg of manufacturing firms and workers in the United States and Japan considers the effects of all of the six work structures on satisfaction and commitment.[28] Consistent with many previous studies, they find that American workers are far more satisfied than the Japanese, even when the effects of the other work structures are taken into account. This finding may surprise many readers now long accustomed to the admiring, even envious, descriptions of Japanese workers that have filled the media. These residual differences in satisfaction could be attributed in part to different cultural tendencies to express contentment; American workers are more likely to do so. They also found that there is little, if any, "commitment gap" between Japanese and American workers; the Japanese productivity advantage, in recent years, can accordingly not be attributed to Japanese workers being more committed to their organizations. Lincoln and Kalleberg also found that work structures were important for explaining differences in satisfaction and commitment *within* each country. For example, union members in both the United States and Japan tended to be less satisfied with their jobs and less committed to their organizations than their unorganized peers. Moreover, correlates of occupations (skills), industries (the automation and standardization of technology), and organizations (size, ranks, and so on) also produced differences in work attitudes.

WORK-RELATED BEHAVIOR

Attitudes are intrinsically interesting, but it occurs to most of us to ask whether they are themselves as consequential as they are interesting. Seasoned readers know attitude-and-behavior issues as old social science chestnuts; they will accordingly be sympathetic to our bypassing questions about the possible causal links between the wide variety of attitudes discussed in the previous section, on one side, and work-related behavior, on the other, in favor of turning directly to a brief review of the behavioral correlates of some of our structures.

[28] See James R. Lincoln and Arne L. Kalleberg, "Work Organization and Workforce Commitment: A Study of Plants and Employees in the U.S. and Japan," *American Sociological Review* 50 (December 1985): 738–60.

Class, State, and Worker Behavior

We have noted that we observe more class-linked behavior in Western Europe than in the United States. The sharpness of class-bound perspectives of Americans was dulled, early on, by the absence of a hereditary aristocracy and by the remarkable cultural, ethnic, and, for many years, linguistic heterogeneity of the emerging industrial work force so thoroughly populated by immigrants from other shores.

Further diversification was organic to our industrial development as well as to our cultural history: craft and industrial unions, religious pluralism, rural-urban antipathies, interregional splits, generation gaps even between the earliest settlers and their children, and racial politics, among other divisions. These divisions were grist for the politicos who operated the mills in our political parties: their coalition politics papered over their members' intramural squabbles.

Add to these, especially to our party politics, the capacity of interest groups more narrowly delineated to use the state to serve the interests of both the propertied haves and the have nots, and one begins to see at least the shadows of an explanation for the fact that classes have been relatively weaker social, political, and economic agents in the United States than in other nations: the potential virulence of class politics—a potential "pressure cooker" rather than a "melting pot"—was well tempered by the social stew served up in several different versions of Americans' beloved (and somewhat romanticized) views of the country as one nation under God.

The image, meanwhile, of an ambitious railsplitter doing homework on the back of a besooted coal shovel on his remarkable way to the White House was not without its contraclass appeal to parents who urged their offspring to "dredge their channels that they may be wide and deep" and to be "unobstructed when their ships came in." A belief in the prospect that one could put meager circumstances behind one contributes little to even class-tinged behavior.

Such clearly class-tinged behavior as we have experienced in the United States has been linked to the operation of the state, to industry segments, and to firms (organizations) in the form of industrial unionism, subjects that we addressed in Chapters 2 and 3.

In marked contrast with the craft unions preceding them, industrial unions seized opportunities to use the state (and the several states) both to legitimize collective bargaining and to achieve fair labor standards in the nation's shops, mills, and factories, and in general to construct the warp and weft of an emerging social safety net. Craft unions were not sympathetic to these welfare-type efforts until well into the years of the

Great Depression, since they had long served up their own welfare menus to their members. What industrial unions did not receive from their bargains with employers, meanwhile, they sought to receive from Uncle Sam. These collectively bargained benefits, of course, accrued to unions' members, not to workers as a class.

Leaving worker-class behavior aside, we must look more closely at two aspects of worker and state interactions in behavioral terms. The first of these aspects in this country turns on national, public, and private (corporate) policies affecting both overall and specific demand(s) for workers; the second turns on public and private (corporate) policies affecting the participation rates of the population and its principal subsets in the nation's labor force. One initial definition: labor force participants are officially conceived for statistical, record-keeping, and index-construction purposes as those at work or seeking work in a given week of a survey by the Bureau of Labor Statistics; workers without work who are not looking for jobs, that is, discouraged workers, are accordingly labeled neither as unemployed nor as labor force participants.

One complex of major public policies affecting the demand for labor in the aggregate (and in many particular sectors and industries) includes those affecting interest rates, (for example, the Federal Reserve Board), banks, large (leveraged) investors, and those affecting public indebtedness (through government deficits to support purchases of goods and services not financed by public resources). Note here that the affected entities are both structures and markets. Collectively these public undertakings are monetary policies.

A second major complex includes the policies of public leaders—executives and legislators—that affect governments' purchases (and therefore their tax and borrowing programs) and are known as fiscal policies.

A third complex does not have a particular label and does not amount to anything like a full-fledged policy but rather involves programs—thousands of them—that are aimed, in accord with one or another effective interest group's values, at improving the "quality of American life." Examples include occupational health and safety reforms, affirmative action and equal opportunity programs, changes in fair labor standards laws affecting hours and compensation (especially regarding nonprofessional and management personnel), and health- and retirement-related programs that affect the labor force participation rates of the population. Each of these programs has been defended as civilized and progressive by one or more protagonists and attacked as offensive intrusions by government into private areas by antagonists.

A fourth complex of public and private policies and programs is directed at problems specifically related to unemployed Americans or at circumstances, such as business cyclical fluctuations, that contribute significantly to increased unemployment (like plant shutdowns). These programs are also promoted by their designers to afford support to victims of economic circumstances. For example, unemployment insurance or ESOP plans are used to save workers' jobs from their owners' plans to sell them off or to relocate them.

These four complexes of policies and programs can each affect both the demand for labor and labor force participation rates especially if one calculates that the policies and programs in question involve national, regional, state, and local institutions as well as the actions of employers, industry groups (like those affected by protective quotas or tariffs), trade associations, and, in recent years, the initiatives and actions of foreign governments and their larger industry groups.

The first two complexes, having to do with monetary and fiscal policies, were considered for several years to be critical determinants affecting the overall economy, particularly the demand for labor and inflation rates. As time passed and we entered a period of stagflation, in which both unemployment rates and inflation rates were high, easy assumptions about a readily calculable trade-off between these two variables—so much unemployment needed for so much reduction of inflation—were challenged.

In particular, analysts began to look at the attributes of the unemployed, having earlier looked at the differential rewards to employed workers with different educational achievements. Since income and education were so highly correlated in studies of income and occupational achievements, as we saw in an earlier chapter, then it seemed logical to extend the analysis on the supply side: if there were degrees of difference in the attributes of economic winners, from high to low, they reasoned, then perhaps the losers were worst case versions of the good case winners.

Three attributes of those with both the most frequent and longest bouts of unemployment were of particular interest in the search for blame for the conditions of losers: their work experience, their educational preparation for the world of work, and their population numbers. The results: the least favored workers—reentering women who came to the market place in droves (54% of all women and 62% of mothers with children under 18 were in the work force by 1985) and new entry workers (and youths otherwise)—had less education and less work experience. And young workers (the last third of the baby boom) were so numerous that they allegedly crowded each other out of an inevitably limited market for unskilled workers.

These findings—which afford a picture of the *structure of unem-*

ployment (a term of art in demography)—were very quickly transmuted into an explanation that blamed victims of unemployment (and the prolific parents of the younger ones) for youths' unhappy fates in the labor market: it would fuel inflation, it was generally argued, if monetary and fiscal policies were aimed (in accord with a continuation of the new Keynesean economics of Kennedy, Johnson, and Nixon) at "heating up" the economy.

The reasoning was straightforward: unskilled and skilled workers are not endlessly substitutable, one group for the other; if employers are prodded into meeting booming demands for their goods and services by Uncle Sam's policies, they will be pushed to hire greater numbers of the least productive workers in the labor markets, many of whose earnings would be protected by putatively too-high minimum wage laws and by the low opportunity costs of not working (by way of welfare-type programs, food stamps, Medicaid, and unemployment payments).

As we have suggested, the early human capital explanations for income differences were more than a little too simplistic: if better educated people earn more than others, one argues, it is because, naturally, they are more productive in the eyes of always rational employers; and we know they are more productive because they are better paid. The extension of the argument to take account of age cohorts' sizes is not less simplistic, as the reader can plainly see, if it substitutes cohort sizes for educational differences in the preceding tautology *cum* algorithm.

In World War II, after all, we employed any and everybody—and it cannot be convincingly argued that our very marginal annual war time inflation rates were entirely attributable to wage and price controls.

The fact is that millions of Americans of modest attributes became very productive very quickly, a fact in which managers took understandable pride! But then it is our central thesis that the interplay and interactions among phenomena in our different structures, different markets, and among markets and structures must all be taken into account. Mainline assessments of unemployment can move from deficiencies in the demand for labor to deficiencies in workers as handily as they do because they focus, after all, on the intersections of prototypal developments in the cells in which only one or two structures intersect with only one or two markets.

We have alluded, in the foregoing overview of the first two policy complexes affecting employment and unemployment, to both straight economic policy and program packages (unemployment insurance, for example) and to quality of life packages (Medicaid, unemployment insurance, and food stamps); we can safely leave it to readers to consider the contributions (or hindering effects) of their own favored (or despised) policies and programs in accord with their own lights. One caution: most program prescriptions designed to be countercyclical— helping victims of recession, for example—take time to design and enact into law and thus, more often than not, are implemented only after the worst is over; they thus become *procyclical,* in that they contribute to exacerbations rather than remissions of the maladies they were designed to ameliorate.

Industries, Firms, and Unions

Given the evolving character of unions in the United States, it is in connection with industries and their member firms that most worker behavior patterns surface and become important. We need not rehearse our discussion of the relevant worker behavior discussed in the lengthy treatment of unions in Chapters 2 and 3, but we can add to those discussions a brief treatment of grievances and strikes.

Unorganized workers unquestionably develop grievances, over work assignments, supervisors' ways and means, work loads, promotion practices, comfort, safety, vacation schedules, wage and salary arrangements, and many other matters involving questions of equity, justice, fairness, and even the civilities (or lack thereof) in their organizations' cultures. Generally, though, these grievances are not "processed" in the stylized fashion observed in organized shops and offices in which: (a) a grievance committee decides whether a grievance formally filed by one or more rank-and-filers will have the group's endorsement; (b) formal steps for the settlement of the grievance occur; and (c) in exchange for a no-strike clause in agreements, unsettled grievances can be submitted to a permanent or *ad hoc* third party arbitrator hired jointly by labor and management.

There are no available measures of the number of grievances filed by workers (or, for that matter, of the initiatives by management that spark most of them) except in case studies. It is apparently the case, however, in study after study, that:

1. Grievances are often "banked" and used as bargaining devices by union leaders who have members' mandates to withdraw them, wholesale, "quids for quos," in return for one or another desired provision in a contract round.
2. The astuteness and thus the success of grievances vary directly with the skill levels of those who file them; more highly skilled workers grieve in what Leonard Sayles has described as more "strategic ways."
3. Just as grievances can be banked against a contract deadline, they can be threatened, filed, and withdrawn, day by day, as part of day-to-day bargaining, in which case (as we noted in Chapter

3) they may be likened to a kind of grease that lubricates the machines of bureaucracies with their sometimes small tolerances; the bargaining process and the grievance process, all thus blended one with the other, are like modern bifocal lenses that have no perceptible lines separating them.

4. Most industrial relationists—labor and management—think highly of their grievance mechanisms; sores are more readily treated before than after they become infections.

5. When managers lose grievance contests, they tend to do so because they violated agreed-upon procedures regarding such things as timely notice and sufficient warning. For a tentative but empirically informed discussion of grievance outcomes following arbitration procedures, 1953 to 1972, see Berg, Freedman, and Freeman.[29]

Strike data afford additional measures of worker behavior in organized settings. In general, these data show that strike activity is more apparent: (1) when workers feel that there is a gap between expectations and achievements in the rates of change in their real wages; (2) in periods of prosperity and tight labor markets (when unemployment is low); and (3) among better heeled workers, that is, workers with resources to help sustain them during their absence from work.

A replication of a classic 1954 study by Kerr and Siegel[30] of the "interindustry propensity to strike" showed that the markedness of the differences declined very considerably between 1949 and 1973. The changes in the earlier patterns reflect, among other things: (1) the fuzziness of industries as "self-contained" (i.e., homogeneous) socioeconomic entities; (2) the increasing decentralization of large national unions whose locals "go it alone"; (3) the economic development of the Sunbelt in which many industries' member companies located plants in areas with fewer unions while keeping unionized shops open; (4) the spread of unions into the public sector (we all know about teacher strikes) just as union strength in the private sector yielded to the pressures of stagflation, the deindustrialization of the Snowbelt region, and foreign competition; and, finally, (5) the up-and-down movements, across industries, of industry members' differential vulnerability to regulation, taxation, subsidization, and competitiveness. These factors affect an industry's health and thus its target value to unionists and at any given time suggest that managers

---

[29] Berg, Freedman, and Freeman, Chapters 10 and 12.

[30] Clark Kerr and Abraham Siegel, "The Inter-industry Propensity to Strike—An International Comparison," in *Industrial Conflict*, ed. Arthur Kornhauser, Robert Dubin, and Arthur Ross (New York: McGraw-Hill, 1954), 189–212.

believe more in the value of mobility than in their organizations' need for loyalty: the turnover rates among 135,000 "truly policy-level executives"—exclusive of retirement—"has risen from close to zero pre–World War II to an estimated 20,000-plus [in 1972]. . . . This 15 percent figure may be compared with the upper limit of 10 percent placed on *labor* turnover as a prerequisite for successful workplace innovations by reputable 'workplace redesigners'."[31]

Studying Work-Related Behavior

Before leaving this discussion of work-related behavior, we should mention the long history of studies beginning in the late 1920s, at the Hawthorne works of the Western Electric Company, culminating in the work reform movement of the late 1960s, and continuing into the present.

Begun by Harvard Business School researchers in cooperation with business firms and interested business leaders such as Bell Telephone's Chester Barnard, the study's original investigators (led by Elton Mayo, Fritz Roethlisberger, and Western Electric's W. J. Dickson) claimed to have discovered what came to be known as the "Hawthorne effect": even if workers are regarded only as research subjects, most of them respond to this putative evidence of managerial interest in their welfare by raising their productivity from lower levels previously fixed by work group members' norms. These norms, requiring that workers restrict output, the investigators reported, were obeyed by workers who, on one side, needlessly mistrusted managers and, on the other, suffered from "anomie" in their industrial world that could be ameliorated by the social psychological rewards of group membership.

According to the model derived from their reading of their data—published six years after the Hawthorne experiment first began in 1933[32]—managers were generally rational whereas workers were often nonrational in response to authority figures. The model's design drew heavily on Sigmund Freud's conceptions of the unconscious; Emile Durkheim's conception of anomie, or rootlessness; anthropologists' studies of ritualized collective behavior; and Wilfredo Pareto's notions of the "social mind" and of equilibrated and disequilibrated social systems.

In an apparently major stride forward in the late 1950s, managers' own behavior came under social psychologists' magnifying glasses; Chris Argyris became the leader of these human relations revisionists with the publication of studies, starting in 1957, of organizations as reflections of

[31] Berg, Freedman, and Freeman, 200.
[32] See, for example, Roethlisberger and Dickson.

managers' personalities.[33] These revisionists concluded that workers were indeed often rational in their pursuit of "self-actualization" but that the needs of mature workers were often thwarted by the means used by managers to exercise their authority. Organizations' structures, meanwhile, especially their hierarchies, were held to be far more valuable to managers' personal needs than to stockholders' putative interests in happy, "self-actualized" (and thus presumably more productive) workers.

As matters turned out, in modern reexaminations of the data from the original Hawthorne studies, the increases in productivity during the classic investigation were evidently less the result of apparent evidence of management's solicitousness than of the fact that "uncooperative" workers (i.e., chronically low producers and work group leaders) had been fired just before productivity increased. It has also been suggested that a study beginning in 1929 might predictably have discovered productivity increases: a desire to comply with a work group's production quotas might understandably have given way to employment insecurity, and thus higher output, following the Great Crash (in October 1929) and its unmistakable portents of layoffs.

Modern enthusiasms about shirt-sleeve managerial applications of social science wisdom to workers have gone up and down cyclically: when managers face low unemployment rates they worry about worker morale; this laudably humane cause knows fewer champions when the economy turns down or slips sideways for extended periods. It is also the case, moreover, that reformers have only very rarely returned to the scene of their virtuous efforts to see whether their innovative interventions have survived the productivity gains that appear, at least in the short run, to be evoked by democratizing the workplace or restructuring work. For a critique of the human relations movement in its several incarnations, see the book by Berg, Freedman, and Freeman.[34]

We now turn, in this chapter's concluding section, to a discussion of jobs and skills.

JOBS AND SKILLS

Jobs differ in various ways. For example, work structures differ in the sheer *number* of job titles associated with them. Thus, Cole[35] com-

---

[33] See, for example, Chris Argyris, *Personality and Organization* (New York: Harper & Row, 1957); and *Understanding Organizational Behavior* (Homewood, Ill.: Dorsey Press, 1960).

[34] Berg, Freedman, and Freeman.

[35] Robert Cole, *Work, Mobility and Participation* (Berkeley: University of California Press, 1979).

pares the job structures of the United States and Japan and notes that American industry is characterized by a much greater number of job titles. In contrast, Japanese managers are less concerned with linking workers to specific jobs and therefore there are fewer job titles. Whereas Cole attributes this difference to the actions of American unions, which have historically been concerned with differentiating the work force with respect to equal work, Piore[36] has argued that unions simply reacted to management's preoccupations with highly differentiated job structures and that unions cannot be viewed as the architects of America's proliferation of job titles. Nevertheless, American unions have been paying the price for management's preferences ever since; indeed, the work reform movement in the United States has been hampered by the great attachment of unions to the detailed job descriptions with which American managers endowed them.

The main correlate of jobs we consider in this section is their *skill* component. This concept is rarely explicitly defined and, indeed, it is very difficult to do so. A basic issue here is whether skills inhere in jobs or in people. That skills are features of jobs is consistent with much sociological research on roles, organizations, and "positional inequality," as well as some work by economists.[37] These writers argue that jobs are associated with different training requirements and can be arranged along a continuum from high-to low-skilled. Others assume that skills do not inhere in jobs but in the individuals who perform them. This reasoning underlies human capital theory in economics: individuals make different kinds of investments in training and hence are more or less skilled and productive. Those who believe that skill resides in people often point to the labor shortages created by World War II, when many presumably unskilled workers were able to perform relatively highly skilled tasks. One distinction: workers own their skills but these skills must be sold to employers whose organizations own the jobs!

As with most such debates, each position has some merit: skill is a characteristic of both jobs and people. Some jobs inherently require more training than others and can be said to be more skilled. On the other hand, highly able individuals may often be able to upgrade the skill levels of their jobs. Therefore, skill must be defined in terms of the *interplay* between individuals and work structures.

Skill is a multidimensional concept and has two major components: *substantive complexity* and *autonomy*.[38] Substantive complexity refers

[36] Piore, "American Labor and the Industrial Crisis."

[37] Thurow.

[38] Kenneth Spenner, "Deciphering Prometheus: Temporal Change in the Skill Level of Work," *American Sociological Review* 48 (1983): 824–37.

to the level, scope, and integration of mental, interpersonal, and manipulative tasks in a job. This dimension is the subject of most research on skills by occupational sociologists, who usually define it in terms of job-learning time or the knowledge base of the occupation. Measures of these characteristics are available for thousands of jobs in the *Dictionary of Occupational Titles*.

The second dimension of skill, autonomy, refers to the amount of control an individual has over the performance of the job. Wright considers this correlate of jobs as defining semiautonomous workers, who possess control over their own work and on this basis are assumed to be a distinct class. The degree of autonomy a person has over the task is closely related to its substantive complexity. For example, the more complex a task, the more difficult it is to supervise closely and routinize, and workers doing complex tasks are more likely to have greater autonomy over these activities. Similarly, the more autonomy associated with the job, the more likely it is that the task will require more training and experience to perform adequately.

Previous studies have measured skill in three major ways. First, the *nonmeasurement* strategy simply infers skill differences from classifications of occupations such as blue-collar, white-collar or skilled, semi-skilled, unskilled. This is not very enlightening, as it assumes what should be explained: skill differences among occupations. Second, some studies measure skill *indirectly*, from information on occupational wage ratios[39] or education levels of incumbents. This approach has some advantages, especially when other measures are unavailable, but leaves open the question of how these proxies for skill are actually related to the content of work activities. Finally, a number of studies (summarized below) measure skill *directly*, from information on actual content of the occupation's activities.

Substantive complexity and autonomy are related to both occupational and organizational differences. Occupational differences are more closely tied to the substantive complexity of jobs, since occupations are groups of jobs with similar complexity and training requirements. On the other hand, organizational correlates may be primarily responsible for differences among jobs with respect to their levels of autonomy since firms are the loci wherein which jobs are directly defined and structured. Two occupations with similar levels of complexity, then, may be structured in very different ways depending on whether organizational leaders seek to enhance their employees' autonomy through structures such as quality circles and participatory management.

---

[39] For example, Wallace and Kalleberg, "Industrial Transformation and the Decline of Craft."

Changes in Skills

Changes in skills are important issues in debates over the consequences of technology. For example, do technological advances *upgrade* skills as the division of labor evolves along lines of greater efficiency and complexity;[40] *downgrade* them, as capitalists use technological advances and other structures to control workers by detailed divisions of labor;[41] or are the consequences *mixed*? Answers to these questions must consider two very different ways in which skill levels of jobs and/or occupations may be altered: there may be changes in the actual *content* of the task and there may be changes in the *composition* of the occupation, such that more or fewer people perform the activity, which may remain similar in content. The choice of one over the other as the object of study is influenced by, among other things, one's theoretical assumptions as to whether skills inhere in jobs or people and the availability of data on the content of occupational activities and/or their composition.

Spenner,[42] in a review of research on temporal changes in skills, concludes that there is little cumulative evidence to distinguish among the upgrading, downgrading, and mixed effects/no change hypotheses. This is the case for several reasons. For example, studies using aggregated and disaggregated data often reach different conclusions. Aggregate studies tend to find greater stability in skills, whereas disaggregated studies often provide evidence in favor of skill change. This may occur because aggregate studies tend to average out important changes within specific work structures and hence mask offsetting patterns of upgrading and downgrading. Studies also differ as to whether they investigate changes in actual work content or composition. Finally, studies differ in the time periods covered.

Most studies of changes in job skills have focused on occupations as the units of analysis. For example, Spenner[43] examined changes in content of work for a sample of matched third- and fourth-edition DOT occupations. He found that, overall, there was little net change but some evidence for slight upgrading. Moreover, Berg[44] studied skill changes

---

[40] Kerr *et al., Industrialism and Industrial Man.*

[41] Harry Braverman, *Labor and Monopoly Capital* (New York: Monthly Review Press, 1974).

[42] Spenner, "Deciphering Prometheus."

[43] Kenneth Spenner, "Temporal Changes in Work Content," *American Sociological Review* 44 (1979): 968–75.

[44] Ivar Berg, *Education and Jobs.* See also Eva Mueller, Judith Hybels, Jay Schmiedeskamp, John Sonquist, and Charles Staelin, *Technological Advance in an Expanding Economy: Its Impact on a Cross-section of the Labor Force* (Ann Arbor, Mich.: Survey Research Center, Institute for Social Research, University of Michigan, 1969).

using both census and DOT occupations and found that significant upgrading in both content and composition occurred during the 1960s. These results were largely substantiated in a subsequent analysis.[45] Note, though, that the upgrading he observed was in the putative *educational* requirements for an endless number of jobs specified by government job analysts and employers; he reserved judgment about how many real changes in actual jobs these credentials reflected.

Others have examined occupational changes within industries. Horowitz and Herrenstadt,[46] for example, studied changes in content in all DOT jobs in five industries (slaughter and meat packing, rubber tires and tubes, machine shop trades, medical services, banking). They found little evidence of any net change, perhaps because of an underlying mixture of upgrading and downgrading. Singelmann and Wright[47] studied changes in the composition of the labor force in census occupations within thirty-seven industry sectors for 1960 to 1970. Overall, they found only small changes. Finally, Wallace and Kalleberg[48] examined changes in skills, operationalized indirectly by occupational wage ratios, within the American printing and publishing industry for the 1931 to 1978 period. They found that hand compositors experienced a loss of skills relative to other occupational groups, which they interpreted as the result of the introduction of capital-intensive technology.

Resolving issues related to changes in skills requires a multilevel approach. Longitudinal data are of course necessary for studying changes in skills, but such data must be collected for a diverse mix of industries, occupations, and organizations. Moreover, it is necessary to investigate changes in both substantive complexity and autonomy, as these could change in very different ways. For example, automation may increase the complexity of tasks but also their interdependence, thereby reducing the autonomy and control allowed individual workers.

---

[45] Berg, Freedman, and Freeman.

[46] Morris Horowitz and Irwin Herrenstadt, "Changes in Skill Requirements of Occupations in Selected Industries," in *The Employment Impact of Technological Change*, Appendix, Vol. 2 (Washington, D. C.: U. S. Government Printing Office, 1968), 223–87.

[47] Joachim Singelmann and Erik Olin Wright, "Proletarianization in Advanced Capitalist Societies: An Empirical Intervention into the Debate Between Marxist and Post-Industrial Theorists over the Transformations of the Labor Process," in *Marxist Inquiries: Studies of Labor, Class and States,* ed. Michael Burawoy and Theda Skocpol (Chicago: University of Chicago Press, 1982), S176–S209.

[48] Wallace and Kalleberg, "Industrial Transformation and the Decline of Craft."

CHAPTER 6

THE DYNAMICS OF MARKETS AND WORK STRUCTURES

INTRODUCTION

Several common themes in the work of those whose multivariate approaches to markets and structures we commended in Chapter 1 have informed the foregoing chapters. Thus we have urged that one's understanding of work and industry structures is improved appreciably by examining:

1. The meetings and "cross-breedings" of phenomena associated with activities within and among the six structures with which we are concerned
2. The intramural intersections within and among our four markets
3. The interactions between the two arrays, structures and markets

Neither of the first two of these sets of interactions are diagrammed either in the front or back endpapers; we have settled instead (and immodestly enough), for a first pass at the third set. The separate interactions within and among markets and those within and among work structures have been alluded to, of course, but they have not been at the center of our attention. Although we will not now move them to the center, we shall pause again to note a set of these interactions before moving on.

When actors in producers' markets sell credit to their customers along with their products, for example—as do the auto and appliance manufacturers and product retailers (such as Sears Roebuck)—they compete directly with the installment credit units of banks although they face fewer federal and state-level restrictions on their practices as creditors than do "straight" financial institutions.[1] Similarly, regulations differ in the cases of brokerage houses, which offer money management accounts, and banks, both of whose activities fall within the capital market rubric. In this chapter, in which our purpose is to assay some features of each of our four markets that figure most prominently in the key changes observable in our work structures, we will continue to stress the interactions among markets and work structures but we do not thereby mean, in short, that the intramural interactions within each of these two systems can be ignored even in the interest of parsimonious modeling. The literature by specialists whose good works focus on only limited clusters of cells in our input–output matrix supports much more synthesis than we accomplish in our perhaps already too ambitious efforts to that end; we are obliged, therefore, to remind readers that ours may be likened to pregame "warm-ups" or a book-length introduction, either to the game itself or to the prospectively definitive volume.

We should add and thereby remind readers also that we regard markets almost in ontological terms, that is to say as the uncaused causes of the phenomena under discussion: "in the beginning, there were exchanges," whether in barter or in monetized terms. Beyond that, our markets become differentiated as the principals therein interact and as they are affected, in turn, by principals who come to these exchange relationships as representatives of structures designed, in good measure, to deal with "marketers"; these structures are themselves reformed and reorganized as their agents deal with different marketers and with principals and agents from other structures who may be competitors or helpmates. In the case of the state, the principals and agents in markets and work structures confront makers of what are commonly regarded as the webs of rules and the basic terms of trade that sometimes limit (and sometimes foster) the freedom of economic actors representing both markets and structures.

As prominent in history, once marketlike exchanges are underway, are nation-states, defined as rulers (and their agents) with significant (or even monopolistic) controls over all relevant means of coercion and with clearly understood capacities to levy and collect revenues.

---

[1] In 1972 Sears Roebuck earned nearly 7 percent of its total net earnings (before extraordinary income) from its retail credit operations alone. For General Electric the figure was 9 percent. See Cleveland A. Christophe, *Competition in Financial Services* (New York: First National City Corporation, 1974), 15–16.

In this chapter, we will first present, in highly schematic but, we hope, suggestive fashion, three cases that will serve reasonably well to illustrate the points implied in this introductory section. These cases involve familiar developments from what is generally called "the real world" in contrast with the world as it may be conceived in abstract and taxonomic terms by economists only slightly more than other social scientists.

Next, with the help of a timely econometric study of the climactic "Great Recession" of 1974 to 1975, we look at the roles of developments in several markets and several work structures that are conceived *implicitly* in our interactional terms; the developments associated with that recession, we argue, can be conceived more profitably in *explicit* interactional terms.

Third, we present a brief treatment of the state *per se* in its impact on markets and on some of our structures.[2]

Next, given the relatively short time perspective in the analysis of the Great Recession, we review several watershedlike developments in America's longer social, political, and economic history (i.e., since the colonial period) to illustrate further how the state impacts on our markets and our structures. Given limits on space and readers' patience, we focus on two of our six structures, industries and firms.

In a final section, we set the stage for our concluding chapter in which we will consider some reasonably palpable sources of stability and change in our markets and structures. Such an exercise leaves us with some confidence that we have indeed identified key variables as deserving candidates for inclusion in the multivariate analyses we urge. The "endgame" exercise also leaves us, though, with a sense of the need to keep our synthesizing models realistically open-ended.

THREE "CANDID CAMERA" SHOTS OF THE STATE'S ECONOMIC ROLES

Consider first the recurrent vexing question of tariffs. If the state protects an American industry against exporters by tariffs (rather than by import quotas), it effectively subsidizes a domestic producer over the short haul. Over the longer haul, tariffs simply encourage victimized foreign exporters to retain or even expand their United States markets

---

[2] We considered the state and markets vis-à-vis unions, jobs, and occupations in Chapter 3.

by making higher quality products and by producing their products more efficiently; they then stand good chances of absorbing the applicable tariff without much pain.

Japanese car makers adopted both of these strategies to very considerable advantage following the imposition of import tariffs against their increasingly popular products in the 1970s. Among the reasons for their products' popularity was the fact that the growing numbers of married women in the labor force left fewer supernumerary family members free at home to pursue warranties on lower-quality American durable goods frequently in need of repair services. The success of higher-priced imports inhered, very considerably, in quality differences and the purchase of quality involved a trade-off by consumers between time, on one side, and the costs of goods for consumers, on the other. The effects on American workers of protection against foreign imports, in the event, would be appreciably different if the state set quotas on exporters' shipments.

All things being equal, quotas on foreign producers' goods help to perpetuate inefficient domestic producers at consumers' expense; in the absence of price competition, American producers protected by quotas lack the added incentive of competition to do their work with weather eyes to costs or to pay rapt attention to foreign sellers' product quality.

In the short term, a protected industry and its workers may well gain at the expense of consumers, lenders, and investors. We may note (and will return to the fact shortly) that one of the first laws enacted by the fledgling republic was a tariff (4 July 1789) designed to protect American manufacturers and agricultural producers. Later, the Smoot-Hawley Tariff (1931) contributed materially to the worldwide crash in the 1930s, but that act was only the more celebrated of not fewer than fifteen *major* tariffs passed by Congress between 1789 and 1930.

Tariffs gain favor in Congress to the extent that interest groups' lobbyists persuade its members that the interests of the lobbyists' clients, the congresspersons' constituents, and the republic, overall, are a trinity. Generally, the period of grace thereby bestowed on an industry is brief and tends to hurt others by the skewing effects on resource allocations— labor, capital, and rawstuffs. Hence, tariffs add to a system that is quite imperfectly competitive even without tariffs. Why? Because tariffs tend to engender retaliatory actions by victimized producers on other shores, with sad consequences for international markets generally and in the United States for producers, workers, and capital sponsors in one or more industries that are situated beyond the parietal walls of the protected industry and against whose products foreign governments regularly retaliate.

Next, consider a few aspects of the limits on horizontal and vertical mergers of so-called antitrust laws. These laws enhance competition to a lesser degree than is their intent: they have relatively little impact on firms the managers of which find that it is easier to draw on capital markets generously disposed to conglomerated firms; these laws impact more essentially on firms seeking to expand on an intraindustry basis. As a handful of large pension funds (among an only slightly larger group of very large investors) seek very short-run increases in the market values of their portfolios, they avidly follow the fortunes of conglomerates in order to cash in on equity prices that have been run up by merger and acquisition bids and even by rumors of corporate takeovers.

And, in a third example, if the nation-state encourages the use of borrowed funds for conglomerators' purchases of acquisitions (for example, by allowing deductions of interest payments on takeover loans from corporate taxes), we observe shifts in the ways that "the market for money" is structured as well as changes in the ways that industries are structured. Furthermore, if the state is itself a substantial borrower, the net effect is to bid up interest rates and thus to cool down sales in product and labor markets. Note the nearly immediate—and somewhat paradoxical—reverberations, in different markets, of laws that discriminate against some types of corporate unification in the name of price competition in an industry while they engender competition for funds supporting other unifications that drive up the price of money.

Note also, in each of these three cases, that noneconomic forces—public opinion; the sagacity, bargaining skills, credibility, and popularity of union leaders and corporate officials; concerns about market concentrations, nationalistic demiurges among the most frequently noted principals and the interest groups they can mobilize; and changing attitudes toward questions about equity and related welfare considerations—play critically important roles. The specifics of such noneconomic forces are grist for sociologists' mills somewhat more often than for those of economists, given the embeddedness of such forces in cultural predispositions and social definitions.

As we will see, Americans' attitudes toward the "positive state" have had a pendulumlike character, the long swing from FDR's "New Deal" to "Reaganomics" being the most recent example. Increases in the concentration of manufacturing wealth, a correlate of merger fever, will, after all, trouble populists and liberal democrats far more than they will disquiet investors who give high priority to short-term economic returns on "run ups" in the value of stocks generated by well-leveraged corporate raiders. The latter groups worry hardly at all about the distribution of manufacturing wealth, whereas the former groups fret about the shrinking number of decision makers affecting the economy; those sympathetic to mergers worry, more narrowly, about the stock prices these decision makers generate.

Normally, the most competent analyses of markets and structures in the published literature focus on relatively few of the intercell articulations and interactions to which we have alluded in our three brief cases. The tendency to avoid looking at the larger picture, in favor of more specialized undertakings, thus exacerbates the problems implied by the familiar adage about forests and trees.

THE STATE AND THE GREAT RECESSION OF 1974–1975: ANOTHER CASE IN POINT

Examinations of the interactions among the exchanges suggested by our matrix, a variation on an input–output table of the type long used in looking at interindustry transactions, are far more frequently applied by investigators to short periods—five or fewer years—than to longer ones.

The results—usually explanations for sudden, radical discontinuities, or "spikes," in the key economic indicators by which we measure an economy's health—are usually impressive. These efforts offer, among other utilities, abundant reasons for being skeptical of "stage theories" of economic causes and effects and of deterministic theories, like those emphasizing technological change, for example.

Consider the analysis by Eckstein of the potential and kinetic forces that generated and reinforced the Great Recession of 1974–1975, an analysis in which the researcher was able to juxtapose data on developments in most of our markets and several of our structures in *intertemporal* terms by specifying the variables in structural equations.[3]

Leaving aside the stabilities and instabilities in each of the markets that long preceded the Great Recession's onset, Eckstein's data highlight the very rapid and widespread effects of the Organization of Petroleum

---

[3] *The Great Recession with a Postscript on Stagflation* (Amsterdam and New York: North Holland, 1979). For an abstract, more explicitly theoretical analysis based on consciously executed differentiations of the intramural operations within multiple markets, see Arthur M. Okun, *Prices and Quantities, A Macroeconomic Analysis* (Washington D. C.: Brookings Institute, 1981). Some of his chapter titles are revealing: "The Labor Market," "Product Markets," and "Asset Markets." Across markets, Okun distinguishes between the different weights of auction markets, search markets, customer-oriented markets, customer–career markets, and classical markets. Interestingly, the *logic* of the distinctions *as such* is unattended; the different types of markets are simply defined and used in the analysis as if there were nothing problematical about the generic idea; the term *markets* thus does not appear in the index, for example.

Exporting Countries' cartel-like embargo on oil shipments to the non-communist industrial nations in the fall of 1973.[4]

Oil price increases immediately affected the markets associated with, for example: petroleum product refiners, petroleum marketers, and distributors; providers of public transportation and those who purvey services to drivers—restauranteurs; theater operators; state toll road managers; owners and managers of popular vacation sites; those who sold small cars and provided auto repair service; unemployed auto workers (who, during the previous summer, ironically, were fighting against compulsory overtime); the managers and owners in the auto manufacturing, steel, glass, tire, and auto parts replacement industries, and so on—and on, and on.

Readers will recall that the recession in question essentially involved the exacerbation of forces, already under way, that generated both higher unemployment and higher inflation rates. Although economies have had problems with one or the other of these trends, 1974–1975 was unique in the degree to which these two rates measured not a *trade off* of one in *exchange* for the other—as in traditional Keynesian notions—but mutually *reinforcing* menaces.[5]

Next, food prices exploded as a result of: (1) the so-called Russian wheat deal of 1972;[6] (2) crop-destroying floods and droughts in many parts of the world; (3) the shift, in the Third World, of these nations' investments favoring heavy industry as against agricultural production; and (4) higher fuel prices facing the majority of farmers whose methods had become increasingly capital-intensive.

And, as we have noted, there was OPEC.[7]

In addition to these proximal causes there were several ominous underlying factors the force of which was exacerbated by the oil and food shocks.

---

[4] See Chapter 2, footnote 11.

[5] Eckstein proposes an inventive index combining the two newly linked sources of popular grief, calling it the Discomfort Index. It is "calculated as the sum of unemployment rate and inflation rate, but not less than zero" (p. 153–55).

[6] The Soviets signed contracts, with Washington's approval, well in advance of harvesting, at prices well below the ultimate market prices. Effectively, the Soviet buyers operated as highly successful investors in grain futures while American families suffered the appreciably higher prices following low-yield harvests internationally.

[7] We did not know, before OPEC, how inelastic was the demand among car owners for gasoline. It turned out that consumer demand in our four-wheeled commuter economy was barely influenced by rising prices until they rose threefold; at that point the need for gasoline yielded to more clearly differentiated dispositions regarding the uses to which personal income might be put.

First, there was the devaluation of the dollar following the uncommon simultaneity of waves of recovery from successive earlier international recessions. Next, there were the equally inflationary pressures of the earlier boom, from 1971 to 1973, arising from the extraordinary excesses in worldwide "demand." Third, there was the worldwide character of inflation attending these changes, changes that were coupled with the earlier collapse of the system of fixed international exchange rates. Note the markets—capital, product, resource, and ultimately labor—that these developments affected.

Collectively, these developments helped fuel the pre–Great Recession boom. Eckstein also notes the disquieting effects of gyrating monetary policies from 1964 to 1974, such that by the early 1970s these policies came to reinforce both growing and inflationary excesses in demand in booming periods and the forces pushing economies deeper into troughs as business cycles bottomed out. Eckstein adds also the effects of price decontrols in April 1974 and the failure, through fiscal policies from 1969 to 1974, to manage demand effectively during that period. (Readers will recall our brief discussion in Chapter 5 of the role of the state in structuring the demand for labor.)

Indeed, politically inspired increases in per capita income through increases in transfer payments sparked by actions of the Federal Reserve Board, in support of Nixon's drive for reelection, subverted earlier intentions to keep an antiinflation lid on demand, a fact we also noted in Chapter 5. We must quickly add that Nixon was by no means the first White House tenant to heat up the economy (by means of transfer payments) in a reelection bid. We will revisit this highly politicized market in our concluding chapter and comment on it a little further on in this chapter in a more relevant context.

Two tables from Eckstein's report (Tables 5 and 6) show the percentage points by which 1974 inflation and 1975 unemployment rates (10.3 and 8.5, respectively) were elevated by the six aforementioned factors.

Eckstein's analysis will be of particular interest to our readers because it is so clearly organized around several of the variables in the rows and columns of our matrix. As his tables show, he is able to account for 60 percent of one of his dependent variables (inflation) and 50 percent of the other (unemployment) by looking, on one side, at movements in two resource markets (energy and agriculture, both in domestic and international terms), two product markets (food and fuel), and several components of capital markets (interest rates in both domestic and international terms). On the other side, the tables, like the analyses underlying them, take systematic account of policies and actions of our

TABLE 5. Impact of Shocks on the Inflation Rate in 1974 (Percentage Points)

Contributing factor	Contribution to inflation rate[a]
1. Energy crisis	1.7
2. Agricultural price explosion	1.5
3. Devaluation of dollar	1.2
4. Monetary policies, 1964–74	0.9
5. Price decontrol	0.8
6. Fiscal policies, 1969–74	0.3
Sum of 1–6	6.4
Rate of inflation, 1974	10.3

SOURCE: Otto Eckstein, *The Great Recession with a Postscript on Stagflation* (Amsterdam: North-Holland Publishing, 1979), 139.
[a] Inflation rate is historical tracking solution of the Data Resources Model minus inflation rate in the alternative solution with the respective shock removed.

structures: the *state*, the financial and agricultural sectors of *industries*, the actions of the larger *firms* in the energy industry, and of *labor unions'* effects on wages and productivity.

Eckstein does not treat consumers' expectations econometrically because they are not actually measurable apart from their assumed roles in the actions that are aggregated in the tables; consumers' expectations are thus viewed indirectly. But Eckstein does make note in his text of the fact that consumer expectations are important, figuring as prominently as they do in the changes in demands for the offerings in several

TABLE 6. Impact of Shocks on Unemployment in 1975 (Percentage Points)

Contributing factor	Contribution to unemployment rate[a]
1. Energy crisis	1.9
2. Monetary policies, 1964–75	1.6
3. Agricultural price explosion	0.9
4. Price controls	0.2
5. Fiscal policies, 1969–74	0.1
6. Devaluation	−0.2
Sum of 1–6	4.5
Unemployment rate, 1975	8.5

SOURCE: Otto Eckstein, *The Great Recession with a Postscript on Stagflation* (Amsterdam: North-Holland Publishing, 1979), 140.
[a] Unemployment rate is historical tracking solution minus unemployment rate in the alternative solution with the respective shock removed.

important product markets beyond agriculture and fuel markets, the markets that more immediately affected prices and labor markets.[8]

Demands for labor in the auto and steel industries, in particular, and in manufacturing generally were obviously affected by fuel prices almost immediately after OPEC's actions. And, we may add, it is evident that the huge reduction in manufacturing employment in ensuing years, and slowdowns in the gains of manufacturing workers' wages and benefits, otherwise, were significantly related to the mutually reinforcing effects of inflation, foreign competition, and managers' growing determination to be "lean and mean." The recovery of manufacturing in recent times has been accomplished by heavily subcontracting manufacturers' orders to employers of lower-wage, unorganized workers in small shops and to employers of workers in other low-wage countries, a practice that has been infelicitously dubbed "outsourcing." The effect has been a marked change in the structure of labor markets in the goods sector.

Eckstein also makes the point that "business expectations can be wrong, and occasional periods of massive error are a major factor in the business cycle." Eckstein generously allows, for example, that it is not easy for firms' managers correctly to anticipate the timing and magnitudes of growth factors, of credit crunches and of recessions, in a volatile period. But he points out that

> the record shows some tendency to [managers'] systematic error, even after the fallibility of forecasting is recognized. The boom of the early 1970's saw numerous excesses of investment, which cannot be entirely blamed on too low a real cost of capital. Expectations became overexuberant. Financial pressures to achieve rising earnings-per-share, building on inadequacies of accounting principles rather than real business success, reinforced those tendencies. . . . Whereas households staged a quick retreat at early signs of increased food prices, business investment and inventory policies operated on a grossly false set of future expectations for the succeeding eighteen months.[9]

Next, Eckstein notes that the presidency (and thus, in some measure, the state) had "deteriorated during the last ten years, and during some crucial periods it collapsed." The references here are to President Johnson's hassles with Congress over the financing of the Vietnam War; the Watergate crisis; and, earlier, price and wage controls. "The United States," he remarks, "is not accustomed to instability in its central government,"[10] an instability that adds very substantially to forecasting difficulties by the principals and their agents in both our markets and in our structures.

[8] Eckstein, *op. cit.*, 148.
[9] *Loc. cit.* 148.
[10] *Loc. cit.*, 148.

"Finally, and perhaps most importantly," Eckstein writes in a section on the system's recovery and survival,

> the Great Recession did not produce social tension or an increased struggle over income distribution. Indeed, more than anything else it appears to have been a sobering experience that helped bring an end to the strife created in the years of affluence in the Vietnam War in the mid- and late-1960's.[11]

Eckstein's explanation for the absence of mass distemper might as well be interpreted in his own more congenial economic terms as in his vaguer social psychological terms. In the "political marketplace," after all, the demand for radical political change is fairly inelastic; even the rapidly rising prices summed up in inflation, together with lamentably high unemployment rates, did not lead to even a small shift in consumer-voter demand for change. A small shift, that is, if one does not a bit later characterize the swing to Reaganomics as a revolution of the *right*.

Eckstein's explanation for the equanimity with which Americans paid the price, captured in the ominous phrase, *the Great Recession,* with its unmistakable allusion to the Great Depression, is not an untenable one. But there are several alternatives, two of which relate to the roles of classes, roles that deserve consideration in fairness to those who stress them. Classes, we may remind ourselves, are among the work structures to which this volume assigns some, if uncertain, weight.

In its most vulgarized form, the class argument holds that large numbers of Americans were "falsely" unconscious of the degree to which the multiple dislocations leading to the Great Recession, like those leading to the Great Depression, made victims of them. Distracted or confused by the interests attaching to multiple roles that they are urged to consider—as producers; savers; investors (generally through pension funds heavily invested in corporate stocks and bonds); members of race, gender, and age cohorts; consumers; and more—the members of the working class did not adequately perceive their fundamental class interests *per se* and thus failed to see the justification for the antagonism toward other less victimized classes that their misery should have inspired.

The partial enumeration, in the previous paragraph, of the large numbers of socioeconomic roles in which even working-class Americans find themselves may, however, afford us clues to the necessarily limited value of class analysis, the vexing question of class members' consciousness quite aside.

The fact of life in the Western democracies is that most workers are consumers, for example, and will inevitably spite themselves as workers

[11] Eckstein, 143–44.

when, at one point, rising inflation rates lead them to ease up on job-generating purchases that were encouraged, at an earlier point, when inflation rates were lower. Eckstein, we will recall, usefully reminds us in this connection that consumers changed their behavior far more quickly and intelligently than did business leaders when inflation rates soared.

Moreover, many organized workers' wages were indexed—rising in fixed proportions to inflation—enabling that subset of the working class to view rising inflation rates with a certain equanimity. And so they did until spiraling rates actually did trade off against their own continuing employment prospects; the indexing of wages was of little comfort, meanwhile, to unemployed workers, since such indexing contributes to inflation by augmenting the disposable income of consumer-bent, organized workers virtually at the expense of unorganized workers—the majority—and of those on fixed incomes.

Add the differentially negative and positive responses to imports among different subsets of workers, sometimes in the same industry, and one begins to sense that consciousness is as consciousness does, neither more nor less. Consider in this regard that there are as many jobs in the United States tied to sales of Japanese and other imported cars as to sales of American-made cars. And, reminding ourselves of the earlier brief discussion of tariffs, we are well aware of the divisions between these two groups of workers in their attitudes toward protectionism.

Given his well-reasoned chapters on the roles of public policy in the genesis of the Great Recession, Eckstein might well have noted another factor tempering the potential for outrage, an explanation that also bears on the matter of class analysis. Thus, it is the case that in the nine to twelve months preceding nearly every presidential election in which a White House tenant has sought reelection, his party has pursued policies that generate increases in disposable income and decreases in unemployment rates. And so it was as we headed into the Carter–Ford campaign. The only exception was during Eisenhower's reelection campaign.[12]

By January 1975 an 8 percent dip in disposable income, beginning in 1973, had been stemmed and reversed; in the months before the November 1976 election, disposable income went up nearly 4 percent. And the unemployment rate dropped more than 1 percent from its 9 percent level 18 months earlier. Although one percentage point seems

---

[12] For a fine, well-documented discussion of the political market in which expansionary policies are offered in exchange for votes (and contribute to political business cycles), see E. R. Tufte, *Political Control of the Economy* (Princeton, N.J.: Princeton University Press, 1978), *passim;* and D. J. Meiselman, "The Political Monetary Cycle," *Wall Street Journal,* 10 January 1984, 8.

small, it represents a great many reemployed workers over and above the hundreds of thousands of new jobs appearing each year.

The members of most classes in America quite apparently feel encouraged, in this fashion, by White House tenants who are comfortable in their government quarters; the ritualized courtship of Americans by political candidates for reelection and their party workers obviously does little to persuade voters that the republic needs fundamental reform. Readers can decide for themselves, meanwhile, whether working-class voters would be better advised to ignore popular economic indicators of the economy's health touted by presidents on the stump, especially since so many of them can urge policies that administer short-run "fixes" to key economic indicators.

We have illustrated in this section some key interactions among events occurring in our structures and markets over a fairly short-run period, the early 1970s. In the next sections we move to a consideration of the state as a primary structure in our drama of structures and markets. We then move, a bit cautiously, to a schematic outline of a series of watershedlike discontinuities in America's economic development overall.

THE NATION-STATE'S ROLE IN ECONOMIC GROWTH AND DEVELOPMENT

We acknowledged some cautiousness in the previous paragraph because able critics have not been especially generous in their assessments of major efforts to explain America's development in accord with a logic attaching to key events and to assertedly prepotent variables.

Charles Beard's *Economic Interpretation of the Constitution*, for example, enjoys little more than passing attention these days; few historians are prepared to regard a few years before and two decades after the American Revolution as nothing much more than a period in which a small number of propertied colonial leaders sought first to make the colonies independent of Britain's mercantile capitalists and thereafter essentially to impose law and order on debtors and workers whose antagonisms threatened their property claims after King George had been routed.

Frederick Jackson Turner's thesis, that cheap land west of the original coastal colonies provided a safety valve for the release of tensions otherwise likely to have festered among urban have-nots, does not enjoy much more favor than Beard's. An updated version of Turner's argument, by Potter, is widely read in American studies programs; he offers a more general analysis of the role of abundance, which, until recent times, was a key factor in America's essentially peaceful development. The argument, however, receives no mention in the work of the new economic historians to whose work we made enthusiastic allusions in Chapter 1.

Thus "simple and sovereign" theses—from Beard's and Turner's to those of W. W. Rostow, for instance, who sees stages in economic development—enjoy little favor. But it is useful to identify key attributes of our markets and structures in each of the segments of American history that have repeatedly been identified as relatively self-contained blocks: the colonial era; the post-Revolutionary era (1790–1860); Reconstruction and the "Age of Big Business" (1865–1914); the twenties; the thirties; the "Liberals' Era" (1946–1976); and, finally, the period from 1976 to 1985, which we may dare to call the Period of Deconstruction. America's economic history is, to a very marked degree, the history of state intervention on behalf of (1) investors, (2) then producers, (3) then workers, (4) and then consumers, have-nots, and users of public goods. As these words are written, finally, a fair segment of the public policies captured in the term *Reaganomics* are, at least putatively, designed to help investors as we appear to revisit the policies of the majority of our earliest patron-leaders.

The two most heavily favored theoretical apparatuses available for assessing the processes of economic growth and development, allowing, of course, for hybrids between them, are those generally identified as Marxist and neoclassical. At their roots they differ fundamentally in the favorable weights they would give to individuals' as contrasted with collective claims to the ownership and disposition of property, and to the rewards that should go to these groups emerging from the economically rational deployment of the factors of production to which property ownership affords access.

Different as the two apparatuses are in most of their detailed analyses, they do converge on the strategic point that the state (a nominal term for those who rule or where "the people shall judge," the people's agents) plays a singularly important role in writing the rules of the politicoeconomic game.

These rules set the terms of the exchanges in our markets and especially the rules governing the ways in which property may be obtained, used, and transferred, and the rights, privileges, and immunities of property owners, including owners of ideas—the holders of proprietary information, trade secrets, patents, and copyrights, particularly.[13]

---

[13] An exomologesis: This discussion borrows heavily and freely from an extraordinarily well-balanced account in Douglas North, *Structure and Change in Economic History* (New York: W. W. Norton, 1981). "May we forgive those who had our best ideas before we did."

The tensions between those who seek to own, exploit, transfer, or otherwise dispose of property and those who seek power or authority and ultimately the taxes that support them were as sharp in ancient times as in more recent eras. If rulers tax too much, indirectly or directly, or limit too significantly, in other ways, the options of property holders to dispose of or use their property, they have regularly provoked their subjects into taking (or undoing) actions the effects of which generally are to restore a balance between the imperatives of the erstwhile adversaries. The principal extreme alternatives available to the parties, of course, are revolution or repression.[14] The former, by subjects, contributes to growth, or has been seen to do so, as the American Revolution may have done to that of the colonial economy;[15] repression by rulers probably does not.

As leaders of the two mainline traditions see it, property ownership in a political environment permissive toward owners affords them incentives to earn, save, and invest and thus to deploy productive factors in economically rational ways. The traditions part company in their antagonistic judgments about the prospects for continuing growth under conditions of mostly public or mostly private ownership associated with planning and market-driven decision making, respectively. They also disagree in theoretical and ideological terms about the implications of markets and plans for egalitarianism, whether in terms of economic opportunity or economic outcomes; neither tradition invests confidence in the other's claims that its ways will lead to greater freedoms.

The realities accessible to us as the result of historians' good work suggest that growth can occur under a variety of balances among collectivized, heavily regulated, or significantly planned economies, on one side, and those in which property owners enjoy very wide latitude, on the other. Between the so-called limiting cases are those economies like our own that are themselves admixtures of purely market-driven components, more or less heavily regulated components and, eventually, planned components. The very words cause one to recall the terms descriptive of one or more social, political, and economic aspects of these cases: *pluralism, declarative planning, imperfect competition,* and that wonderful

---

[14] The cases of Peter the Great's policies and of Leninism-Stalinism, in Russia and the USSR, are more complicated ones. Growth clearly occurred in both of these notorious periods, but this is not an occasion for a rehearsal of these complexities.

[15] The empirical evidence that resentment of middle-class colonists against England's Navigation and Stamp Acts truly fettered colonial merchants and slowed growth has not overly impressed our new economic historians. See Lee and Passell, *op cit.* The argument that Hitler's repressive regime helped German recovery in the 1930 to 1940 period must take account of the degree to which he left the business leaders of Germany to their own devices while generating markets for their output through construction and rearmament.

euphemism for the socioeconomic salmagundi that is the United States, *the mixed economy.*

In abstract analytical terms, the space between rulers and the ruled (the latter often consisting of a plurality of interests in transactions among our structures and markets as a society becomes more industrialized and thus more highly differentiated) is not a vacuum. On one side, both rulers and their agents—the state—and the ruled are differentially perceptive about the limits on their freedom of action. But their actions are also more or less shaped by the limits placed upon them by social institutions and the prevailing ideologies (or tapestries of ideologies) that give these institutions their legitimacy.

In North's words:

> Institutions are a set of rules, compliance procedures, and moral and ethical behavioral norms designed to constrain the behavior of individuals in the interests of maximizing the wealth or utility of principals [and their agents]. . . . Constitutional rules, operating rules, and normative rules are frequently overlapping[;] . . . [the first] are the fundamental rules designed to specify the basic structure of property rights and control of the state. They are intended to be more costly to modify than are operating rules, which either as statute laws, common law, or voluntary contracts, specify terms of exchange within the framework of the constitutional rules. Normative behavioral rules are codes of behavior aimed at legitimating the constitutional and operating rules. . . . Personalized exchange—repetitive dealings and personal contracts—minimizes the need for formal rules and compliance procedures since reciprocity and consensus ideology . . . constrain behavior. Where operational exchange occurs, competition plays the key role in constraining behavior of the parties to exchanges.[16]

Moral and ethical norms are an essential part of the constraints that make up institutions. They are derived from the constructions of reality (ideology) that individuals develop to contend with their environment.[17]

Voluntary contracts are of particular importance, especially the prospect that they are sufficiently binding that the signatories can make plans in accord with their stipulations of mutual obligations; although many uncertainties will confront economic actors, their risks mount as uncertainties grow.[18]

---

[16] D. North, *op. cit.*, 201–3.

[17] *Ibid.*, 204.

[18] One possibility: that voluntary contracts contain conspiratorial attacks on valued institutions, as when pricing conspiracies or trusts develop. In these instances, as in the United States in the 1880s and 1890s, one observes the emergence of laws designed to protect competition and to measure its presence or absence with the help of economic evidence.

North's analysis represents a most thoughtful synthesis of old-fashioned institutionalism with the two main lines of economic inquiry drawing from the neoclassical and Marxist traditions, both of which were discussed briefly in Chapter 1. As such, his analysis suits us very well indeed in a brief discussion of the American case as a historical one: While Marxists helpfully make much of ideology—especially the putative ideologies of those with and without property—and of the state as an instrument of the propertied classes, North applies an economic model to the state that helps to clarify the literal *give and take* that occurs among rulers, their agents (whose agendas may not be precisely the same as the rulers) and the larger numbers of ruled peoples in a society.

North's calculus is a straightforward one: rulers must weigh the costs of interferences—regulations and taxes, for example—that generate hostility among those who seek to conduct commerce in one or more of our different market contexts. Property holders subject to the state authority, in turn, seek ways of demonstrating that the fewer the fetters on their freedom of action, the more likely it is that the state will be stable and capable of self-defense.

Property holders are also inclined to argue that the state is less likely to be challenged by propertyless claimants in systems in which the less fortunate can share in the benefits of economic growth. This growth, they argue, will be sparked by property holders' reasonable expectations that, with initiative, incentives, a predictable legal order, and a good deal of pluck, they will be able to earn private returns that approach social returns, an expectation that encourages investment to the extent that risks are reduced and in proportion to the degree to which uncertainty is reduced. The unpropertied earn shares in the proceeds, they are regularly (almost monotonously) advised, by working conscientiously.

It will take no leap of imagination to recognize that there are many kinds of equilibrium among rulers, on one side, and the propertied and unpropertied on the other; some equilibria are more stable than others. In the Western democracies, these equilibria have shifted as the three types of interest groups have vied with each other for maximum freedom of action for themselves or for constraints on the freedom of action of the others, as the case may be.

The three interest groupings are not internally homogeneous, however; indeed, their memberships can actually overlap, as when workers own income-producing apartment houses, becoming landlords, and hold vested pension rights. Similarly, large property owners become dependent on what has become an army of professional managers and technicians. Managers alone increased by 9 percent, despite two back-to-back recessions, from 1980 to 1982 while overall employment declined by 1 percent and blue-collar jobs dropped by 12 percent![19]

Ideologies that legitimate a given equilibration, moreover, can contribute significantly to reasonably high orders of social consensus and the level of social harmony Eckstein observed to have mitigated what might have been social unrest in the United States during the most pained months of the Great Recession, discussed earlier.

Such ideologies are far more readily defended where the interests of large groups overlap; the more interests that large numbers of citizens (the middle class, say), can identify favorably with the status quo the less sharp the conflicts among status, race, sex, and age groups within the larger class groups. The growth of a black middle class in the United States, for example, is a source of both pride and frustration to sizable numbers of black leaders.

Many members of each of these separate reference groups simply have too much in common in their pension funds, in their tax-deductible interest payments on homes, in their need for asphalt and concrete ribbons on which to drive their beached whales. These groups also have too many distinguishable but not terribly different yearnings for welfare (whether grants, food stamps, protective tariffs, tax shelters, or countless other benefits the state may be persuaded to bestow, naturally, as incentives) to engage in enduringly vicious intergroup conflict.

With this brief discussion of the state and social classes as background, we may move to an equally schematic review of developments in American history.

THE AMERICAN CASE

The American case, in historical terms, is an instructive one precisely because, at the outset, there were misgivings among property owners about the economic and other disadvantages inhering in so loosely knit a political system as existed after the Revolution.

Beyond the need for a common defense, better ordered interstate relationships, and a system of coinage, there were obvious needs, for example, to come to grips with war debts; the latter concern was of especially great interest to the first new nation's creditors and not a trivial number of scare-mongering speculators who trafficked in these obligations. A nation honors its debts to the very considerable advantage of those who have longer-term interests in establishing those "rules of the

[19] "Management's Ranks Grow," *New York Times*, 14 April 1983, D1.

game," as North puts it, that have to do specifically with property ownership.

The rest of the next segment of the story is, as some like to say, history. The period 1778 to 1789 was marked by a succession of conventions ordering progressively more integrated (i.e., centralized) political institutions until the nearly anarchic contempt for central authority that suffused the Declaration of Independence gave way entirely to the constitutional system essentially as we know it today, with the establishment of the rights of property holders clearly a priority matter.

Shays' Rebellion (by debtors) in 1786 helped considerably in persuading the rebels of 1775 that hostility toward King George's "law and order" was one thing and our *own* need for law and order quite another! Masterful newspaper essays the same year on the subject were published in book form the following year, as *The Federalist*; one of the principal themes (of Hamilton, Madison, and Hay) in that book was the need for a strong government.

In the decades prior to the Revolution, we were, in terms of markets and structures, a nation of farmers, with some regional differences in the degree of interest in (or opposition to) England's mercantilist economic policies, and of a smaller number of city-dwelling artisans, exporters and importers, fisherfolk, timbermen, and seaport entrepreneurs (chandelers, boatwrights, and riggers). Our export traders were both helped and constrained by the Crown's trade policies: on one side, they protected our exporters against competitors for customers in English markets; but, on the other, these policies reduced the colonists' profits on American goods and resources reexported, at a profit for British leaders, to Englishmen's own overseas customers.

The principal markets were organized around raw materials (exported), producers' goods (imported), and some urban commerce related to these activities and to distributional activities in intramural economic transactions.

Slave labor, mostly in the South, involved a market for that labor resource as slaves were sold and bought, to be sure, but it was not a market resembling that linking labor and management under conditions in which, as Max Weber described it, workers are "formally free." Nor, of course, did slaves have trade unions.

Capital markets existed essentially only in a primitive form, although trading companies—Maryland and Massachusetts, for example, were in fact born of Crown corporations—like the Hudson Bay Company, were visible manifestations of the crafts of capitalists in league with their kings and their kings' agents. Otherwise, there were borrowers, mostly farmers, and creditors, a market relationship that was later fraught with tensions.

Ideological considerations at least as much as fundamentally economic ones fed growing resentments against the Crown as the pages in calendars turned to the mid-1770s, a period in which heroic statements about the evils of tyranny attracted many readers. Once independence was theirs, however, the colonists' highly charged ideological rhetoric calmed down quite significantly.

In January 1790, not even two years after the requisite ninth state (Maryland) had ratified the Constitution (21 June 1788), our founders "hit the ground running," as Reagan's preinaugural team put it nearly two centuries later.

Washington was sworn into office on 7 January 1789, and only seven days later Hamilton, the first secretary of the treasury, issued his first report on the public credit in which he recommended federal funding of the inherited foreign and domestic debts at par and the assumption by the federal government of up to $21,500,000 of debts incurred by the states during the Revolution. Such an arrangement surely would elicit confidence, home and away, in the new nation-state as a fundamentally stable and thus a stabilizing agency. As noted in the *Encyclopedia of American History*, the funding and assumption of debts would "strengthen and stabilize the central government by fostering a consciousness of national solidarity of interest among those business and commercial groups holding the greater part of the domestic debt."[20] Orderly capital markets are far more of a *sine qua non* than other sorts of orderly markets, for other markets can be regulated by laws or coercive methods, or else they are derivative of confidence on the part of investors that the state will reduce some of the uncertainties that inhibit investment.

There was southern opposition to the domestic portion of Hamilton's funding proposals; northerners held the largest portion of the unpaid debts and understandably favored assumption, a turn that left southerners (most of whom had already settled with their creditors or sold the debt they held, at discounts, to northerners) with shared responsibilities for a large increase in the national debt.

Hamilton's plan was finally passed only a few months later when he arranged with James Madison of Virginia, at a party given by Jefferson, a compromise whereby the secretary would advocate a transfer of the national capital from Philadelphia to the banks of the Potomac. In return, Hamilton's proposed plans for the debt would benefit from the Virginian's artful lobbying with his fellow southerners. Northern debtors, as such, lost nothing in this horse trade; southerners literally paid for the desired

---

[20] Richard Morris, ed., *Encyclopedia of American History* (New York: Harper & Row, 1961), 122.

relocation of the capital through subsequent taxes in support of debt assumption and through the discounts they had absorbed earlier in the sales to speculators of their claims to payment on the obligations they had bought during the war. Nicholas Biddle, a Philadelphia man of many, many parts, an intimate of Monroe (and later, perhaps for his virtues, a president of the Second United States Bank), probably helped "grease the skids" back in his Philadelphia Washington Square neighborhood wherein stood the Capitol; Independence Hall and the Liberty Bell were not included in the bargain. This transaction, among different types of property holders with differentiated economic interests, is a quintessentially paradigmatic American one; "logrolling" bills among legislators who represent different economic constituencies, as their critics see them, are as American as any swap sanctified by the values of consummate pragmatists.

Note that not a few of the members of the new nation's first Congress, themselves, were busy, once the ratification of the Constitution seemed assured, buying up the debt at discounted value. As it turned out, these venturers gambled wisely on the prospects that there would be a continuing urge to restore and maintain the law and order disrupted by Shays and his fellow debtors prior to the final Constitutional Convention!

It is the case, moreover, that private investments are indeed less fraught with risk in a politically stable system. And, although Charles Beard may have underestimated the purely ideological or patriotic interest of the majority of our Founding Fathers in his interpretation, one cannot simply gainsay the more mundane economic interests that Beard described, in persuasive detail, in his 1913 classic, *An Economic Interpretation of the Constitution.*[21]

In 1790, Hamilton also urged the chartering of a national bank, appealing to the federal government's implied powers and introducing thereby the "loose constructionist" philosophy in American constitutional law; these loose constructionist interpretations have enabled both liberals and conservatives, ever since, to fashion laws serving their respective constituencies. Indeed, this legal philosophy has enabled contending parties who seek to gain political means—the state—to serve economic ends of very different colors. The bank was chartered, early on, in 1791; shifts among capitalists of different kinds caused the bank's subsequent ups and downs as the new republic's structural differentiations continued.

The Constitution's emphases on the separation of powers and of federalist principles regarding the general character of the powers of the

---

[21] Charles Beard, *An Economic Interpretation of the Constitution* (New York: Free Press, 1965). This book is still in print.

state vis-à-vis the several individual states clearly reflected a desire to control the central state. Anti-federalists (mostly southern landholders) remained essentially loyal to this demiurge, but it did not take long for others to see benefits in the state's becoming a major force in the structuring of the rules regarding property in ways that favored investors, manufacturers, and other persons of commerce.

Such factionalist aspirations had been anticipated, especially by James Madison, in *The Federalist*. But the separation of powers, a bicameral legislature, and the states' reservation of rights not specifically accorded to the federal government (which were designed in part to limit factionalism) slowed—but only slowed—those who saw prospects for redistributing rights, and thus to a very marked degree the distribution of opportunities and economic prospects, by political means.

European wars (and wars of our own with England and the Indians) also slowed the fulfillment of Hamiltonian ambitions in the early 1800s. But the federal purchases of land and the movement westward involved more than a few of the aspirations of aggrandizing Americans. The United States Bank's charter expired in 1811 but it was rechartered in 1816, putting the state squarely back in the capital markets with a vehicle for making money; the Second Bank became a critical component in the state's capacity to help fund both the roads and the canals that became the prerailroad sinews of the expanding nation and its growing economy.

There were two other key developments: Chief Justice Marshall's opinions, on behalf of the Supreme Court and the Hamiltonian-Federalist position, in the Dartmouth College case and in the case of *McCulloch v. Maryland*.

In the first of these, in February 1819, corporate charters granted by the states were held to be protected by the Constitution's contract clause against impairments by the chartering state. Apart from Marshall's assertions of the supremacy of federal over state law in the area of contracts, as in other areas of constitutional law, the case reached back into natural law and afforded corporate entities the same rights in contracts that the Constitution, in literal terms, had granted to natural persons; the court thus reaffirmed the natural law conception of the corporation as *persona ficta*.

The other case, *McCulloch v. Maryland*, one month later, involved the constitutionality of the Second United States Bank and the rights of a state to tax one of the bank's branches. The Supreme Court, once again, vigorously upheld federal supremacy. The Federalists, who were parties, earlier, to the *construction* of a limited state power—with separation of powers and the rest—thus came, early on, to stand foursquare behind the *use* of the power of "the positive state" to assure traditional property rights.

The only major property right of the time, to which northern Federalists began more and more frequently to object (for both economic and ideological reasons), was the right to own slaves. These nearly paradoxical attitudes of the Federalists were not really paradoxical at all: with increasing structural differentiation, in what was a developing country, antagonisms began to develop among *different types* of property holders. The widespread ownership of one type of property, once basic ownership claims enjoy legal protection, does not assure that property owners will forever thereafter have shared interests, as students of zoning ordinances, for example, know very well. Few homeowners like to live next to the gas stations, shopping malls, pizza parlors, bowling alleys, supermarkets, and bars in which they spend so much of their time away from home. Years of political compromise over slave ownership in the new states that signed on with the Union delayed the denouement over slavery. It "took a civil war," as North points out, regarding emancipation (p. 189), to effect the single largest change in property rights, "and [the] consequent redistribution of wealth in America's 19th Century."[22] The judgment is as significant to an understanding of the role of property rights as it is bold.

Attentive readers will recognize, in this brief review, the competitors in different markets (land settlement, agriculture, financial markets, the manufacturing sector, labor markets, and even in political markets) championing their own views of what the state should and should not venture to do. The use of the state as both a guarantor and redistributor of property rights and as the agent that ultimately writes the rules *within a constitutional-legal* framework was accordingly well developed long before we became a developed nation in the current sense of the word.

And structures—like corporations—beget other structures, unions, for example, labor parties, and trade associations in search of tariffs, like those that supported the so-called American System (of tariffs, 1824) that Hamilton anticipated in his Report on Manufactures in 1789.

Collections of individuals who pooled their property (investments) in corporate entities, meanwhile, became duly constituted *personae fictae*. Unions—nascent in the early 1800s, but making themselves notable by the 1830s—remained conspiracies of individuals against persons-as-legal-corporations. Indeed, from 1819 (the Dartmouth College case) until 1863 (emancipation), some things (corporations) were people and some

---

[22] North, *op. cit.*, 191.

people (slaves) were things. The property ownership qualification for voting, meanwhile, did not begin to be eroded until 1821 (New York) and lasted (in Rhode Island) until 1834, nearly half a century after the Constitution was ratified. And unions, though they could still be legally ignored for practical purposes thereafter by employers, remained conspiracies under the law until 1842 (*Commonwealth v. Hunt*), *one-half* of a century after ratification and *one-quarter* of a century after stockholders became collective *personae fictae.*

Note, here, the interplay of developments urged at somewhat different times by principals (and their agents) in different markets—agriculture, manufacturing, import–export, labor, capital, and political. And note, on the structural side, the emergence of associational and other types of nonbusiness agencies. Patent law had its origins in the Constitution—hence the beginning of encouragement for the marriage of technology with science, a development aided by land grant colleges (the Morrill Act, 1862) which was also the fundamental beginning of the "production of human capital," as it is now called, in institutions of higher education. Thorstein Veblen's 1919 volume, *The Higher Learning in America,* an institutionalist's version of the human capital approach (and never footnoted therein by this tradition's ahistorical scholars) largely anticipated the approach by Gary Becker by forty-four years.

There is no easy way to summarize the differentiations among and within markets, on one side, and the differentiations of American structures that formed, shaped, and modified these markets on the other. The Age of Big Business was so much the stuff of American history, in this regard, that there is scarcely a university worthy of the name that does not offer an entire course—an economic history course—on the fifty years between 1860 and 1910.

The clearest analytical lines, from Charles Beard to Samuel Huntington (*American Politics and Promises of Disharmony,* 1981), to Douglas North (1981) and Robert Solo (*The Positive State,* 1982) focus on larger, pendulumlike swings between the state as an instrument of redistribution to the state as an instrument for the restriction of the capacities of groups to use the state as a mechanism for the reform of propertied principals (and their agents) in markets and structures.

Thus, North writes pointedly about the move toward greater government intervention in the United States economy originating in the last quarter of the nineteenth century but notes very emphatically that it had "long antecedents."[23] He recounts the emergence of "government by commission" and the use, by evolving interest groups, of other organ-

[23] North, *op. cit.,* 192.

izational mechanisms that would reduce the cost of utilizing the political process to alter property rights.

In recent times, Congress has passed so many laws annually that its members have, to an increasing degree, written only general principles for which a host of regulatory agencies—OSHA, EPA, FCC, among the most deplored or celebrated—would write the regulations. And presidents have written thousands of executive orders (such as two controversial executive orders concerning affirmative action). These orders have most of the force of laws passed by the people's legislators, through the enforcement apparatus of executive departments like the Justice Department.

Solo reminds us that when a Congress has been liberal—"redistributive"—in its dispositions (as in the New Deal), the Court has regularly been conservative (as when one of FDR's New Deal agencies was declared unconstitutional) in restoring a kind of equipoise between the propertied and the nonpropertied. He also outlines American economic history as embodying the transformation of the state as an agent, writ large and longitudinally, as an instrument that first established the rights of investors, then those of producers (manufacturers), then those of labor, and, in the 1960s and 70s, those of consumers and the users of public goods and services.

All along, farmers have been served with support systems and price guarantees. Tradesmen (from the several states) have been given rights to plumb and electrify buildings; to teach, to operate, eviscerate and medicate; to crop and paint the women members of our tribe; and to protect the arcane arts whereby attorneys and accountants live in a litigious and calculating population of rights-minded persons, corporate and natural.

In each case, competitors vie to use, or to protect themselves abundantly within, a well-developed system of propertied and proprietary rights, privileges, and immunities: city denizens have tenant laws and rent control; Yuppies are aided in negating their dealings with the creditors who sponsored their job-gaining education by bankruptcy laws very much like those further protecting the limited liability of corporate shareholders; and the UAW and the United Steelworkers share in lobbying efforts with their members' employers to secure protective tariffs. An insurance company's familiar urgings on the picture tube that we buy "a piece of the Rock" is but a variation on a wide-going and historically favored exhortation that we should seek, each after our own fashion, to secure "a piece of the action."

The action, in the event, is the state, and we rearrange our markets and our structures to assure ourselves the safekeeping of "ourselves and sacred fortunes" while insisting that competition is a wonderfully chastening challenge—to the other guy.

CONCLUSION

One inference that might reasonably be drawn by readers, in a romantic mood, from the materials discussed in this chapter is that the state really has been the instrument of the vast majority of the citizens, specifically in the ways that it has generated rules pertaining to property.

Consider, in company with romantics, that these rules have responded neither to radicals' entreaties to collectivize nor to hyperconservative arguments that ownership of property concentrated in the hands of a very few should be viewed with equanimity. Rather, we have regularly redefined property rights to the point where we have created a kind of modern yeomanry; the sharpness of our political conflicts has been tempered, in this view, almost precisely as Jefferson hoped it would be. And to the extent that the state is useful to the many different segments of an elaborated middle class and is recognized as a state available to all there is widespread loyalty, as romantics see things, to its doings and most of its creatures, corporations and unions among them.

Jefferson, in de Tocqueville's terms, believed that "if a state of society can ever be founded in which every man shall have something to keep and little to take from others, much will have been done for the peace of the world."[24] Modern romantics, in a tradition that goes back to Aristotle in its belief in the stabilizing roles of a middle class, would see in our materials that the state has been used, in fairly basic political terms, to extend rights by linking them to new forms of property rather than by simply redistributing property, as such. And, as we noted from North, the only truly radical redistribution of property in the United States—the freeing of American slaves—was indeed associated with a major—and bloody—conflict. Critics of a middle-class society, meanwhile, will never make peace with romantics because, as realists they cannot. Seeing, it appears, is not believing.

Another inference would generate controversy of a somewhat different sort. Thus, this chapter gives little support to a widely shared commitment in the sciences, the social sciences increasingly included, to Galilean, Newtonian, Lockean, or Cartesian versions of reductionism. A moment's reflection will help us recall that a great many of our inves-

[24] Alexis de Tocqueville, *Democracy in America*, Vol. 2 (New York: Vintage Books, 1954), 266.

tigations are informed, usually implicitly, by Descartes's metaphor of the world as a machine not less than by a social version of Newtonian mechanics according to which the natural state of society—equilibrium—is order and we therefore must account for disorder.

The alternative view, holism, that gains from this chapter's discussion, is that the world is disorderly and we must account for historically rarer periods of orderliness. Social arrangements cannot be reduced, in accord with the Cartesian paradigm's constraining assumptions of metaphors, to smaller and smaller units—from the state to the firm, for example—that are internally homogeneous.

Rather, it is exactly our position that our system's parts—markets and structures in our parlance—are differentially constituted and that they mesh only with help, institutionally, from the web of rules that is made and remade; laws governing contracts of all types, from marriage to real estate, for example, are regularly revised. Further, new social technology is created—unions, and their grievance and bargaining mechanisms, for example, or the New York Port Authority, or Comsat, or political parties (frowned upon in *The Federalist* and deliberately ignored in our Constitution), or third-party health payment plans—to facilitate the evolution of *modi vivendi* that enable reasonable people to disagree in reasoned ways.

By augmenting the Cartesian, Newtonian, and neo-Pythagorean world of economists with that of institutionalists, historians, political scientists, and legal historians, we can apprehend the collective contents of the cells in our matrix as they are: special cases of parts the interactions of which will be unruly unless they are reasonably well managed by rulers whose tenure endures only to the extent that they make valuable—that is, acceptable—accommodations such that the benefits to the majority outweigh the costs.

On this tentative note we turn to our final chapter, in which we look ahead in an effort to identify a few continuing sources of stability and change that will affect the long-term vitality and survival capacity of our markets and structures in their intramural evolutions and their interactions with each other.

CHAPTER 7

CHANGES IN MARKETS AND WORK STRUCTURES

Several key themes have guided our efforts in this book. One is that analysts studying one or another of the multidimensional work structures we have limned can profit from close considerations of those emphasized by other analysts. Thus, those who focus on a row, a column, or small clusters of cells will find clues to the residual variances left unexplained by the predictors with which they have been working.

A second common thread is that the origins of work structures are to be found, essentially if not entirely, in the various types of markets that characterize industrial societies. Markets are themselves multidimensional, including those in which exchanges of products, services, capital and credit, endless varieties of resources, and, of course, labor occur.

In previous chapters, we have sought to identify some key dimensions along which markets and work structures differ, and we have suggested that many utilities are derived from paying close attention to the interplay between markets and structures and among their respective subsystems; we hinted at some of these relations in the matrix printed on the front endpaper.

We chose to discuss the particular markets and work structures we did because of their enduring quality, as reflected in the attention paid to them in the past by researchers in diverse disciplines. However, rapid changes are occurring in each of the four markets: they have become internally more complex, more volatile, increasingly interdependent, and more heavily influenced than ever before by developments, political not less than cultural and economic, in Latin America, Southeast Asia, and the Middle East. The organizational and economic changes that are now occurring in American society and the world have important implications for both the stability and coherence of our work structures. Importantly, these changes in markets and structures may well reduce the salience of some structures (e.g., industries and unions) for shaping the nature of work and magnify the importance of others (e.g., the state and firms) as we head into the twenty-first century.

In this final chapter, we attempt to identify a few—only a few—continuing sources of stability and change that will likely affect the long-term vitality and survival capacities of the markets and structures upon which we have focused. Our examples are organized around some of the key cells of the matrix of interrelations between markets and structures printed on the back endpaper; readers will note that the matrix in the back endpaper goes beyond the one in front in that it contains suggestions about some of the key *subsystems* in our markets. The cells illustrate some of the major interdependencies between markets and structures that will become increasingly important in the future. Our aim is not to forecast or to join in the games played by futurists, however. Rather, we are simply extrapolating from what we take to be trends that are already well underway. Moreover, we confine our discussion primarily to the United States: while many of the changes to which we allude (e.g., conglomeration) are also taking place throughout much of the industrialized world, the vast cultural and institutional differences among countries necessitate that we hold in abeyance the forecasts we make to other nations.

We first discuss some actions by the state that will continue to transform the markets that we have discussed and that in our judgment will increase the importance of a fifth type of market: that for political influence. We then describe some changes in product, capital, resource, and labor markets that are likely sources of stability and changes in their associated work structures. We next consider some implications for markets and structures of the increasing internationalization of production and the growing interdependency among the world's political economies. Finally, we briefly outline some key elements of a research agenda suggested by our discussion; the pursuit of these issues would make it possible to go much farther on the road to a synthesis of understandings regarding work and industry than we have traveled in these pages.

THE NATION-STATE AND MARKETS

As we have noted at various points in previous chapters, the policies and actions of the state have profound consequences for the operation of all our markets and structures. In addition to being a work structure in its own right, the state apparatus is also a superstructure, so to speak, that shapes many component parts of the contexts that in turn shape all the other markets and structures and their patterns of stability and change. We consider the impact of the state on each market in turn.

Product Markets

As the experience of the auto industry during the 1970s and 1980s illustrates, product markets have become increasingly internationalized. Accordingly, changes in the United States government's policies in recent years with regard to product markets have been aimed at increasing the competitiveness of American companies in world markets. In the past, "government by commission" and by agencies like the FTC (in its antitrust roles in product markets), OSHA (in labor markets), and the EPA (in both resource and product markets) has apparently made it difficult for American firms to compete in world markets. The difficulties of American producers were compounded by regulations based on standards—so many acceptable emission units from smokestacks, for example—rather than on incentives (such as offering tax advantages prorated to link with degrees of compliance), which has further reduced their competitiveness.[1]

During the Reagan Administration, an era of deregulation has been ushered in; some critics think of it as the Period of Deconstruction. Thus, the Justice Department has been denied, for example, the mandate to encourage or join in class action affirmative action–equal opportunity suits and other initiatives in labor markets. And in cases wherein the government has been hindered by legislators in efforts to deregulate certain agencies, the Reagan Administration has reduced their potency by simply reducing their budgets.

Not surprisingly, this deregulation has not been without its critics, and some former heads of regulatory agencies—such as Michael Pertschuk, former commissioner of the FTC—have openly expressed their anger in strongly accusative language.[2] Given the broad support for Reagan's policies generally, it does not seem likely, absent a crash as serious as the Great Depression, that we will soon see a reversal in the direction

---

[1] See Charles L. Schultze, *The Public Use of Private Interest* (Washington, D. C.: Brookings Institution, 1977).

[2] Michael Pertschuk, *Revolt Against Regulation* (Berkeley: University of California Press, 1982).

liberals would prefer. Reinforcing Reagan's policies are the roles of foreign states in product markets—Japan's, especially—and we appear to be countering by using a lighter hand on the levers of our antitrust machinery, thereby encouraging business consolidations and interindustry cooperation.

Capital Markets

As we have also previously noted, the state's fiscal policies toward credit markets have been largely responsible for the boom in conglomeration in recent years. These policies have favored those who borrow money for short-term gains, produced by the bidding up of stock prices, far more than they have favored those who create jobs. Firms have naturally sought to increase their earnings by taking advantage of the tax breaks offered to those who acquire companies rather than to those who start new ones, tax breaks that are not affected by proposals for the reforms that are likely to be enacted in 1986. Moreover, these policies have encouraged short-term perspectives on the part of managers, who must keep a close eye on quarterly movements of stock prices. It is true that many takeover targets have not been well managed—one of their vulnerabilities as they try to defend themselves—but it is far from clear that the raiders have reformed the companies they have acquired. T. Boone Pickens, Jr., one of the major raiders, claims that "investment-grade companies"—mostly Fortune Five Hundred companies—have lost three million jobs since 1965 while the "below-investment-grade companies"—those who finance takeovers with so-called junk bonds—"created 38 million jobs" in that twenty-year period.[3]

At the same time, the increasing complexity and volatility of credit markets have made it more difficult to anticipate the consequences of one governmental policy as contrasted with another, and the state is relatively ineffectual in changing the operation of capital markets either speedily or in reassuringly predictable ways. Hence, the implications for particular groups of changes in tax laws, or of higher or lower interest rates, are difficult to anticipate. Debates about tax reform in 1984–1985, for example, have left all of us in doubt about outcomes because the proposals have been so divergent. These constraints on the actions of government leaders vis-à-vis capital markets suggest that we must monitor their policies very carefully, both domestically and in the Third World.

---

[3] In "Management Interest vs. Shareholder Rights," *Beta Gamma Sigma: Interview,* December 1985, 4.

Resource Markets

The state has become increasingly involved in resource markets, which have at the same time also become highly internationalized in recent years, posing additional dilemmas for political leaders.

It may not be possible, for example, for the United States to maximize the acquisition of both natural resources, so many of which are located primarily in the Third World, and necessary nonnatural resources (skilled labor and modern plants), which are found in the developed world. Should the state help the Third World countries through investment, thus running the risk later of their nationalization (as in Libya, which nationalized Occidental Oil's facilities, or in Cuba, which nationalized the property of United States oil and sugar producers)? Or should the government support further the formation of multinational corporations that, in the process, become relatively independent and may not act in the state's interests?

Within the United States, actions by government agencies in resource markets have had substantial impact on firms and industries. For example, when the EPA documented and publicized the pollution hazards inhering in the burning of coal, the resource (and product) market for coal decreased drastically. Moreover, there is an upper limit to the growth in the Sunbelt imposed thereon by the lack of water needed for manufacturing and other key industries. This is particularly true for states outside the area in the Southeast served by the TVA.

Labor Markets

The state has helped businesspeople in the South in recent years by a series of NLRB rulings that have been significantly antiunion in their consequences. And current changes suggest that state policies will continue to hurt labor, at least as union leaders see it, through the rulings of the board. For example, in addition to appointing conservatives to the NLRB, whose members have destabilized unions already reeling and writhing from deindustrialization, Reagan has been openly hostile to unions as in the remarkable case of PATCO, the one-time air traffic controllers' union, and the airline pilots' union, both of which *supported* his initial election bid.

The state has recently affected labor markets in many other important ways. For example, the government has allegedly helped California businesses to hire undocumented aliens by unenergetic enforcement of immigration laws. Such policies may indeed alleviate emerging labor market pressures produced by the current baby bust (see later discussion), even as Mexican authorities welcome some relief afforded them by émigrés' relocation to the United States. State policies have also in the past increased competition in labor markets: for example, income tax policies, which gradually increased the deductibility for dependents at the time, probably helped fuel the baby boom during the post–World War II period (1945–1962). This demographic event has generated considerable competitiveness among job-seeking youths and women reentering the labor market during the last twenty years. The stabilization of these deductions coupled with income erosion by inflation—"tax creep"—has effectively made childbearing and child rearing more expensive.

POLITICAL MARKETS

A common thread in these examples is the growing competition among actors in markets and structures for the help of the state. This trend points to the growing importance to American political economy of *political markets* and of the *interest groups* that seek to exchange power and influence in them. Among the key issues in these competitive situations perhaps the most salient is: Given that the state will indeed redistribute, how and in whose interests will it redistribute economic and other important resources? The scrap over the state's resources will continue to be an important feature of the American political economy. Moreover, this competition is likely to become even more complex in the future, as the political marketplace as well as the economy are becoming increasingly internationalized and penetrated by foreign companies. Foreigners' ownership of American assets has gone up sixfold since 1973, according to government studies described on page one of the *New York Times* on 29 December 1985. According to these studies, foreigners may already own as much as 1 percent of all our assets, 1 percent of our real estate, and perhaps 5 percent of our public securities. Individual industrial foreign corporations have spent as much as three quarters of a million dollars in efforts to defeat bills of which they disapprove before California's and Utah's legislatures.

A theory of political markets requires a well-developed specification of exchanges and relations in these arenas, tasks we cannot undertake here. We simply note that the examples of the deconstruction of work structures to which we allude below are partly a result of changes in the political marketplace.

For example, since the Campaign Reform Act of the early 1970s, it has become more difficult for political parties to discipline their members; parties simply do not control the purse strings and thus have lost considerable control over their elected members. This weakening of the potency of political parties has contributed to the emergence of a multiplicity of interest groups anxious to curry candidates' favor, and considerable instability as representatives from diverse work structures have sought to buy or sell influence in the political marketplace.

The greater instability in political markets and the rise of single-interest groups have been especially damaging to organized labor. For example, industrial unions have been closely aligned with the Democratic Party since the presidency of Franklin Roosevelt. Labor's strength was rooted, in large measure, in its ability to mobilize its members to support Democratic candidates. Unions' political clout has deteriorated in recent years, as they have been less successful in raising money for candidates and in "getting the vote out."

We now take a closer if brief look at how some changes in each of our four key markets are likely to lead to future changes in the various work structures.

PRODUCT MARKETS

Since they produce and sell many different products, conglomerates tend to foster the deconstruction of industries as a work structure. By reducing the overlap between industries and product markets, the current age of conglomeration has made it much more difficult than in the past to define industrial concentration, competition, and the other key correlates of industries that we discussed in Chapter 3. For example, oil as an industry was "deconstructed" as a number of unrelated producers (such as U.S. Steel) entered into it by their acquisitions of oil companies with wells, oil resources, exploration technology, and refineries.

Periods of conglomeration are followed by cycles of divestiture (for example, divestitures have exceeded acquisitions in the past five years). However, the product-specific firms that result from such divestitures are unlikely to resume their former place in familiar, old, orderly industrial structures because the structures of industries have themselves changed in fundamental ways: for example, many mass markets have been displaced by customized, specialized consumer markets (see Piore and Sabel)[4] in which there is great demand for high-quality, nonstandardized goods. This change may, of course, *forestall* or even reverse the deconstruction of some industries; the building trades in the housing industry, for example, were rapidly moving toward greater standardization, a move-

---

[4] Piore and Sabel, *The Second Industrial Divide.*

ment that may be stinted by the demand for less "tacky" suburban dwell-ings and for renovated town houses.

CAPITAL MARKETS

Changes in capital markets, resulting in greater conglomeration, have also led to a progressive deconstruction of industries as coherent aggregations of pooled interests. Although representatives of a large in-dustry used to be able to extract favorable treatment in credit market exchanges, the present lack of unity within industries has made it difficult for them to act as coherent interest groups to secure long-term invest-ments and publicly secured loans.

Developments in capital and credit markets have also pitted subsid-iary firms of conglomerates against each other. The decisions by investors as to which of their subsidiary firms will be supported and which are destined to be milked as "cash cows" and perhaps divested are intimately related to developments in capital and credit markets, which determine which activities receive financial and other resources. For example, U.S. Steel bought into oil with borrowed money and used their oil earnings to service the new debt instead of making steel; debt service affected the allocation of this company's funds in substantial ways. This occurs in part because many stockholders or agents of stockholders have no es-sential interest in the actual workings of the firms whose securities they hold. Rather, they are more concerned with the market values of stocks, values which are more often drummed up by the demands of merger-minded bidders as by the performance of a company as a production entity. Other mergerers, recognizing that the stock market undervalues many firms' assets, buy them in order to make gains by selling off some of the acquired company's assets.

Conglomeration has also decreased the autonomy of local managers. For example, since more and more firms are managed by impotent man-agers who cannot make basic decisions associated with the running of their business,[5] aspiring "captains of industry" are fast becoming the "corporals of bureaucracy." Mammoth retailers like Sears Roebuck have centralized their advertising as well as decisions about which products are to be sold or discontinued, for example. These relocations of authority deprive local managers of mandates to run their stores based on their intimate knowledge of local market conditions and their sense of cus-tomers' needs and wants.

[5] See Berg, Freedman, and Freeman.

Conglomeration and other correlates of credit market policies have also affected rates of innovation and economic growth. For example, since customers for machine tools are spread among many conglomerates, the machine-tool industry, serving smaller customers, is less likely to be a source of innovations, a situation that is different from the one in the United Kingdom (see Sabel).[6] Moreover, the greatest source of innovations, the small business, would be injured more critically than conglomerates and large organizations by credit market policies such as changes in tax laws to prohibit the deduction of state and local taxes on federal returns, a proposal that did not survive in either the House or the Senate in 1986 (prior to a reform bill sent to joint committee) in part because small business helped resist such a change. The slack in innovation may perhaps be picked up by large companies that are trying new methods to encourage entrepreneurial activity; this has been dubbed by some writers as "intrapreneurship."[7] In this case, innovation is affected by a "credit/capital allocation market" *within* the large firm.

Unions can be decimated by the way capital is allocated when it results in conglomeration. Since credit market policies may discourage the creation of new jobs, they reduce the potential pool of future recruits that unions can draw upon. Conglomerates also have the resources and the motivation to encourage decertification of unions and otherwise to reduce their potency by playing their organized plants off against their unorganized ones.

Some of the changes in capital markets have also directly and indirectly produced changes in occupations. Due to the conglomeration process demand has been heightened for financial wizards and specialists in takeovers (e.g., accountants, lawyers, financial analysts) as well as white-collar supporting staff. Indirectly, the allocation of capital has facilitated the rise of the service sector, often at the expense of occupations in manufacturing and retail trade. Consider that the credit card industry—with leave to charge higher interest rates than banks can charge—serves an infinitely larger number of customers for services and customized retail products than they serve customers for cars, refrigerators, and homes.

Changes in capital markets have also further reduced the efficacy of class as a viable work structure. Older workers, who want to increase

[6] Sabel, *Work and Politics.*

[7] For discussions of "intrapreneurship," or entrepreneurship within large corporations, see Rosabeth M. Kanter, *The Changemasters: Innovation for Productivity in the American Corporation* (New York: Simon & Schuster, 1983); and Gifford Pinchot III *Intrapreneuring: Why You Don't Have to Leave the Corporation to Become an Entrepreneur* (New York: Harper & Row, 1985).

the value of their pensions by having portfolio managers bid up their value through short-term investments, are pitted against younger workers, whose future jobs are threatened by the artificial bidding up of stocks. Class appears unlikely to reemerge as a salient work structure in American society, even to the limited degree it did during the Depression, unless we experience a renewed period of political crisis, like another worldwide depression triggered in part by, say, Third World countries defaulting on their debts. This may make employees forget their differences and perceive more clearly their putatively shared interests.

RESOURCE MARKETS

One of the main resource problems in the United States involves the availability of water and soil, which are necessary for the production of our biggest export, agricultural products. Since the agribusiness lobbies in political markets have invested heavily in soil-related food production technology (pesticides, fertilizer), alternative technologies such as hydroponics (growing food in water or air) are not likely soon to be developed. At the same time, the internationalization of agribusiness has weakened America's position in these markets. For example, longtime steady customers, like India and the Soviet Union, are devoting more of their resources to agriculture. Since American farmers are thus increasingly limited in their efforts to sell their crops, their land purchased with borrowed money becomes less valuable and as a consequence more farmers are going bankrupt. The stories of suicides and murders in small farm towns by our television newscasters afford dramatic evidence of the despairing state of things down on the family farm. The return of Third World countries to agriculture will take some of the pressure off the shortage of the worldwide supply of raw materials, but it will do so at the expense of producers who benefited from the inadequate supply of foodstuffs.

Changes in other resource markets have also affected occupations. For example, the decrease in oil prices due to the present oil glut, if that indeed is what has developed, has reduced the demand for refinery workers, as owners of oil companies will refine less oil if they cannot sell more of it profitably. These events have already generated ripples throughout the economy, affecting nominal industries such as machine-tool makers who supply the oil and other mass manufacturing industries and tanker operators who move these products.

Developments in other markets affect the ways in which firms deal with the problem of obtaining raw materials from resource markets to produce their products and services. For example, increases in sugar prices in product markets in the 1970s led companies such as Coca-Cola to substitute the cheaper corn syrup in their original recipe; real Classic Coke disappeared well before the "new formula" Coke appeared in 1985. The "New Coke" and "Classic Coke" were just the latest events in the roller-coaster experiences of sugar refiners in the economy since the events surrounding the Molasses Act of 1733. One accordingly wonders whether Coca-Cola's enormous advertising expenditures for the reintroduction of Classic Coke will change if sugar prices fall, enabling them to make real classic Coke, and thus whether we have seen the last salvo in the resource market-based war among soft-drink makers.

LABOR MARKETS

A major change that will very likely affect labor markets and their work structures for at least the next twenty years is the baby bust. Barring changes in immigration laws and other external shocks, it is clear that there will be shortages of new-entry workers during the next two decades.

Many occupations will benefit from the declining size of the youth cohort in this current baby bust, since there will be less competition among young people for jobs than there was in the second half of the postwar baby boom cohort. Coupled with the absence of a military draft and the growing size of the public sector, the competition for scarce manpower should continue, strengthening the ability of some occupations to obtain greater rewards for their members. In particular, this competition will increase the chances for college students majoring in the arts and social sciences to receive greater income returns on their educational attainments; not only is the cohort smaller than it was in 1963, but the shift to a service economy will raise the premium for adaptable workers with high-level white-collar skills in speaking, writing, computing, and researching.

In comparison, this baby bust has uncertain effects on unions. For example, the presence of fewer workers could make them feel that they do not need unions, since they may be better off relying on individual market exchanges. At the same time, the presence of relatively few but highly educated workers may make them want to flex their muscles through unionization. It was very clearly the more educated air traffic controllers, for example, who made PATCO into the militant union it became in 1980.

Another key trend in labor markets that will increasingly affect the occupational structure is the growing vulnerability of white-collar occupations to unemployment. This trend is likely to continue, since these workers are more likely than their blue-collar counterparts to be shelved during a divestiture than in days gone by: fewer office personnel are needed in the smaller firms that are spun off from larger ones. This is keenly illustrated in the first new industry (next to high tech) in recent years—financial services. Divestments in this industry are analogous to plant closings in the blue-collar world, and if companies in the financial services industry start divesting, which seems likely given the inability of some of these conglomerates to deal successfully with the range of services that they are now providing, white-collar unemployment should continue to rise. These changes, in turn, will increase the opposition of white-collar workers to unemployment—the trade-off argument—as a way of fighting recession and provide the potential bases for a more unified "working class."

On the more general issue, and with the same "bottom line," James Kuhn has reported that:

> White-collar workers today are more subject, and blue-collar workers are less subject, to the pain and costs of unemployment than ever before. In 1958, blue-collar workers absorbed over 57 percent of all unemployment, whereas in 1977, when the unemployment rate was higher, they accounted for 39 percent; their share of unemployment had decreased three times faster than their share of employment. The white-collar share of unemployment rose from 18 to 29 percent, more than three and a half times faster than the white-collar share of employment. Thus the extension of unemployment to occupations that had been relatively immune has no doubt increased opposition to policies that use unemployment to mediate economic activities.[8]

Conglomeration has also affected labor markets and the ways in which large firms deal with organized labor. For example, important segments of labor relations are often highly centralized in large conglomerates; hence, a local plant manager is often unable to deal directly and authoritatively with unions. Such centralization of collective bargaining enables conglomerates to play off one of the locals of a union against another (or others) by exploiting the lack of common contract expiration dates for different locals and multiple sources of supply for the same product. Moreover, local union lawyers are almost never a match for the "hot shot" corporate lawyers on the payrolls of the large conglomerates. This reduces the efficacy (from labor's point of view) of arbitration and

[8] Kuhn, 105.

distorts arbitration as an alternative to the right to strike, as Berg and Shack-Marquez have reported in a case study of a small Midwest industrial city.[9]

These changes in labor markets have also contributed to the weakening of class as a work structure. Nevertheless, class-oriented univariate structuralists continue to try to reconstruct the role of the working class as a significant work structure in labor markets. A recent example is Ronnie Steinberg's *Wages and Hours*,[10] in which she argues that the working class was responsible for improvements in fair labor standards and wages in the twentieth century. However, even her own data suggest that the working class did not really do this. Rather, these reforms were enacted because a lot of people, managers prominently among them, were attracted to reforms for many reasons, including a desire to reduce workers' dependence on unions. Indeed, unions initially opposed these reforms; there is accordingly little evidence in her own volume to suggest that the working class was a moving force behind them. In fairness, the unions involved were generally *craft* unions the members of which were very much dedicated to the use of their unions to secure improved working conditions and specifically not to use the state (or states) to such ends.

THE INTERNATIONALIZATION OF WORK AND INDUSTRY STRUCTURES

As we have noted, markets and work structures have become increasingly internationalized: product, credit, resources, and labor are now commonly traded on markets that span country boundaries.

Moreover, occupations, multinational corporations, unions, and industries are increasingly crossing national borders. Within the United States, markets and structures are also now more affected than ever by developments originating in the rest of the world. In some cases, this internationalization reflects domestic changes; for example, the labor

[9] Ivar Berg and Janice Shack-Marquez, "Corporations, Human Resources, and the Grass Roots: Community Profiles," in *The Impact of the Corporation,* ed. Betty Bok, Harvey J. Goldschmid, Ira M. Millstein, and F. M. Scherer (New York: Columbia University Center for Law and Economic Studies, 1984), 219–54.

[10] Ronnie Steinberg, *Wages and Hours: Labor and Reform in 20th Century America* (New Brunswick, N.J.: Rutgers University Press, 1982).

market in the United States would not have become as internationalized in recent years if the baby boom had not ended. In others, as when union and occupational leaders complain about the loss of jobs to overseas producers, or when corporations, for competitive reasons, can no longer pass on costs to consumers and lay off workers, the members of work structures are simply reacting to foreign developments.

These changes underscore the fact that there was never as much need as there is now for explanations of work and industry rooted in considerations of political economy. Domestic markets are becoming increasingly fragile. For example, the large investments in capital equipment by American farmers made them very vulnerable to a problem originating in resource markets, the shortage of oil in the mid-1970s. Work structures are also increasingly vulnerable: American corporations are now commonly bought by foreign firms; unions are threatened by immigrants willing to work more cheaply; and key American industries are losing the competitive battle to foreign ones. These problems are exacerbated by the increase in the salience of ideology, whether Islamic, or Soviet and Chinese versions of Marxism, in other climes.

Our earlier observations that foreign ownership is expanding, that the management work force is expanding, and that managers are so often at loggerheads with well-financed corporate raiders hold special interest. The United States is not terribly anxious to slow foreign investment—we need their capital—and raiders will not become fonder of reluctant managers of the companies they seek to acquire (and vice versa). It will be interesting—one hopes not frightening—to observe the internecine struggles of the managing and owning classes that are already palpable and could readily grow more intense. Readers will recall the uproar, just a few years ago, over the sales of intelligence aircraft, "AWACS," to Saudi Arabia that were encouraged by holders of Arab petrodollars, resisted by prominent American Jews, strongly favored by defense contractors, and admired by pension fund managers (and owners) with interests in aircraft stocks.

Two of the "Big Three" automakers, meanwhile, were about as enthusiastic about General Motors' joint venture with a Japanese automaker in Southern California (to build an essentially Japanese car) as were the United Auto Workers, whose members' jobs at General Motors could be threatened by the new joint venture's sales at the same time that the union's pension fund could benefit thereby.

It is likely that these conflicts among and between managers, different kinds of owners, worker-owners, owner-managers, and investors not elsewhere classified will become more, not less, interesting.

FUTURE RESEARCH ON WORK AND INDUSTRY

These trends point to the need for future research on work and industry to be more explicitly comparative and to study the operation of work and industry structures in a variety of nations. This kind of research is necessary to understand the interdependencies between work structures and markets, on the one hand, and nation-states on the other. Such research would better sensitize us to societal and possibly cultural differences in the nature of markets and work structures. Studying work and industry structures much more consciously in comparative terms than in the past, and than we have been able to do in this volume, will also enable us to better understand the American political economy.

Comparative research, however, must take into account the multidimensionality of work structures. Whereas some work structures are declining in importance in the United States (e.g., industries and unions), others are becoming more prominent (e.g., firms). Moreover, the decline in the salience of some work structures here does not mean that they are not still key structures in other countries. For example, industries are likely to continue to be coherent and important work structures in countries such as Japan, largely because of support provided by the state, and unions will continue to be significant structures in Western Europe.

At the same time, the changes to which we have alluded have contributed to the growing importance of political markets and interest groups. Such interest groups are sometimes formed along the lines of the work structures we have identified, such as firms or occupations. In other cases, single-interest groups recruit members and support from the broad spectrum of work structures. This implies that we must continue to be sensitive to the creation of new work structures and to their relations with older, more traditional ones. The matrix printed on the back endpaper illustrates the kinds of relationships in and among the cells that must be considered in future investigations of the structure of work and industry.

SUMMARY OF SOURCES

In our discussion of work structures, markets, and processes, we have attempted to incorporate relevant materials from several disciplines, including sociology, economics, history, industrial relations, business, and political science. The complexity and diversity of phenomena related to our broad topic demand such electicism, hazardous as that practice may often be. We have also tried to include in our discussions of various topics both the older, classic statements of these issues as well as the major recent treatments. Fortunately our forebearers, like our contemporaries, have been attending to relevant segments of each others' disciplines, a fact that imposes some significant orders of discipline that reduce the risks of dilettantism.

In this section, we summarize those studies that have been of greatest use to us in addressing our main themes. Our summary is illustrative rather than exhaustive, and many of the sources that we classify under a particular heading have been relevant as well at other points in our discussion.

Several writers have tried to integrate work structures and markets in ways similar to our own. A major early attempt at such a synthesis in the post–World War II era was the research program of Kerr, Dunlop, and their associates (see, e.g., the brief concluding statement found in John T. Dunlop, Frederick H. Harbison, Clark Kerr, and Charles Myers, *Industrialism and Industrial Man Reconsidered: Some Perspectives on a Study Over Two Decades of the Problems of Labor and Management in Economic Growth* [Princeton, N.J.: The Inter-University Study of Human Resources in National Development, 1975]). More recent efforts to integrate sociological and economic approaches to the problems of distribution, production and consumption include: Neil J. Smelser, *The Sociology of Economic Life* (Englewood Cliffs, N.J.: Prentice-Hall, 1976); and Charles F. Sabel, *Work and Politics: The Division of Labor in In-*

dustry (New York: Cambridge University Press, 1982). In addition, several notable syntheses of economic and sociological theories related to work and industry appeared too recently to be incorporated in our discussion: Oliver E. Williamson's *The Economic Institutions of Capitalism* (New York: Free Press, 1985), which elaborates and extends his earlier argument in *Markets and Hierarchies: Analysis and Anti-trust Implications* (New York: Free Press, 1975); and Mark Granovetter's essay, "Economic Action and Social Structure: The Problem of Embeddedness," *American Journal of Sociology* 91 (1985): 481–510. Two much earlier classics that dealt with these issues are Karl Marx's *Capital* and Max Weber's *General Economic History*.

The notion of "multivariate structuralism" owes a considerable debt to writers in several related traditions in the social sciences. The first group is the "new institutionalists," a variety of economists, sociologists, industrial relations specialists, and legal scholars who are concerned with the legal, social, political, and economic dimensions of structures and markets. The boldest statement of this approach is Charles Lindblom's *Politics and Markets* (New York: Basic Books, 1977). The most detailed empirically informed—and richest—statements of the new institutionalist position are found in two books by Irma Adelman and Cynthia T. Morris: *Economic Growth and Social Equity in Developing Countries* (Stanford, Cal.: Stanford University Press, 1973); and *Society, Politics and Economic Development* (Baltimore: Johns Hopkins University Press, 1971). A distinct institutional tradition focuses on the legal issues related to work and industry, among them the implications of differences between the capacities of "corporate" and "natural" persons to serve themselves well. The most complete and suggestive modern statement of the asymmetry between these types of persons is James S. Coleman's *The Asymmetrical Society* (Syracuse: Syracuse University Press, 1982).

In their classic, A.A. Berle and G.C. Means explored the implications of "corporate persons" being "controlled" by professionals, rather than by owners, as the former was increasingly separated from the other. A somewhat updated version was issued by Harcourt, Brace in 1968. According to their analysis, we now have a secular trinity: corporate persons, managers, and natural persons with different social and thus legal roles.

A second group of writers whose work illustrates a "multivariate structuralist" approach is the "new economic historians," who focus on the history of trade, regulation, public policy, finance, and economic and industrial organization. They are especially concerned with the role of the nation-state in shaping the correlates of work structures and markets. An excellent example of this approach is the comparison of state and private sector investments in the United States's growth from a neo-orthodox point of view as presented by Douglas C. North, *Structure and*

Change in Economic History (New York: W. W. Norton, 1981). We relied heavily on North's study in Chapter 6 of this volume. Another brilliant and influential overview—a compendium, really—of American economic history that is informed by considerations of the development of markets and the evolution of private strategies and public policies that have affected them along social, political and economic dimensions, is S.P. Lee and P. Passell's *A New Economic View of American History* (New York: W.W. Norton, 1979), a volume already in its fourth printing.

The seeds of a multivariate structural approach are also found in the research of a number of "comparative analysts." Major early exemplars include: Clark Kerr, John T. Dunlop, Frederick H. Harbison, and Charles A. Myers, *Industrialism and Industrial Man* (London: Penguin Press, 1973); and Reinhard Bendix, *Work and Authority in Industry: Ideologies of Management in the Course of Industrialization* (New York: John Wiley, 1956). More recent examples of a comparative multivariate structural approach include: Sabel's attempt to develop an historical and comparative sociology of workplace relations in industrial capitalist societies in which he contrasts the United States, the United Kingdom, Germany, France, and Italy; a comparative study of manufacturing plants and employees in the United States and Japan by James R. Lincoln and Arne L. Kalleberg, *Culture, Control Systems and Commitment: A Study of Work Organization and Work Attitudes in the United States and Japan* (in progress); and Craig R. Littler's comparison of the nature of work organization in the United States, Britain, and Japan, *The Development of the Labour Process in Capitalist Societies* (London: Heinemann, 1982).

A final multivariate structural tradition is represented by the "new structuralists" in stratification research. These sociologists have tried to modify the individualism of the status attainment and human capital approaches by focusing on how work structures generate economic and thus social inequality. Examples include: James N. Baron and William T. Bielby, "Bringing the Firms Back In: Stratification, Segmentation and the Organization of Work," *American Sociological Review* 45 (1980): 737–65; and the analysis of the structure of income inequality by Arne L. Kalleberg, Michael Wallace, and Robert P. Althauser, "Economic Segmentation, Worker Power and Income Inequality," *American Journal of Sociology* 87 (1981): 651–83.

WORK STRUCTURES

A useful discussion of the contrast between orthodox economists who regard work structures as "given" and those who seek to explain their correlates is provided in David M. Gordon's *Theories of Poverty and Underemployment* (Lexington, Mass.: D.C. Heath, 1972).

Our discussion of how the *nation-state* affects markets and work structures relied heavily on the account by Douglas North as well as on the illustrations provided by Otto Eckstein, *The Great Recession with a Postscript on Stagflation* (Amsterdam: North Holland, 1979). Analyses of the role of the state in shaping markets and structures are also found in: Samuel Huntington, *American Politics and Promises of Disharmony* (Cambridge: Harvard University, 1981); and Robert A. Solo, *The Positive State* (Cincinnati, South-Western Publishing Co.: 1982). An informative comparative treatment of the impact of nation-states on markets, legal and political systems, as well as of the nonmarket provision of goods and services is provided by Frederick L. Pryor, *Property and Industrial Organization in Communist and Capitalist Nations* (Bloomington, Ind.: Indiana University Press, 1973). Finally, the often inconsistent relationships that characterize American industrial programs (as opposed to policies) are discussed in Robert B. Reich, "An Industrial Policy of the Right," *The Public Interest* 73 (Fall 1983): 3–17. For those who would like to be reassured about the constant involvement of the American state in the republic's economy, we recommend reading any ten randomly selected pages in Richard Morris, ed., *Encyclopedia of American History* (New York: Harper & Row, 1961).

The univariate *class* approach is well represented by Erik Olin Wright's Marxist analysis of problems related to work and industry. See, for example, his *Class Structure and Income Determination* (New York: Academic Press, 1979); "Class Boundaries in Advanced Capitalist Societies," *New Left Review* 98 (July–August 1976): 3–41; and *Classes* (London: Verso, 1985). Another influential Marxist analysis of the ways in which class relations shape the organization of work is Richard C. Edwards's *Contested Terrain* (New York: Basic Books, 1979). The classic statement of the Weberian view of class is found in Max Weber, 1922, *Economy and Society,* edited by Gunther Roth (New York: Bedminster Press, 1968). A more recent extension of this position is Anthony Giddens's *The Class Structure of Advanced Societies* (New York: Harper & Row, 1975). In our discussion of class as a process, we drew upon E.P. Thompson's *The Making of the English Working Class* (New York: Pantheon, 1963).

We illustrated the univariate *occupation* approach by the research program of Melvin L. Kohn and Carmi Schooler, summarized in their *Work and Personality: An Inquiry into the Impact of Social Stratification* (Norwood, N.J.: Ablex Publishing, 1983). The classic statement of occupational mobility and the role of occupational status in socioeconomic attainment is Peter M. Blau and Otis Dudley Duncan's *The American*

Occupational Structure (New York: John Wiley, 1967). A useful discussion of power differences among occupations is found in William H. Form and Joan A. Huber, "Occupational Power," in Robert Dubin, ed., *Handbook of Work, Organization and Society* (Chicago: Rand McNally, 1976), 751–806.

The univariate *industry* approach is represented by Robert Blauner's *Alienation and Freedom: The Factory Worker and His Industry* (Chicago: University of Chicago Press, 1964). The best summaries of a highly technical literature on the correlates of industries (market structures, concentration, and so on) are found in F.M. Scherer, *Industrial Market Structure and Performance* (Chicago: Rand McNally, 1980). See also: Richard Caves, *American Industry: Structure, Conduct, Performance* (Englewood Cliffs, N.J.: Prentice-Hall, 1967); Joe S. Bain, *Industrial Organization* (New York: John Wiley, 1959); and the six updated editions of *The Structure of American Industry* (New York: Macmillan, 1950–1982), edited by Walter Adams. Moreover, a now classic (though not uncontroversial) description of the changes in industrial structure that are thought to accompany the continuing development of the "post-industrial" society is Daniel Bell's *The Coming of Post-Industrial Society* (New York: Basic Books, 1973).

The univariate *organization* approach is illustrated by the "closed system" tradition of organizational analysis: see, for example, Jerald Hage, "An Axiomatic Theory of Organizations," *Administrative Science Quarterly* 10 (December 1965): 289–320; and Derek Pugh, David Hickson, Robert Hinings, and Chris Turner, "Dimensions of Organization Structure," *Administrative Science Quarterly* 13 (1968): 65–104. A classic statement of organizations as "corporate groups" is found in Max Weber's *The Theory of Social and Economic Organization,* translated and edited by A.M. Henderson and Talcott Parsons (New York: Oxford University Press, 1947). An early (1932) and basic discussion of the separation of ownership and control in organizations, as we noted above in a different context, was provided by Adolf A. Berle and Gardiner C. Means, *The Modern Corporation and Private Property,* rev. ed. (New York: Harcourt, Brace & World, 1968).

Our discussion of the distinction between so-called formal and informal organizational structures draws upon Alvin W. Gouldner's essay, "Organizational Analysis," in Robert K. Merton, Leonard Broom, and Leonard S. Cottrell, eds., *Sociology Today* (New York: Basic Books, 1959), 400–28. A useful review of research on the consequences of (formal) correlates of organizations is James N. Baron's "Organizational Perspectives on Inequality," *Annual Review of Sociology* 10 (1984): 37–69. One of the few systematic discussions of the history and significance of trends in the size distribution of business organizations is provided by Mark Granovetter, "Small is Bountiful: Labor Markets and Establishment Size," *American Sociological Review* 49 (1984): 323–34. In addition, an influential statement of the dual economy perspective as it applies to organizations is Robert T. Averitt's *The Dual Economy: The Dynamics of American Industry Structure* (New York: Norton, 1968).

Excellent overviews of the impacts, on a variety of outcomes, of *unions* in the United States are found in Richard B. Freeman and James L. Medoff's *What Do Unions Do?* (New York: Basic Books, 1984); and in the collection of papers edited by Thomas A. Kochan, *Challenges and Choices Facing American Labor* (Cambridge: M.I.T. Press, 1985). A concise but insightful discussion of some of the major challenges currently facing labor in the United States is Michael J. Piore's "American Labor and the Industrial Crisis," *Challenge* (March–April 1982): 5–11.

MARKETS

A central concept in the analysis of *labor markets* is that of the "internal labor market." An influential treatment of internal labor markets is Peter B. Doeringer and Michael J. Piore's *Internal Labor Markets and Manpower Analysis* (Lexington, Mass.: D.C. Heath, 1971), which extends arguments anticipated by John T. Dunlop (e.g., "The Task of Contemporary Wage Theory," in G. W. Taylor and F. C. Pierson, eds., *New Concepts in Wage Determination* [New York: McGraw-Hill, 1957], 3–30). A more recent collection of papers dealing with internal labor markets is found in Paul Osterman, ed., *Internal Labor Markets* (Cambridge: M.I.T. Press, 1984).

An historical analysis of labor market segmentation from a Marxist perspective is provided by David M. Gordon, Richard Edwards, and Michael Reich, *Segmented Work, Divided Workers* (New York: Cambridge University Press, 1982). Some of the recent research on labor markets being undertaken in different countries is summarized in Frank Wilkinson, ed., *The Dynamics of Labor Market Segmentation* (New York: Academic Press, 1981). Moreover, an early, empirically informed analysis of the criteria used by employers in selecting workers in the labor market which is highly critical of neoclassical economic explanations, is Ivar Berg's *Education and Jobs: The Great Training Robbery* (New York: Praeger, 1970).

Our discussions of the implications of the changing nature of *product markets* parallel those of Michael J. Piore and Charles F. Sabel, *The Second Industrial Divide: Possibilities for Prosperity* (New York: Basic Books, 1984); and Robert B. Reich, *The Next American Frontier* (New

York: Penguin, 1983). These are insightful analyses of the consequences of changes in product markets for the structure of industries and for America's relative position in the world economy. The impacts of the nation-state on competitiveness in product markets, through regulations based on "standards" rather than on incentives, are also discussed by Charles L. Schultze, *The Public Use of Private Interest* (Washington, D.C.: Brookings Institution, 1977).

Many of the studies by the "new institutionalists" and the "new economic historians" examine the correlates and consequences of *capital markets*. We have focused on a key outcome of changes in capital markets: the growth of conglomerates. Many of the (negative) consequences of conglomeration are summarized by Barry Bluestone and Bennett Harrison in *The Deindustrialization of America* (New York: Basic Books, 1982). A more positive picture of the impacts of mergers on job creation is provided in an interview with T. Boone Pickens, "Management Interest vs. Shareholder Rights," *Beta Gamma Sigma: Interview* (St. Louis, Mo.: December 1985), 4. We also considered some changes occurring in the kinds of institutions that provide credit. For example, in our discussion of competition in credit markets between producers who sell credit to their customers along with their products, on the one hand, and financial institutions, on the other, we relied on: Cleveland A. Christophe, *Competition in Financial Services* (New York: First National City Corporation, 1974).

A striking illustration of the far-reaching implications of changes in *resource markets* was provided by the oil crisis in the 1970s. Our discussion of this event is based in part on Jack Anderson, *The Great Fiasco* (New York: Times Books, 1983); and Robert Engler, *The Politics of Oil* (New York: New American Library, 1977).

Finally, well-documented discussions of the *political market*, in which expansionary policies are offered in exchange for votes, are provided by: E. R. Tufte, *Political Control of the Economy* (Princeton: Princeton University Press, 1978); and D. J. Meiselman, "The Political Monetary Cycle," *Wall Street Journal*, 10 January 1984, 10.

PROCESSES

For a discussion of *interest groups* that closely conforms to our own, see Graham K. Wilson, *Interest Groups in the United States* (Oxford: Clarendon Press, 1981; published in the United States by Oxford University Press, 1981). A useful treatment of one important type of interest group—business lobbies—is provided by Sar A. Levitan and Martha R.

Cooper, *Business Lobbies: The Public Good and the Bottom Line* (Baltimore: Johns Hopkins University Press, 1984). A consequence of the activities of business lobbies has been the deregulation of many key industries; this trend has accelerated in recent years and has led to considerable controversy. This debate is illustrated by the reactions to President Reagan's efforts to dismantle the regulatory apparatus in the United States delivered in Michael Pertschuk's *Revolt Against Regulation* (Berkeley: University of California Press, 1982).

NAME INDEX

SUBJECT INDEX